The Student
Newspaper
Survival
Guide

The Student
Newspaper
Survival
Guide

Rachele Kanigel

San Francisco State University

Blackwell
Publishing

Blackwell Publishing Professional
2121 State Avenue, Ames, Iowa 50014, USA

Orders: 1-800-862-6657
Office: 1-515-292-0140
Fax: 1-515-292-3348
Web site: www.blackwellprofessional.com

Blackwell Publishing Ltd
9600 Garsington Road, Oxford OX4 2DQ, UK
Tel.: +44 (0)1865 776868

Blackwell Publishing Asia
550 Swanston Street, Carlton, Victoria 3053, Australia
Tel.: +61 (0)3 8359 1011

Cover design and book design by Betsy Brill.
Cover photo by Jordin Thomas Althaus. Reprinted with permission.

Library of Congress Cataloging-in-Publication Data
Kanigel, Rachele.
  The student newspaper survival guide / Rachele Kanigel.
    p. cm.
  Includes bibliographical references and index.
  ISBN-13: 978-0-8138-0741-6 (alk. paper)
  ISBN-10: 0-8138-0741-7 (alk. paper)
  1. College student newspapers and periodicals. I. Title.

LB3621.65.K36 2006
378.1′9897—dc22
                                    2006003139

The last digit is the print number: 9 8 7 6 5 4 3 2

To the students at San Francisco State University and
California State University, Monterey Bay, who inspired me,

To the members of College Media Advisers and the CMA-L listserv subscribers,
who guided and counseled me,

And to my family—Laird, Dashiell, and Trevor—
who put up with me while I wrote this book.

Table of Contents

Preface

In 2002, I started teaching journalism and advising the student newspaper at California State University, Monterey Bay. The staff of *The Otter Realm* newspaper—which numbered less than a dozen students then—was bright and eager to learn. But most of them knew little or nothing about putting out a newspaper.

I had been a journalist for 20 years and had advised one other student paper, yet I realized I didn't have the answers to all of their questions. Did a photojournalist need permission to photograph students in a classroom? What should a newspaper's media kit include? How should a college newspaper cover a student's suicide?

I looked for a book that would help me train my students and expand my own knowledge base. What I sought was more than a newswriting or editing text; I wanted a guide to all aspects of producing a student paper. The only one I could find was out of print and woefully out of date.

So I set out to write my own.

To research *The Student Newspaper Survival Guide* I studied campus newspapers from around North America—struggling publications with small staffs as well as impressive, professional-quality newspapers that routinely sweep awards contests. I interviewed professional journalists, journalism educators, student newspaper advisers and business managers.

I also talked to students—hundreds of reporters, editors, photographers, columnists, ad sales people and Webmasters—asking each of them what challenges they faced and what advice they had for the next generation of student newspaper staffers. This volume is a compendium of their suggestions.

If you've picked up this book, you're probably part of a student newspaper staff, or soon will be. You may be an editor or reporter, a photographer or designer, an ad salesperson or a business manager. Or perhaps you're a student newspaper adviser looking for new ways to train, motivate and inspire your staff.

Whatever your role, welcome. Whether you're doing this for a class, checking out a potential profession or just want to have fun, working for a student newspaper is one of the most eye-opening and empowering experiences you can have in college.

It also can be one of the most challenging. Over the months or years you work on a newspaper, you will encounter many obstacles. People you need to interview won't want to talk with you, subjects will decline to be photographed, businesses will refuse to buy ads. People you depend on will let you down. Heated debates will break out in the newsroom over photos and stories and headlines and ads. You'll face ethical and legal issues you don't know how to deal with.

This book is designed to help you cope with these challenges and to give you the resources you need to make reasoned decisions.

The first chapters of the book focus on editorial issues—everything from recruiting and training a staff, to photographing sports and campus events, to steering clear of legal minefields. Here's where advisers, editors, reporters and photographers can look for guidance and ideas on the issues they deal with on a day-to-day basis.

Later chapters address design and production—how to put out a readable and attractive paper that invites readers to pick it up and a Web site readers will turn to.

The last chapter deals with advertising, including training and motivating your sales staff and keeping your revenue flowing.

Each section includes tipsheets, checklists, Q&As and essays from professionals, some of them well-respected leaders in their fields, others who are just barely out of college themselves. At the end of each chapter is a list of projects, readings and Web sites you can explore to deepen your understanding of your craft and make your papers run more smoothly.

My inspiration for this book comes from my students at *The Otter Realm* and at *Golden Gate [X]press* at San Francisco State University, where I teach now. On both staffs, students were always hungry for ideas to make their papers better. I hope they and other students will see this book as a valuable resource. I thank them for their help, advice and support in preparing these pages.

One thing to remember: Student newspapers are training grounds for journalists, yes, but they are also boot camps for life. Your campus newsroom may end up the most valuable classroom you have during your college years. Take full advantage of your rights. But be mindful, too, of your responsibilities. As a journalist you have the power to help and to harm, to expose wrongs and ruin careers. If you understand this power and use it wisely, you can change your corner of the world.

Rachele Kanigel

Acknowledgements

When I set out to write this book, I knew I'd need help. I wanted this to be a compendium of advice from student journalists, college newspaper advisers, advertising and business managers, media lawyers, professional journalists and others dedicated to sustaining and nurturing the student press.

But I had no idea how much help I would receive. Now, as I think back over the two years I worked on this book, I'm overwhelmed by the generosity of my colleagues in journalism and journalism education. What touched me most was how much people were willing to share. Often I'd post a query to the College Media Advisers listserv on some esoteric topic (Who owns the copyright to material your student newspaper publishes? Does your paper have a mission statement? Can anyone recommend a good student sex columnist?) and within an hour I would have half a dozen helpful responses, most from people I'd never met in person. Thanks to all the advisers who contributed tidbits of information. I promise not to bombard the list with questions for a while—at least not until I start working on the second edition!

It's hard to imagine this book would exist without the help of my mentor, friend and colleague, Kenneth Kobré, whose wise insights, demanding criticism and rousing pep talks kept me going when I felt overwhelmed. Thanks, too, to his wife, designer Betsy Brill, who helped me envision how the book should look and who brought her design expertise to these pages.

My tireless research assistant Eugenia Chien was a tremendous help in many different ways—from her technical expertise to her youthful perspective to her sharp eye for math mistakes. Daniel Jimenez proved to be an adept copy editor. Thanks to San Francisco State University, the College of Humanities and Dean Paul Sherwin for the Affirmative Action Faculty Development Grant that made their contributions possible.

Several people read chapters and provided much-needed feedback: Amy Emmert, Nils Rosdahl, Cynthia Mitchell, Dave Waddell, Sylvia Fox, Joe Gisondi, Mike Spohn. Thanks for your encouraging words and helpful criticism. In addition, Mark Goodman's legal advice—for my readers, my students and for me as an author—was invaluable.

My colleagues at San Francisco State University, many of whom have co-advised student publications with me, have all taught me useful lessons about teaching and advising: Cristina Azocar, John Burks, Yvonne Daley, Andrew DeVigal, Lesley Guth, Tom Johnson, Dottie Katzeff, Barbara Landis, Edna Lee, Austin Long-Scott, Jim Merithew, Raul Ramirez, Erna Smith, Scot Tucker, Venise Wagner, James Wagstaffe, Yumi Wilson.

Sylvia Fox and the board of the California College Media Association—Paul Bittick, Amy Emmert, Rich Cameron, Michelle Carter, Melinda Dudley, Tom Clanin, Tim Hendrick, Tom Nelson, Jennifer Poole, Dave Waddell, Jenifer Woodring—helped me understand the needs of college newspapers. Their passion for student publications was a constant source of inspiration.

And when I was stuck on what to do for graphics, Bradley Wilson saved the day.

I am thankful to Mark Barrett, Dede Pedersen, Judi Brown and the others at Blackwell Publishing who believed in this book and helped bring it to publication. Tracy Petersen not only proved to be a crackerjack copyeditor, but an astute and sensible adviser on the text.

Thanks to my brother, Robert Kanigel, who always asked how the book was going, and to my mother, Beatrice Kanigel, who reminded me not to work too hard.

To Dashiell and Trevor, I pledge to be a better, more attentive mommy, now that this book is done. I am enduringly grateful to my husband, Laird Harrison, who provides me with time, writing and editing advice, a ready ear and love. I can't imagine a more perfect life partner.

Finally, thanks to my students, who each day remind me why I love journalism.

The following journalists and journalism educators contributed material or information to this book. (Affiliations are current as of when I was last in touch with them.)

Robert Adams, *College Heights Herald*, Western Kentucky University

David L. Adams, *Indiana Daily Student*, Indiana University, Bloomington

Jordin Thomas Althaus, photographer

Kaylene D. Armstrong, *The Daily Universe*, Brigham Young University

Michael Arrieta-Walden, *The Oregonian*

Harry Austin, *Chattanooga Times Free Press*

Nate Beeler, *The Washington Examiner*

Paul Bittick, *Mustang Daily*, California Polytechnic State University, San Luis Obispo

Robert Bohler, *The Daily Skiff*, Texas Christian University

Ed Bonza, *The Sentinel*, Kennesaw State University

Timothy Michael Bowles, *Orbis*, Vanderbilt University

Ralph Braseth, *The Daily Mississippian*, University of Mississippi

Elinor J. Brecher, *The Miami Herald*

Jerry Bush, *The Daily Egyptian*, Southern Illinois University, Carbondale

Steve Buttry, American Press Institute

Dan Carino, cartoonist

Chris Carroll, *The Vanderbilt Hustler*, Vanderbilt University

Emery Carrington, *The Daily Mississippian*, University of Mississippi

Brian Cassella, *The Daily Tar Heel*, University of North Carolina at Chapel Hill

Steven E. Chappell, *Truman State University Index,* Truman State University

Nathaniel Christopher, *Toast*, Trent University

Betty Clapp, Cleveland State University

Mac Clemmens, *The Otter Realm*, California State University, Monterey Bay

Aly Colón, The Poynter Institute

Michael Conti, *The Harvard Crimson*, Harvard University

Autumn Cruz, *Sacramento Bee*

David Cuillier, Washington State University

Tonya Danos, *The Nicholls Worth*, Nicholls State University

Juanita Darling, *The Otter Realm*, California State University, Monterey Bay

Christopher Dinn, Canadian University Press

Mike Donoghue, *The Burlington* (Vt.) *Free Press*

Roger Ebert, *Chicago Sun-Times*

Joel Elliott, *The Toccoa Record*

Amy Emmert, *The Daily Bruin*, University of California, Los Angeles

Mark Fainaru-Wada, *San Francisco Chronicle*

Vincent Filak, *The Ball State Daily News*, Ball State University

Annette Forbes, *Iowa State Daily*, Iowa State University

John Frank, *The Post and Courier*, Charleston, S.C.

Sean Gallagher, photographer

Jessie Gardner, Primo Advertising

Matt Garton, *Cleveland Plain Dealer*

Lloyd Goodman, *The Shorthorn*, University of Texas at Arlington

Mark Goodman, Student Press Law Center

Jeremy Gragert, *The Flip Side*, University of Wisconsin-Eau Claire

Andy Guess, *The Cornell Sun*, Cornell University

Shannon Guthrie, *State Journal-Register*

Gerry Lynn Hamilton, *The Daily Collegian*, Pennsylvania State University

Terrence G. Harper, Society of Professional Journalists

Christy Harrison, *The Exponent*, Purdue University

Tim Harrower, design consultant

Elaine Helm, *The Daily Northwestern*, Northwestern University

Sarah Hemus, *Golden Gate [X]press*, San Francisco State University

Brant Houston, Investigative Reporters and Editors, Inc.

Megan Irwin, *The State Press Magazine*, Arizona State University

Eric Jacobs, *The Daily Pennsylvanian*, University of Pennsylvania

Joe Jaszewski, *Idaho Statesman*

Lee Jenkins, *The New York Times*

Tyler Kepner, *The New York Times*

Jim Killam, *Northern Star*, Northern Illinois University

Harry Kloman, *The Pitt News*, University of Pittsburgh

Kenneth Kobré, *Golden Gate [X]press*, San Francisco State University

Brian Krans, *The Dispatch/Rock Island Argus/The Leader* newspaper group

Jill "J.R." Labbe, *Fort Worth Star-Telegram*

Jack Lancaster, *Daily O'Collegian*, Oklahoma State University

Al Lanier, *Chicago Tribune*

Kathy Lawrence, *The Daily Texan*, University of Texas at Austin

Ira David Levy, *Diversity*, Wilbur Wright College

Scott Lindenberg, *The Gamecock*, University of South Carolina

Charles Little, *el Don*, Santa Ana College

Mark Ludwig, *The State Hornet*, Sacramento State University

Sherrie Mazingo, University of Minnesota School of Journalism

Sean McCourt, freelance writer

Michael G. McLaughlin, *The Daily Evergreen*, Washington State University

Melvin Mencher, *News Reporting and Writing*

Jim Merithew, *San Francisco Chronicle*

Derek Montgomery, *The Badger Herald*, University of Wisconsin, Madison

Miguel M. Morales, *The Campus Ledger*, Johnson County Community College

Nick Mrozowski, *The State News*, Michigan State University

Erika B. Neldner, *The Sentinel*, Kennesaw State University

Ashley Nelson, *The Orion*, California State University, Chico

Michael Newsom, *The Daily Mississippian*, University of Mississippi

Jeremy Norman, *Northern Star*, Northern Illinois University

Jared Novack, *The Daily Orange*, Syracuse University

Christopher Null, Filmcritic.com

Andrew O'Dell, *Student Life*, Washington University, St. Louis

Jake Ortman, Utterlyboring.com

Rob Owen, *Pittsburgh Post-Gazette*

Pat Parish, *The Daily Reveille*, Louisiana State University

Perry Parks, *The State News*, Michigan State University

Jason Perlmutter, *The Cornell Sun*, Cornell University

Mandy Phillips, Missouri State University

Cera Renault, *Golden Gate [X]press*, San Francisco State University

Alison Roberts, *The State*, Columbia, S.C.

Josie Roberts, *Pittsburgh Tribune-Review*

Tom Rolnicki, Associated Collegiate Press

Amy Rolph, *The Daily*, University of Washington, Seattle

Ed Ronco, *South Bend Tribune*

Nils Rosdahl, *The Sentinel*, North Idaho College

Mike Rosenberg, *Detroit Free Press*

Misha Rosiak, *Golden Gate [X]press*, San Francisco State University

Adam Rubin, *New York Daily News*

Kenneth Rystrom, *The Why, Who and How of the Editorial Page*

Leigh Sabey, *Northern Colorado Business Report*

Peter S. Scholtes, *City Pages*

Lauren Schuker, *The Harvard Crimson*, Harvard University

Kevin Schwartz, *The Daily Tar Heel*, University of North Carolina at Chapel Hill

Becky Sher, Knight Ridder/Tribune

Emmet Smith, *The Plain Dealer*

Kami Smith, *The Daily Barometer*, Oregon State University

Lance Speere, *The Daily Egyptian*, Southern Illinois University, Carbondale

Ron Spielberger, College Media Advisers

Mike Spohn, *The State Press*, Arizona State University

George Srour, *DoG Street Journal*, College of William and Mary

Brian Steffen, *The Simpsonian*, Simpson College

Robert F. Stevenson, *The Forunn*, Lander University

Scott Strazzante, *Chicago Tribune*

Sean Patrick Sullivan, Canadian University Press

Patricia Tisak, *The Philadelphia Inquirer*

Brian Vander Kamp, *The Flip Side*, University of Wisconsin-Eau Claire

James M. Wagstaffe, Kerr & Wagstaffe, LLP

Dave Waddell, *The Orion*, California State University, Chico

Brian Wagner, *The Daily Herald*

Matt Waite, *St. Petersburg Times*

Tom Warhover, *The Columbia Missourian*, University of Missouri-Columbia

Megan Watzin, *The Diamondback*, University of Maryland

Denny Wilkins, St. Bonaventure University

David Williams, Oregon State University

Bradley Wilson, *Technician*, North Carolina State University

John K. Wilson, Collegefreedom.org

Carie Windham, *Technician*, North Carolina State University

Mark Witherspoon, *Iowa State Daily*, Iowa State University

Tom Whisenand, photographer

Kelly Wolff, Educational Media Company at Virginia Tech, Inc.

Stacy Wynn, *The Daily Tar Heel*, University of North Carolina at Chapel Hill

Christine Yee, *Contra Costa Times*

John Zeratsky, *The Badger Herald*, University of Wisconsin- Madison

The Student
Newspaper
Survival
Guide

Figure 1.1. A fraternity house fire at the University of Mississippi in August 2004 highlights the many roles a student newspaper serves. *The Daily Mississippian,* University of Mississippi

 Howard Stone

 William Townsend

 Jordan Williams

INSIDE...

Campus-wide memorial set for Thursday
● Page 6

Community lends support
● Page 7

Timeline of Friday's events
● Pages 8-9

MONDAY
AUGUST 30, 2004
Vol. 96, No.006

THE DAILY MISSISSIPPIAN

The University of Mississippi   Serving Ole Miss and Oxford since 1911.   www.thedmonline.com

Bound as brothers

J.D. Johnson The Daily Mississippian

An **Alpha Tau Omega member** comforts friends outside his fraternity house Friday morning. The ATOs spent most of the early hours in the Beta Theta Pi house.

Fire scene investigation concludes, memorial service set for Thursday

MICHAEL NEWSOM
DM CAMPUS NEWS EDITOR

Fire scene investigations at the Alpha Tau Omega house ended over the weekend as the community prepares to say goodbye to three of its members.

Federal, State and local agencies have wrapped up their on site look into the cause of the fraternity house fire that killed three Ole Miss students early Friday morning. All the while, memorials were being planned.

The investigation into the fire that killed William Townsend, Jordan Williams and Howard Stone has been turned over to the University Police Department.

The investigators said that they found no evidence of foul play and no evidence the fire was intentionally set.

The starting point of the fire has been isolated to one of the basement bedrooms along the south side of the structure on the east wall.

Investigators found several possible points of origin for the fire, therefore samples must be sent to the Alcohol, Tobacco, Firearms and Explosives (ATF) laboratory in Maryland to be analyzed to help determine the cause of the fire.

Joey Hall, an ATF special agent assigned to the Oxford bureau, commented on the samples.

"It will be a priority for them to turn it around, get some answers," Hall said.

Hall said that about 25 agents trained to investigate the cause of fire were summoned to campus.

He said that it is common for his office to deal with on-the-scene fire investigations.

"It is kind of what we do every day. With the amount of loss, along with the fatalities, once we got the calls, we jumped in with open arms," Hall said.

He also said the samples would be analyzed today, and more will be known about the cause of the fire after the results are returned.

Hall worked with ATF agents, the Mississippi Bureau of Investigations, University Police, Lafayette County Sheriff's and Oxford Police Departments.

Investigators took pictures, collected physical evidence at the scene and interviewed witnesses throughout the community.

The fire investigation has been turned over to UPD, so that engineers can be brought in to determine if the structure of the ATO house is sound enough for students to go in and collect any of their belongings that are salvageable.

Stone was the last casualty of the fire to be identified. Authori-

See THURSDAY ➤ page 5

The Role of the Student Press

Chapter Contents

It was about 6:15 on a Friday morning when Michael Newsom, the campus news editor for *The Daily Mississippian* at the University of Mississippi, got a wake-up call from Elizabeth Ogden, the paper's former photo editor.

"Michael, I heard that the ATO (Alpha Tau Omega) house is on fire. It's probably nothing, but you should check it out," she said.

Newsom rolled over and went back to sleep. But five minutes later the phone rang again. It was Ogden.

"Michael, it's bad. Get down here," she said.

Newsom dressed quickly and drove toward Fraternity Row at the Oxford, Miss., campus. As he neared the neighborhood of Greek residences, he saw smoke billowing around the Alpha Tau Omega house, a once stately, brick building with white columns in front.

As firefighters battled the blaze, dazed fraternity members milled about, looking for information about their missing brothers.

Newsom set to work interviewing students, fraternity members, the fraternity's adviser—anyone who would talk, anyone who could help him piece together the facts of the story.

Later that morning, *The Daily Mississippian* reported the grim news on its Web site: Three students had died in the fire.

Over the next several hours and through the weekend, the staff posted updates—stories and photos, as well as radio and video reports from the newspaper's sister student broadcast stations—about the fire on the newspaper's Web site (Figure 1.2). On Monday, the print edition of the paper was filled

Figure 1.2 Though news of the fire breaks after the Friday edition of *The Daily Mississippian* is printed, the staff is able to post updates throughout the weekend on the newspaper's Web site. *The Daily Mississippian,* University of Mississippi

Tips from a Pro

■ Susan Goldberg

The college newspapers where you now work don't need to look like the city newspaper in the nearest town. In fact, they shouldn't. They should be laboratories for cutting-edge journalism.

In addition to the late nights and pizza and camaraderie, make the most of every assignment. Do things that help make your college paper indispensable to readers. Don't be afraid to try new, unconventional approaches.

What kind of approaches? Here are a few you might consider:

1. **Make sure to reflect your community.** Is your front page attuned to what college students are talking about—music, sex, stress, the job market? Do those boring and often inconsequential student government stories really belong out there?
2. **Make use of the latest technology.** Can you podcast your news so students can download it and listen to it when they want to?
3. **Make other people do your work.** Provide a platform for a series of different Web logs—a dorm blog, a Greek blog, a rate-the-prof blog.
4. **Make a local mark.** Leave national and international stories to someone else. It's not your area of expertise and folks can get that information off any number of national Web sites. Instead, focus on news that is local and useful for your campus readers.
5. **Make the stories you write accessible.** Use everything in your toolbox of tricks—lists, charts, highlights, summaries, tips—to help quickly usher people into your content.

6. **Make watchdog stories your hallmark.** Your on-campus location puts you in the catbird seat to see what the university is up to. Exploit that advantage. How is the administration spending money? Who gets a free car? Whose lover just got a high-paying job? Nothing you do will be more compelling to your readers than revelatory and exclusive local content.
7. **Make change; be a crusader.** Editorial pages too often are boring. Set out to make your pages provocative. Take up a cause. Work in concert with the news side. Get some action!
8. **Make some hard choices.** Newspapers are drowning in dull, turn-of-the-screw 12- to 20-inch stories. Figure out the handful of stories you are going to tell really well on a given day—stories where you can really add value. Brief everything else.
9. **Make hearing your readers a priority.** Ask your readers what they'd like to see you cover. I'm sure you *think* you know—but do you really? Invite them to tell you, and actually listen to their answers. Maybe you'll learn something that will surprise you and suggest a ground-breaking avenue of presentation or coverage.
10. **Learn your craft.** Newspapers are the public trust. Be proud of that responsibility, and take it seriously. But don't shy away from being bold about it.

Susan Goldberg is executive editor of the San Jose Mercury News. *She got her start at* The State News *at Michigan State University, where she was a general assignment reporter, county reporter and assistant editor.*

These tips are adapted from a speech she gave at the National College Newspaper Convention in San Francisco in 2005.

with in-depth coverage of the tragedy, including profiles of the victims, a timeline of events and information about how to help the surviving fraternity brothers.

The August 27, 2004 fire challenged *The Daily Mississippian* staff in many ways. Official sources were tight-lipped, making it difficult to get information. Photographers were shooed away from the scene. Reporters and editors, just settling into their new roles on the fourth day of classes, grappled with unfamiliar equipment and difficult decisions.

But the fire reminded the University of Mississippi of how essential the paper, along with its affiliated radio and television stations, were to the campus and larger community.

"The nation wanted to know exactly what was going on in Oxford, Miss., and we told them," says Emery Carrington, the newspaper's editor in chief that year. "Ole Miss parents, alumni, fellow fraternity members, the media and the general public created an unprecedented amount of traffic on our Web site—over 1 million hits within the first 24 hours of the fire, 2 million by the end of the weekend."

The Role of the Student Press

The tragedy at the University of Mississippi highlights the vital role a student newspaper plays on a college campus. Whether it's a stapled sheaf of photocopied pages distributed every couple of weeks or a professional-looking daily broadsheet, a college newspaper serves many functions:

- It's a chronicle of campus life that informs the campus about everything from scientific research and protest demonstrations to championship basketball games and out-of-control fraternity parties.
- It's a community forum where students, faculty, administrators and staff can debate issues of common concern.
- It's a watchdog that barks when a cafeteria is cited for health code violations or hale athletes drive around with handicapped parking placards.
- It's a training ground for the next generation of journalists.

Let's look at these roles and the responsibilities and challenges that come along with them.

The Chronicle of Campus Life

Every campus has its events, issues and personalities, and a student newspaper is often the only unbiased vehicle for reporting on the life of a college community. While the primary audience for college papers is students, a good paper covers the whole campus.

"One of the responsibilities of a newspaper is to reflect the nature of the community it serves," says Melvin Mencher, a longtime journalism educator and author of *News Reporting and Writing*, a leading journalism textbook. "A student newspaper should be able to understand and display all dimensions of a campus community, not just student life but the concerns of the university employees, faculty, administrators and staff."

The Community Forum

A college campus can be a fragmented place. Freshmen and transfer students may feel lost and alienated. Seniors and commuters may be so wrapped up in their majors and school-work that they're unaware of what's happening on the rest of the campus. And students can feel overwhelmed at times by a monolithic entity that can raise their tuition, their rents and their health care costs with little warning.

"The student paper can be a unifying force," says Mencher. "It should represent students from around the campus. And it should establish some kind of leadership, demanding the highest quality education for students, so students have an outlet for their frustrations, their excitements, their passions."

In the days and weeks after the University of Mississippi fire, for example, the opinion section and the Web site comment boxes overflowed with letters and e-mail messages expressing prayers, sadness and outrage (Figure 1.3). The wounded community needed to vent, and *The Daily Mississippian* provided a place to do that.

ATO fire leaves three students dead		
Post your feedback on this topic here		
Date	**Subject**	**Posted by:**
08/27/2004	God bless and be with you, men of...	Candy
08/27/2004	All the Taus in Western Michigan wish...	Kurt Pease
08/27/2004	God be with the families of these...	Missy
08/27/2004	I am so saddened about this and my...	Julie
08/27/2004	First I want to let the ATO...	Mike
08/27/2004	I heard about this tragedy on the...	Lindsay
08/27/2004	I feel terrible for all of those...	Josh Loper
08/27/2004	Were the 3 dead before the fire?	M
08/27/2004	Thoughts and support are with you...	Brother Leighton Mohl
08/27/2004	As the father of an Ole Miss Student,...	Charley Cook
08/27/2004	Pray for these kids and their...	prayers
08/27/2004	As a Beta alum, my prayers go out to...	Tom Rice
08/27/2004	The loss of our interfraternal...	Stephen Rupprecht
08/27/2004	My heart goes out to the families of...	Sympathy

Figure. 1.3. As news of the fire spreads, students, faculty, alumni, parents of students and members of the community share prayers and messages of mourning on *The Daily Mississippian*'s Web site. *The Daily Mississippian*, University of Mississippi

Journalism and the Movies

■ **Eugenia Chien**

Movies about journalism are great for inspiration, motivation and illumination. Stick a video in the newsroom's DVD player, throw some popcorn in the microwave and gather the staff for an evening of fun flicks and discussion.

The Front Page (1931) What are you willing to do to cover a big story? In this classic comedy, an editor convinces a top reporter to put off his marriage long enough to cover the hottest story in town. The original film stars Pat O'Brien, Adolphe Menjou and Mary Brian. B&W, 99 minutes. (A 1974 remake features Jack Lemmon, Walter Matthau and Susan Sarandon. Color, 105 minutes.)

Foreign Correspondent (1940) A crime reporter turned foreign correspondent is caught up in the espionage and danger of World War I. Alfred Hitchcock's famous scene of an assassin escaping into a sea of rippling umbrellas is just one of the unforgettable images from this movie. Joel McCrea and Laraine Day star. B&W, 120 minutes.

His Girl Friday (1940) In a clever remake of "The Front Page," the tables are turned when an editor (Cary Grant) tries to stop his female star reporter (Rosalind Russell), who happens to be his ex-wife, from leaving the newspaper business. Howard Hawks directs. B&W, 92 minutes.

Citizen Kane (1941) If you don't know what "Rosebud" refers to, you've got to check out this thinly disguised biopic about newspaper publisher William Randolph Hearst. Orson Welles writes, directs and stars. B&W, 119 minutes.

Teacher's Pet (1958) Clark Gable plays a tough city editor who doesn't believe in college-taught journalism. He goes head to head with a journalism professor, played by Doris Day, when he pretends to be a student in her class. B&W, 120 minutes.

All The President's Men (1976) This riveting movie tells the story of how two journalists brought down President Richard Nixon in the Watergate scandal. Dustin Hoffman and Robert Redford play *The Washington Post's* Carl Bernstein and Bob Woodward. Color, 139 minutes.

Absence of Malice (1981) A Miami reporter, played by Sally Field, unknowingly ties an innocent man (Paul Newman) to the murder of a union leader. Color, 116 minutes.

The Year of Living Dangerously (1982) A group of journalists grapples with the political upheaval of the Indonesian government in 1960s Jakarta. Linda Hunt becomes the only actress ever to win an Academy Award playing a man—with no cross dressing or gender confusion involved. Mel Gibson stars. Color, 117 minutes.

Under Fire (1983) A photojournalist finds himself on a mission to photograph a rebel leader in war-torn Nicaragua. Along the way, it becomes difficult for the journalist to stay neutral. Nick Nolte, Ed Harris star. Color, 128 minutes.

The Killing Fields (1984) Based on a true story, this movie explores the relationship between *New York Times* journalist Sidney Schanberg and his Cambodian assistant Dith Pran when Schanberg is unable to help Pran escape the Khmer Rouge. Sam Waterston, Haing S. Ngor star. Color, 142 minutes.

Salvador (1986) A freelance journalist leaves his out-of-control life in San Francisco to cover the bloody civil war in El Salvador. James Woods and James Belushi star. Oliver Stone writes and directs. Color, 122 minutes.

The Paper (1994) This movie captures 24 hours in a hectic New York newsroom, after two young black men are arrested for the murder of two white businessmen. Ron Howard directs. Michael Keaton, Glenn Close and Robert Duvall star. Color, 112 minutes.

Welcome to Sarajevo (1997) American and British journalists find an orphanage in Sarajevo and walk past the line of ethics when they decide to rescue the children. Stephen Dillane, Woody Harrelson star. Color, 102 minutes.

Fear and Loathing in Las Vegas (1998) Legendary gonzo journalist Hunter S. Thompson (Johnny Depp) takes a dizzying, hallucinogenic road trip to Las Vegas with his sidekick, Dr. Gonzo (Benicio Del Toro). Color, 128 minutes.

The Insider (1999) Russell Crowe plays a scientist who violates his contract with a tobacco company when he exposes addictive ingredients in cigarettes. Ethical quandaries arise when broadcast veteran Mike Wallace (Christopher Plummer) and producer Lowell Bergman (Al Pacino) report the story. Color, 157 minutes.

Live from Baghdad (2002) CNN made television news history when it became the only news network remaining in Baghdad on the eve of the first Gulf War. Michael Keaton and Helena Bonham Carter star. Mick Jackson directs. Color, 108 minutes.

Shattered Glass (2003) Stephen Glass, a young journalist at *The New Republic*, had everything: talent, a coveted job and adoring friends. This movie explores how Glass betrayed everyone by fabricating stories. Hayden Christensen, Chloe Sevigny and Peter Sarsgaard star. Color, 94 minutes.

Capote (2005) Philip Seymour Hoffman plays the young Truman Capote as he reports on the murder that inspired his true-crime classic *In Cold Blood*. Color, 114 minutes.

Reflections of a College Newspaper Editor

■ Ed Ronco

Shortly before I graduated from Michigan State University, I had a conversation with my mom about what I had learned. You know, the "how was it?" discussion. College was great, and my professors and classes taught me innumerable things about academic subjects and life in general.

But I had to admit that my most valuable lessons came from working on the student newspaper, *The State News*. Filling the pages of that paper as a reporter, a news editor and finally editor in chief my last year gave me insight into every aspect of journalism, and, also, every aspect of humanity.

I had the chance to write about people who were grieving and celebrating, frustrated and elated. I talked to countless readers on the phone, some who said nice things and others who told me I was a buffoon. (That's fine; maybe I was.)

I got to cover—or lead the coverage of—hundreds of stories, from the formation of a graduate student labor union to the departure of the university president to the war in Iraq.

When some students on our campus rioted in March 2003, our offices were half-newsroom, half-triage unit. As reporters and photographers ran out the door to gather more news, others came back with red and swollen eyes, seeking relief from the tear gas.

When the United States invaded Iraq, we had stories written 30 minutes after President Bush announced the invasion. After watching Bush's statement, our reporters conducted reaction interviews, calling university administrators, local politicians and others, and then returned to the newsroom to assemble it into something coherent, all with lightning speed.

And then there was election night 2004. I'll never forget the scene of that full newsroom in the early hours of the morning, with more than 80 people throwing papers and yelling election totals across the room.

Those were the big successes. The big stories. But it's the smaller things that I hope you get to experience.

I hope you see the lights burning late in your newsroom and hear the crackle of the police scanner that's always on.

I hope you see people going in and out at all hours of the day, forgoing social lives and sometimes academic lives for the sake of an informed campus.

I hope you get to see the presses roll—blurs of gray and black and red and blue that shoot by at astronomical speeds. Our presses were in a warehouse 60 miles away. I'll never forget the smell of the ink.

I hope you see your staff step up to the plate for some of the biggest stories of their lives. And when they do, I hope they hit it out of the park.

I hope you feel the thrill of getting on Page One for the first time, or if you're an editor, I hope you see the look on the face of a rookie reporter you help get there.

I hope you hear the sadness in your co-worker's voice after he's interviewed friends and family members of someone who just died.

I hope you talk to each other at 4 a.m., when one of you can't sleep because you're worried about a story in the next day's paper.

I hope you see a really talented photographer hard at work. I still remember driving one of ours down a two-lane highway in rural Michigan as she snapped photos of a runner from the back of my pickup truck.

I hope you watch your copy desk kick into action—these people actually argue about commas—and see your page designers turn raw text and photos into works of art.

I hope you take time to get to know the people who prepare your paper for press and troubleshoot your technical problems. Ours were the finest and smartest bunch of people I have ever met, and modest, too—they never once stood up and took a bow or even asked for the opportunity.

And I hope you get to know the people who get up before the sun, the ones who complete the miracle. We had a group of 12 carriers who rose at 5:30 every morning to distribute 28,500 copies of our newspaper around the campus and city by 8 a.m.

When the time comes for you to walk away from it all, I hope you leave secure in the knowledge that people will continue to sweat and toil over keyboards and continue to produce good journalism night after night so your campus can read it morning after morning.

And when you get out into the professional world, I hope you can say to an editor, "Oh yeah, I've done that before."

Ed Ronco served as editor in chief of The State News *at Michigan State University in 2004. During his previous years at the paper he was also deputy managing editor, campus news editor, administration reporter and graduate issues reporter. He graduated in December 2004 with a bachelor's degree in journalism and went on to do internships with the* St. Louis Post-Dispatch *and the* Grand Rapids (Mich.) Press. *He is a business reporter for the* South Bend (Ind.) Tribune.

The Watchdog

Colleges and universities may be institutions of learning, but they can also be hotbeds of corruption and scandal. Some undertake questionable research; some misuse state funds; some employ sexual predators.

And on many campuses, the student newspaper is the only institution able to investigate and report such matters.

The Daily Mississippian took its watchdog role seriously after the fraternity house fire. When fire investigators seemed to be holding back information about the cause of the blaze, a *Daily Mississippian* editorial demanded answers. Reporters filed several Freedom of Information Act requests to find out what investigators knew. When government officials finally turned over the investigation report more than six months after the fire, Carrington, the editor in chief, posted the entire document on the newspaper's Web site.

"People really wanted to know what happened," she says. "We felt the community could use it to gain some closure on this tragedy."

The Training Ground

Countless professional journalists got their start at college newspapers. Broadcast journalists Bill Moyers and Walter Cronkite worked at *The Daily Texan*, the student newspaper of the University of Texas at Austin. Michael Isikoff, who broke the Monica Lewinsky story for *Newsweek*, reported for *Student Life* at Washington University in St. Louis. James Fallows, David Halberstam, Michael Kinsley and Susan Faludi all served as editors of *The Harvard Crimson*. Columnist Molly Ivins began to hone her razor-sharp pen in the pages of *The Sophian* at Smith College, and Garry Trudeau created the prototype for Doonesbury for the *Yale Daily News*.

Many believe student newspapers, more even than journalism degree programs, are the best way to launch a career in the field. The clips and experience you get at your college paper can pave the way to internships and jobs.

Challenges of Student Newspapers

Putting out a student paper can be one of the most exciting parts of your college career, but it can also be filled with frustrations. Student journalists often don't feel the power and confidence that professionals do. Among the common problems:

Lack of respect. "As a student journalist, it can be tough to get readers and sources to take you seriously," says Becky Sher, managing editor of special sections at Knight Ridder/Tribune in Washington, D.C., and former editor in chief of the *GW Hatchet* at George Washington University in Washington, D.C. "Off-campus sources can present a particular problem." Administrators and faculty also sometimes fail to give students due consideration.

Conflicts of interest. Even more than professional journalists, student journalists face the challenge of covering the community in which they live. That sometimes means writing about the health violations at the dining hall, the melee after your friend's dorm party or the tenure battle of your favorite English professor. "There are times you can recuse yourself from a story you're too close to, but there are other times that you can't," says Sher. "After all, the latest tuition hike affects you, too."

Inexperience. The most seasoned college newspaper staffer may have three or four years under his belt, but many start writing stories, shooting photographs, selling ads, or designing pages with little or no training. That lack of experience can lead to serious mistakes that are on display for the whole campus—or, in the case of an error picked up by the mass media, the whole world.

Interference. While some student newspapers exist in a climate of complete respect for their First Amendment rights, many don't. Every year, administrators at colleges across the country challenge student newspapers that stir up trouble or embarrass the campus.

Getting Help

Fortunately, there are resources to help. Most college newspapers have an adviser to guide students through the sometimes-choppy waters of newspaper publishing. If yours doesn't, find a professor or professional journalist you trust to become a mentor or unofficial adviser. Take advantage of local press clubs, Society of Professional Journalists chapters and other media groups in your area that can offer advice.

Several national organizations exist solely to support the student press. The Student Press Law Center in Arlington, Va., a tireless advocate for student-press rights, offers free legal advice to student newspapers. Associated Collegiate Press, a nonprofit educational membership association in Minneapolis, Minn., and College Media Advisers, a professional association of advisers, sponsor contests, conventions and advocacy services for member newspapers. And many states have statewide student press associations to support student media.

To Do:

1. Many people on college campuses—especially administrators—don't understand the role of the student press or the basic tenets of press freedom. Early in the school year, plan a meeting with key campus officials to discuss the various roles your paper plays and the importance of press freedom.

2. Plan an open house to acquaint the campus community with your paper. Create displays of major stories and photos. Explain how the paper works, how students can join the staff or contribute material on a freelance basis, how people can send in press releases and letters to the editor.

3. Invite a marketing class on campus to organize a focus group of students to critique your paper. (If you can't get a class to do it, organize a focus group yourself.) Ask participants what they see as the role of your student paper and how well you serve that role. Find out what they like and don't like. Then analyze the responses and see how you can better fulfill their expectations.

4. Conduct a reader survey to find out what readers like about your paper and what they don't like. Develop an action plan to address their concerns.

To Read:

Kovach, Bill and Tom Rosenstiel. *The Elements of Journalism*. New York: Crown Publishers, 2001.

Dardenne, Robert. *A Free and Responsible Student Press: An Ideal Vision of How Community and Communication Can Preserve Scholastic Journalism*. Poynter Paper No. 8. St. Petersburg, Fla.: Poynter Institute for Media Studies, 1996.

Available for free downloading at http://poynteronline.org/shop/product_view.asp?id=689

To Click:

Associated Collegiate Press
http://www.studentpress.org/acp/

College Media Advisers
http://collegemedia.org/

Columbia Scholastic Press Association
http://www.columbia.edu/cu/cspa/

Society of Professional Journalists
http://www.spj.org/

Student Media Sourcebook
http://studentpress.journ.umn.edu/sourcebook/

Student Press Law Center
http://www.splc.org/

From the chancellor's censure to the Wolfpack's Gator Bowl victory –

Technician was there.

As N.C. State's daily student newspaper, the Technician has been the voice of N.C. State students since 1920. Each day, more than 15,000 copies are picked up by faculty, staff and students from some 60 dropboxes on campus.

The largest student publication on campus, the Technician reporters cover university news, people and events. They have the front seat to Wolfpack athletics and give voice to student opinions. Each issue is the place to fi nd the latest campus happenings, as well as student reviews, the crossword puzzle and campus classifieds.

But Technician is more than just the paper to pick up on the way to class – it's a great way to get involved in university life.

From the chancellor's censure to the Wolfpack's Gator Bowl victory over Notre Dame – Technician was there.

Technician Open House
Sept. 2, 7 p.m. • 323 Witherspoon Student Center

Figure 2.1. The *Technician* at North Carolina State University in Raleigh, N.C., hosts an open house every fall to recruit staff. *Technician*, North Carolina State University

Chapter 2

Recruiting and Training Your Staff

P rofessional newspaper editors are always grumbling about the difficulties of recruiting, retaining and training a staff. But compared to student editors, they've got it easy. Most managing editors have a stack of resumes on their desks from young journalists eager to work for them. A phone call to the local college journalism program or a listing on

Chapter Contents

- Recruiting a Staff
- Training Your Staff
- Tips for Organizing Staff Training Sessions
- Checklist: Planning a Training Seminar
- Creating a Staff Manual
- Mentoring
- Training Exercises
- Diversity Training
- Motivating Your Staff
- Q&A: Miguel M. Morales

a journalism jobs Web site will yield even more qualified applicants. Most have a seasoned reporter or two willing to show the newbies the ropes. And while pay for journalists is relatively low, professional newspapers can offer enough compensation to keep people coming to work every day.

Now think of the typical student newspaper editor trying to put together a staff. Where is she going to find a group of talented people willing to work for little or no pay? How will she train them if her most experienced staffers have only a couple of years—or sometimes only a few months—on the job? And how will she keep them motivated when they can make more money washing dishes in the cafeteria?

The key is to make working for your newspaper the best experience it can be.

Recruiting a Staff

Well-established newspapers at large universities usually have systems and traditions for recruiting staff. At the University of California, Los Angeles, for example, *The Daily Bruin* recruits with an open house every quarter and information tables during orientation week. Application forms are posted on the newspaper's Web site along with information about how the newspaper works. Media Adviser Amy Emmert says about 200 students apply for positions on the paper every fall. "We accept about half of those," she says.

At smaller schools, however, recruiting enough students to put out even 12 or 16 pages every week or two can be a formidable task. Commuter schools, where most students live off campus and many students work, may find recruitment especially difficult.

Nils Rosdahl, adviser to the award-winning *Sentinel* at North Idaho College, a community college in Coeur d'Alene with about 4,000 students, starts recruiting at the high school level. Each October, he organizes a high school media day that attracts about 300 young journalists from 15 high schools in three states. Journalists from the two professional newspapers in town lead most of the sessions, but Rosdahl takes a few minutes at the beginning of the day to introduce his journalism program and the biweekly student newspaper. He also schedules annual visits to many of the high school newspapers in Idaho and neighboring Montana and Washington.

"I give a constructive critique of their paper and then I let them know what we offer," says Rosdahl, who worked as a sports writer and editor for newspapers in Chicago and Seattle before he started advising in 1986.

The first week of school Rosdahl visits photography, journalism, graphic design and

Tips for Organizing Staff Training Sessions

Student newspapers should schedule training sessions each time the staff turns over. If you have a large staff, you may want to organize special sections for reporters, editors, photographers and designers. If your staff is small, you'll probably want to have one training for editors and another for the staff as a whole. Here are some tips for making training sessions effective.

1. **Survey the staff.** Ask both returning and incoming staffers what skills they'd most like to learn.
2. **Get organized.** Assign a person or a committee to organize the training. Typically, advisers and top editors or teams of editors create training programs.
3. **Find time.** Decide how much time to devote to training. Some newspapers sponsor multi-day or even multi-week seminars. Others can only spare a day or two.
4. **Arrange the date early.** That way students can plan vacations and work schedules around it. A week or two before the term starts is usually best, although some papers find they get better attendance if they schedule training a day or two before classes start.
5. **Set a budget.** If your newspaper has the money, you may want to arrange for meals or a special venue for the training, such as a hotel, restaurant or conference center. If your budget is tight, you can hold the training in your newsroom or in classrooms and have students handle lunch on their own. If meals are too pricey, provide drinks and snacks to keep people's energy up.
6. **Recruit local journalists.** Invite pros to lead workshops. Alumni of your newspaper who are now working in the field can be especially effective and inspiring.
7. **Learn the law.** Invite your newspaper's attorney, a law professor or other media law expert to offer a session on legal issues, such as libel, copyright and open meetings and records laws.
8. **Break the ice.** If the staffers don't all know each other, open the training with introductions or ice breakers so people can get to know each other.
9. **Mix it up.** Make sure some of the activities are interactive; intersperse large-group sessions with small-group discussions or exercises.
10. **End on a high note.** Conclude the training with an informal social gathering, such as a pizza party. Encourage veteran staffers to mingle with new people.

marketing classes on campus to recruit potential staffers. "I let them know this is really good for developing their portfolio. Working for *The Sentinel*, they can get their work published and get their name in print. It's also a good opportunity for getting scholarships and internships."

Rosdahl believes the best recruiting tool is developing the reputation of the paper as a fun and satisfying place to work. During his two decades as an adviser, Rosdahl has created an inviting newsroom that many students come to think of as a second home. "We have lockers where they can keep their bookbags, a microwave oven, dishes, a refrigerator, a couch, comfortable chairs—everything to make them comfortable. It's really a homeroom atmosphere. They hang out there, their friends hang out there and then we recruit their friends."

In recruiting, take advantage of campus intranet services, bulletin boards, video announcement boards, radio stations and other communication devices—as well as your own paper and Web site—to put out the word you're hiring. Some college career services offices also post on-campus jobs.

Training Your Staff

Once you've assembled a staff, it's important to orient the new players and make your expectations clear. Most newspapers schedule staff trainings in the late summer before the new term starts or at the beginning of each semester, trimester or quarter. Some newspapers organize distinct sessions for reporters, photographers, editors and designers, as well as orientation events for the entire staff.

The Daily Bruin at UCLA has one of the most sophisticated and well-organized training programs around. All new editorial staffers are required to attend a series of four four-hour Saturday training sessions in one of eight departments—news reporting and writing; sportswriting; copyediting; design; photojournalism; online media; arts reporting and writing; and graphics/illustration. The sessions are led by professional journalists from *The Los Angeles Times, Orange County Register* and other Southern California news organizations.

Editors are required to attend summer training sessions—four weeks of sessions in leadership, management and editing skills. Throughout the term the paper offers optional training workshops in specific skills such as accessing public documents, headline writing, feature writing and creating complex graphics.

Most student newspapers don't have such extensive resources, but every paper should have some kind of orientation for new staffers and leadership training for editors. If yours doesn't, talk to your adviser or editor. (For more on training see Tips for Organizing Staff Training Sessions).

Patricia Tisak organized a leadership seminar for her editors when she was editor in chief of *The Daily Collegian* at Pennsylvania State University in 2000. "We played the requisite cheesy bonding games, but we also discussed story ideas, major goals for the various departments, newspaper policy and motivation techniques for our staff," says Tisak, who became a copy editor for *The Philadelphia Inquirer* after graduating in 2001. "Because the dynamic of a college newspaper changes so quickly with the graduation of each class, it's important for editors to get together and have a discussion on the newspaper's standards. It's important to set the tone early so that the staff is on the same page."

Training workshops should also include team-building exercises. *The Nicholls Worth*, the newspaper at Nicholls State University in Thibodaux, La., for example, ends its three-day staff training each summer with a treasure hunt. Teams of student newspaper staffers are instructed to comb the campus looking for clues, which have been set up in advance. The hunt doesn't just build team spirit; it also introduces students to people and parts of the campus they may not have encountered before.

Training should continue through the term. If someone on the staff has done exemplary work, invite her to speak about how she got that story or photo. Organize periodic brown-bag luncheons and invite professional journalists, journalism professors or others to speak. A time management expert on campus might be tapped for a workshop on handling deadlines; ask a meditation or yoga teacher to offer some tips on stress management.

Students can also take advantage of regional, statewide and national training programs and conventions offered by College Media Advisers, Associated Collegiate Press, the Cox Institute for Newspaper Management Studies, Investigative Reporters and Editors and other groups listed at the end of this chapter.

Creating a Staff Manual
One of the most important tools for orienting your staff is a staff manual that includes all the rules and procedures by which your newspaper operates.

If your paper is still using the same old staff manual that's been hanging around for years, it's probably time to update it. And if you don't have one at all, start work on one right away.

A good staff manual can:

- Give the paper a foundation and sense of continuity, even in the face of high turnover
- Serve as a newsroom reference book
- Orient new staffers and help them understand what's expected of them
- Help staffers resolve conflicts

"I view the handbook as a bible—the highest ranking document in the newsroom," says Ira David Levy, adviser to *Diversity*, the monthly college newspaper at Wilbur Wright College in Chicago. "A handbook serves as a point of reference for continual newsroom policies. It also teaches new staff members how things work and what to expect."

The staff manual can also be used to educate your readers about how your newspaper works. Some student newspapers, including *The Cavalier Daily* at the University of Virginia, prominently post their staff manuals on their Web sites for all to see.

Most staff manuals have several of the following sections:

- A list of staff positions and job descriptions
- An ethics policy
- Policies about letters to the editor, anonymous sources, deadlines, freelance contributions, advertising and other issues relevant to the working of the publication
- A stylebook (which may be a separate document or included in the staff manual)

Some staff manuals also include tips on reporting, writing, photojournalism, conflict resolution and avoiding libel.

Mentoring
Mentor relationships are vital in journalism—both for learning the ropes and snagging jobs and internships—and the best student newspapers have systems to cultivate such relationships. A mentor is a more experienced person who can nurture, teach and counsel a young journalist. It can be a fellow reporter on the student paper who has been around a little longer, an editor, an adviser or a professional journalist.

Some student newspapers have a buddy system that links incoming reporters to more experienced staffers; others assign a senior staffer to act as a writing coach.

Miguel M. Morales became a writing coach for *The Campus Ledger* when he was a student at Johnson County Community College in Overland Park, Kan., after serving as a staff reporter, features editor, managing editor and editor in chief for the biweekly paper. "I try to work with reporters in all stages of the process," Morales says. "I provide tips and introduce new skills for the stories they may have to write. I don't force my coaching on staff members, though sometimes their editors make them meet with me."

The Daily Bruin lines up professional journalists to serve as writing coaches. The Center for Integration and Improvement of Journalism at San Francisco State University pairs interested students with writing and photo coaches, most of whom work for local news organizations. Students are encouraged to meet with their coaches every week to discuss assignments and review copy.

Training Exercises

#1: Story Idea Hunt

Break participants into groups of three or four. Make sure each group has people in a variety of positions—editor, reporter, photographer, designer etc.

Send the groups out on campus for half an hour and instruct them to come back with at least three story ideas. You may assign each team to go to a certain building or part of campus or allow them to go wherever they choose.

When the groups return have them pitch the story ideas to the whole staff. Make a list of the story ideas on a board and then discuss which would make good stories for the paper.

#2: Project Planning

Arrange participants in two concentric circles: In the smaller, inner circle place the editor in chief, opinion editor, photo editor or chief photographer, news editor, art director or lead designer, graphics editor, online editor (and possibly two or three other editors). The rest of the group should sit in a circle around them.

Then propose a news scenario—the adoption of new smoking restrictions on campus, flooding in the student health center, a visit to campus by the president of the United States.

Have the inner group spend 15 minutes planning how the paper will cover the story. Then have the outer group critique the planning process by addressing these questions:

1. Did anyone dominate the conversation?
2. Did everyone get a chance to speak?
3. Did the group discuss photos as well as text?
4. Did the group come up with good ideas for graphics?
5. Did the group come up with innovative ideas for presenting the story on the Web?
6. Did the group miss any important angles on the story?
7. What was productive about the discussion? What wasn't productive?

Then break the rest of the staff into small groups to discuss real upcoming stories and how they can enhance those stories with graphics, photos and special online features such as discussion boards, links, polls, slide shows and multimedia reports.

#3: Interviewing

Break participants into groups of three. In each, one person plays the role of a reporter and one the role of a source. The third person is an observer who will take notes on the interaction.

Have the reporter interview the source for five minutes for a short biographical profile.

Next, have members of the group rotate. The observer becomes the reporter, the reporter becomes the source, the source becomes the observer. Have the new reporter interview the source for five minutes.

Then switch one more time. By now, each person has played every role.

Finally, have the groups discuss the interactions.

1. What did the observers notice? Did the reporters establish rapport with the sources? How were the reporters at drawing out their sources? Did they follow up on interesting things the sources said?
2. How did the sources feel about the interaction? Did the reporters make them feel comfortable? Did they feel heard?
3. How did the reporters feel about the interaction? What do they think they did well? How do they think they could have improved?

If time permits, you could expand this exercise by giving each reporter time to write a brief profile of the source and then discuss the stories.

#4: Scavenger Hunt

During a training workshop for editors or for the whole staff, divide participants into groups of four or five. Try to group people with others they don't know well or with whom they don't normally work.

Hand each group a campus map, then tell the groups to come back in a set amount of time (an hour and a half works well) with as many of these items as they can collect (or come up with your own list):

- A bus schedule for a line that goes to campus
- Three fliers for different campus events
- A brochure from the student health center
- A menu from a campus restaurant
- A brochure from an academic department
- A game schedule for an athletic team
- A library map (or some other handout readily available at the library).

Reward the winning team with a gift certificate or coupons to a campus eatery and encourage them to celebrate their victory with a meal together.

Ralph Braseth, director of student media at the University of Mississippi, recommends editors at *The Daily Mississippian* contact their counterparts at a local professional newspaper to seek advice. Obviously, the top editor at a big-city newspaper may not have time to meet with the college paper's editor in chief, but many professional editors are more than happy to mentor up-and-coming journalists. Students should also look for mentors in advisers, journalism faculty members or other writing teachers.

Diversity Training

Is it appropriate for a female reporter to shake hands with an Orthodox Jewish man? Will a person who uses a wheelchair be offended if you stand during an interview? Should you refer to a transgender person as he or she—or is there a preferable term?[1]

---

1. Orthodox Jewish men generally don't shake hands with women who are not their wives. A person in a wheelchair probably will not be offended if you stand for an interview, but it's better to sit if you can. Transgender people generally prefer the pronoun that relates to how they are living their lives, regardless of surgical status. A female-to-male transsexual, for example, should be referred to as "he." Some use the pronoun "ze" for he/she and "hir" for his/her.

Covering a diverse community can enrich you as a journalist and a human being. But it can also raise uncomfortable challenges. In recent years professional newspapers have started to train staffers in cultural competency and student newspapers are beginning to follow suit.

When she was on the staff of *The Daily Collegian*, Patricia Tisak organized a mandatory diversity training program for all new staff members. "During this training, I led discussions on race and ethnicity issues and went over *Collegian* guidelines and policies," Tisak says. "For example, I inevitably encountered at least one new staffer who didn't understand why the term 'Oriental' might be offensive to some when applied to a person of Asian heritage."

To organize a diversity training program, invite professors in ethnic and religious studies departments or student leaders of cultural or religious groups to meet with your staff. Have someone from your campus disability resource center and the gay, lesbian and transgender organizations on campus discuss issues pertinent to those groups. Professional journalists from mainstream newspapers and the ethnic or gay and lesbian press can also offer insights about covering various groups.

Be sure to incorporate what you learn into your newspaper's stylebook and staff manual.

For more ideas about diversity training, check out the Web site of the Poynter Institute for Media Studies, listed in the resources section at the end of this chapter.

Motivating Your Staff

It's the middle of the semester. Everyone's studying for mid-terms and frantically trying to catch up in the classes they've been ignoring in their devotion to the newspaper. The newsroom is virtually empty—except for that guy fast asleep on the couch. How are you going to put out a newspaper this week?

Motivation is a chronic problem at all newspapers, but student newspapers suffer most of all. With little or no pay and competing interests (classes, jobs, spring break, the Big Game, love, graduation, the bar down the street), work for the school paper often gets pushed down the priority list a month or two into the term. How can you keep your staff motivated?

Stroke them every way you can. That means rewards and awards, free food and drinks, pats on the back and shoulder massages. Everyone wants to feel appreciated.

Though *The Sentinel* at North Idaho College doesn't pay writers and photographers, Rosdahl provides lots of incentives to keep staffers committed. He's arranged for his seven editors to get full-ride scholarships "just as if they were on the basketball team. Not only are they doing the school a service

but they're actually going to use the skills they learn when they get out of school, whereas a basketball player probably isn't."

The Sentinel's journalism club raises about $4,000 each year through a book swap the first week of each semester. That pays for trips to national conventions as well as food and other perks. The paper also arranges a lot of ads in trade "so instead of money we get free food, free bowling, free car washes," Rosdahl says. "Students who do a good job win these prizes."

As a student, you probably can't arrange for such enticing perks as full scholarships. But you can make working for the newspaper fun. When you see morale flagging, organize a party or invite the staff out for drinks.

Awards are effective motivators, too. Advisers and editors shouldn't wait for the end of the semester to honor exemplary work. Best-of-the week awards lift staff morale. Dave Waddell, adviser to *The Orion* at California State University, Chico, gives out mugs emblazoned with the paper's name each week to reward good work. Don't have money for promotional mugs? Even paper citations and applause will keep staff members coming back for more.

To Do:

1. Take a look at your current recruiting practices. If your staff isn't as large or as committed as you'd like, try some new recruitment techniques such as those suggested in this chapter. Schedule an open house at the beginning of the term with tours of your newsroom (and don't forget munchies—there's nothing that brings in the crowds like free food).
2. Review your staff training program. Is it sufficient or could you be doing more? Discuss options for more extensive training with your editor or adviser.
3. Invite local journalists to lead workshops on various topics such as photojournalism, headline writing, investigative reporting and page design.
4. Plan a field trip for your editors or your entire staff to a local newspaper. Ask to sit in on an editors' meeting. As an alternative, arrange for individuals or small groups of students to shadow a person or spend time in a department, such as the copy desk, sports department, graphics department or editorial board.
5. If you don't already have one, set up a coaching program. Enlist reporters, editors, photographers, designers and graphic artists from local media organizations to meet on a regular basis with students. You may set up one-on-one relationships or ask a professional to hold regular office hours once or twice a month. Alumni working for local profes-

sional news organizations may be particularly helpful.
6. Find out about local, regional and national conventions and training programs (see Web sites below). If your newspaper cannot afford to pay the expenses, see about getting funding from a local news organization, student government, your journalism or communication program or other source. Or organize a fund-raising event to send staffers to training events.

To Read:

Clark, James C. *Newspaper Training Editors Guide*. Arlington, Va.: The Freedom Forum, 1999. (*This book is out of print but is available for downloading at* http://www.freedomforum.org/templates/document.asp?documentID=13829).

To Click:

American Press Institute
http://www.americanpressinstitute.org/

Associated Collegiate Press
http://www.studentpress.org/acp/

College Media Advisers
http://www.collegemedia.org/

Cox Institute for Newspaper Management Studies
http://www.grady.uga.edu/CoxInstitute/

Journalism Association of Community Colleges
http://www.jacconline.org

Journalism Training.org
http://www.journalismtraining.org

Newsroom Leadership Group
http://www.newsroomleadership.com

No Train No Gain
http://www.notrain-nogain.com/

Poynter Institute for Media Studies
http://poynter.org/seminar/

Society for Collegiate Journalists
http://www.scj.us

Western Association of University Publications Managers
http://www.waupm.org/

State College Press Associations
Many states have press associations or student media associations that offer training opportunities for student journalists. Among them are:

Arkansas Collegiate Press Association

California College Media Association
http://calcollegemedia.org

Florida Community College Activities
   Association
http://www.flccaa.org/StudentPublications.html

Georgia College Press Association
http://www.gapress.org/gcpa.html

Iowa College Media Association

Illinois College Press Association
http://titan.iwu.edu/~jplath/members.html

Indiana Collegiate Press Association
http://www.indianacollegiatepress.org/

Kansas Associated Collegiate Press
http://www.kacponline.org/

Kentucky Intercollegiate Press Association
http://www.kycollegepress.org/

Michigan Collegiate Press Association
http://www.michiganpress.org/index/40

Missouri College Media Association
http://www.mcmachronicle.com/

Nebraska Collegiate Media Association

New Jersey Collegiate Press Association
http://www.njpa.org/collegepress/

Texas Intercollegiate Press Association
http://www.texasipa.org

Question & Answer

What do you do as a writing coach?

My job is to act as a back-up editor in chief, a back-up managing editor and a front-end adviser. I catch things that fall through the cracks when reporters, section editors, the copy desk, the managing editor and the editor in chief don't. I anticipate problems and their solutions. I provide skills training and counseling. I am the personal and professional conscience of the newsroom.

I advocate for the staff. I give them what they need to do their jobs successfully. Sometimes it's a pep talk or a shoulder to cry on, or I research a problem to find a handout or Web site that can help. Other times it means talking with the editor in chief and the managing editor about issue planning, motivating the staff or disciplinary action.

My job changes with the needs of the newsroom. Some days I am the peace keeper, other days I light the fire, other days I bring down the hammer.

How did you prepare to become a writing coach?

I approached it the way I approach a story, through research. I found the best sources and interviewed them. They made time to help me, so I make time to help others.

Since writing coach is a new position, one I haven't seen another college paper institute, I take my lead from professional coaches like Steve Buttry (former writing coach for the *Omaha World-Herald*), Don Fry (co-author of *Coaching Writers: Editors and Reporters Working Together Across Media Platforms*), and other members of Newscoach (a discussion list for newsroom trainers sponsored by the Poynter Institute).

How do you coach reporters?

Whenever I am in the office and a reporter or photographer has come back from an inter-

■ **Miguel M. Morales**

After serving as a reporter, features editor, managing editor and editor in chief of The Campus Ledger *at Johnson County Community College in Overland Park, Kansas, Miguel Morales became the newspaper's writing coach. At a student paper, Morales says, a writing coach can facilitate student journalists' transition from the classroom to the newsroom.*

view or shoot, I stop whatever I'm doing. I ask them how it went and what they covered. Reporters and photographers need to debrief. They need to talk about how the subject was a jerk or about something funny that happened. I also ask questions: What did he (or she) mean by that? Does that answer make sense based on the other interviews you've done? What did their office look like?

This helps them crystallize aspects of the interview they need for the story and identify follow-up questions.

Do you also coach editors?

Yes. Students find it difficult to go from being a reporter, where he or she is strictly responsible for his or her story, to a section editor responsible for five or more stories they didn't write.

I have three goals when coaching editors:

1. Help them learn the reporter's voice.
2. Help them edit in the reporter's voice.
3. When possible, have the editor and the reporter edit together. If not possible, the editor needs to inform the reporter of needed changes and give the reporter the opportunity to make the changes before publication.

What resources have you found that may be useful to other college newspapers?

Every college paper has "trades." The trades are papers we receive from other schools in exchange for ours. I use these as coaching tools. I go through them for story ideas to see what other campus papers cover and how well (or badly) they do it. I tear out examples of good photography, graphics, layouts, headlines, ledes and even ads. I post these at the desk of the appropriate staff member.

The papers I haven't chopped up I distribute at a staff meeting (usually once a semester) and have the staff pick three things the paper does better than our paper and three things we do better than them. We gain insight on our paper. I can't believe we used to throw them away. Now they are teaching tools. That's what I call recycling newspapers!

I constantly search for online resources for my staff. Obitpage.com offers examples of how to write an obituary. The American Copy Editors Society (copydesk.org) offers AP and style quizzes. Glossarist.com offers a searchable directory of glossaries and topical dictionaries. I also use No Train, No Gain and Edward Miller's Reflections on Leadership. I constantly rely on their insights in coaching my newsroom. Professional organizations like the Society of Professional Journalists, American Society of Newspaper Editors, National Association of Hispanic Journalists, National Association of Black Journalists, Asian American Journalists Association and Native American Journalists Association offer scholarships, student membership and/or programs targeting student journalists. These organizations introduced me to coaching and professionalism in the newsroom.

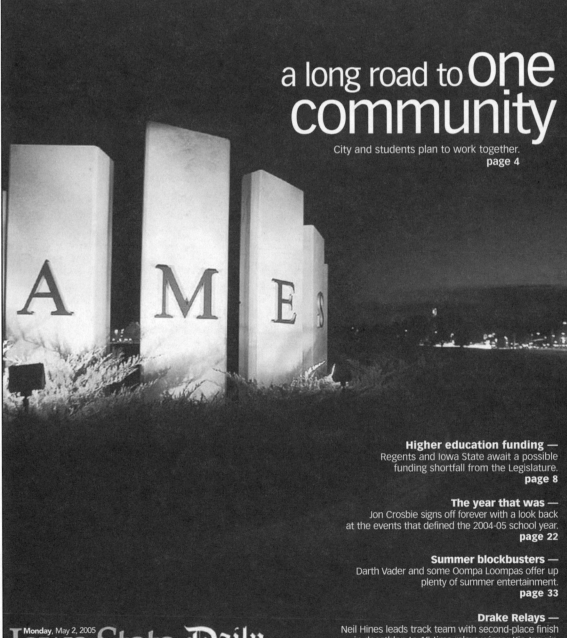

a long road to **one community**
City and students plan to work together.
page 4

Higher education funding —
Regents and Iowa State await a possible
funding shortfall from the Legislature.
page 8

The year that was —
Jon Crosbie signs off forever with a look back
at the events that defined the 2004-05 school year.
page 22

Summer blockbusters —
Darth Vader and some Oompa Loompas offer up
plenty of summer entertainment.
page 33

Drake Relays —
Neil Hines leads track team with second-place finish
in decathlon to 15-time relays winner Kip Janvrin.
page 60

Monday, May 2, 2005
Iowa State Daily

Figure 3.1. Covering a campus means covering a community—students, faculty, staff, as well as the city or town where your campus makes its home. *Iowa State Daily,* Iowa State University

Chapter 3

Covering a Campus

A college campus, even a small one, is like a miniature city. It has its own political establishment (the administration), policy makers (faculty senate, student government), merchants (campus bookstore, food vendors, and other on- and off-campus businesses that serve the college community), residents (students, as well as the faculty and staff who spend their days there). It has its local celebrities (the president, university police chief, noted professors) and its disenfranchised (janitors, restaurant workers, and, some might argue, teaching assistants). Most schools have some kind of health care system and police force.

The typical college campus also has the legal battles, crime, capital improvement projects, union disputes and political entanglements that every small city has, but on top of that, it has fervent intellectual discussion and ground-breaking research that may reach far beyond the borders of the campus. Add to that a dynamic cast of characters—with new faculty, staff and students joining the community every year—and you've got the makings of a darn good news town.

Any student journalist who says, "This campus is so dull. There's no news here," simply isn't looking.

But knowing where to look and how to look isn't second nature.

As we discussed in Chapter 1, your paper may be the only consistent and unbiased vehicle for campus news. Even if local media organizations report on your college, they probably don't have the time, space and contacts to cover your school community as thoroughly as you can. With a staff of reporters dedicated to covering your campus, you should be able to snoop out stories even the most experienced professional reporter would have a hard time finding.

Developing a Beat System

The most efficient way to cover a campus is to develop a coordinated beat system. "The whole idea of reporting on a community is to place people at what I call 'surveillance points,'" says Melvin Mencher, a longtime journalism educator and author of the classic journalism textbook *News Reporting and Writing*. "That way they're apt to find out what's happening."

Virtually all professional news organizations and many college newspapers assign reporters to cover a particular subject area, or beat. Beats may be organized by:

- Subject matter (e.g. crime, politics, health)
- Institution (campus police department, student government, student health center)
- Academic unit (the law school, the political science department, the school of medicine)

Or they may be organized by some combination of these three. The crime reporter, for example, may cover the campus police department as well as the department of criminology; the politics reporter may cover student government, the faculty senate, and the political science department. (For examples of beat structures see Beats for Newspaper

Staffs. Also see the Beat Form at the end of this chapter.)

No single beat system will work for all campuses. Yours should be based on the size of your staff, the type of campus you cover and the issues that are most relevant to your community. A small paper might have one student covering science, health and technology, while a large paper on a big, research-oriented campus may have a team of six reporters assigned to life sciences, medicine, agriculture, nursing, technology and astronomy. A major campus issue, such as budget cuts or the search for a new university president, may warrant its own beat. Some student papers that cover racially diverse campuses assign reporters to diversity or race relations beats.

If drinking is a major part of life on your campus you could even assign a reporter to an alcohol beat. Stories that could come out of such a beat: news on changes in enforcement of drinking laws or drinking-related injuries, profiles of local bartenders, features on the oldest bar or most popular bar in town or on special events like trivia or karaoke nights. One year *Golden Gate [X]press*, the weekly paper at San Francisco State University, created a sex, drugs and rock 'n' roll beat that gave rise to a front-page story on students hooking up in bathrooms in the Humanities Building. To be sure, it was one of the best read stories of the year.

Other papers have created special beats for senior reporters. *The State News*, the daily student paper at Michigan State University, has a "news enterprise" beat. "This has allowed one of our most experienced reporters to pursue more in-depth news and news-feature stories without the pressure of daily deadlines," says Editorial Adviser Perry Parks. During the war in Iraq, the reporter wrote about a former Iraqi nuclear scientist who attended Michigan State and a local company that produces the anthrax vaccine. He also produced an in-depth feature about a center on campus that researches and investigates identity theft.

Reporters aren't the only ones who can benefit from having a beat. Some newspapers assign photographers to beats, as well. At *Golden Gate [X]press*, photographers have been assigned to cover particular buildings or physical areas on campus. A photographer responsible for the Creative Arts Building, for example, may poke around rehearsal rooms and theaters, while a photographer assigned to the Science Building may happen upon interesting experiments and scientific research.

One year a photographer covering the campus athletic fields discovered the university had spent a staggering $19 million on a new baseball field—this at a school that was cutting classes in response to a budget crisis.

The photographer brought the story to a reporter and the two produced an impressive investigative piece, complete with a photo essay on the construction of the field.

Cultivating Sources

Once you've been assigned a beat, your first job is to start developing sources—getting to know people who can clue you in on the issues and personalities you'll be covering. You want to meet the major players—the department chairs, administrators, coaches, club leaders—and other official sources. But you also want to get to know the other players, such as student employees and teaching assistants, janitors and secretaries, any of whom may tip you off to good stories.

Try to build relationships with your sources by developing rapport and letting them know you want to hear what they have to say. "Beat coverage involves a lot of talking that isn't formal interviewing," says Parks. "Part of your work is not just reporting specific stories but looking for your next story, or your next scoop."

With each potential source you meet, ask lots of questions. What are you working on now? What new programs or projects are you developing? What problems do you face? What would you like to change in your department or at the school? Most important, ask for ideas about what your paper *should* be covering. Keep in mind, journalism is a two-way street. You want story ideas; many of your sources want the publicity only you can offer.

After you've met a source, take note of the person's name and vital information, including title, phone numbers (when possible, get home and cell phone numbers as well as office numbers), e-mail addresses and campus address. You may also jot down story ideas and other information the person gave you. Develop a system for keeping track of your sources. Some reporters plug such information into a computer database; others use a PDA. Some prefer an old-fashioned Rolodex or a card file. Whatever the system, make sure you're consistent about updating it and refer back to it regularly.

In addition to developing sources, beat reporters are expected to keep on top of significant events on their beats. A reporter assigned to cover the faculty senate or student government, for example, should cover all of that body's meetings. Even if a meeting seems to have a dull agenda, interesting stories may come out it. Sometimes a seemingly boring or bureaucratic issue will spark a heated debate. And interesting topics may come up during discussions or in before- and after-meeting informal chats.

Police or crime reporters should stop in at the campus police or public safety office on a

Beats for Newspaper Staffs

How beats are divvied up depends on the size of your staff and the type of campus you cover.

Beats for a Small Newspaper Staff

Here's a beat structure that might work for a staff of 10 or fewer reporters:

- **Crime and safety:** campus and city police, crime, safety-oriented organizations
- **City/community:** city politics, neighborhood issues around your campus
- **Academics** (one or two reporters): all academic departments
- **Administration:** school policies and administration officials
- **Campus politics:** student government, faculty senate, political organizations on campus
- **Sports** (one or two reporters): intramural and collegiate sports, physical education
- **Arts and entertainment:** music, dance, theater, film, art, etc.
- **Lifestyle:** clubs, activities, recreation and housing
- **Science and health:** personal health, scientific research

Beats for a Medium or Large Newspaper Staff

Here's a sample beat structure that might work for a medium to large staff. Note that beats can be divided for a larger staff or combined for a smaller staff.

News Beats

- **Administration:** administration, budget, top campus administrators, admissions
- **Crime and safety:** campus and city police departments, may include an academic criminal justice or criminology department if you have one
- **City/community:** city politics and community issues (you may assign several reporters to this beat if your newspaper covers the city as well as the campus)
- **Faculty/staff:** academic senate, staff and faculty unions
- **Student government:** student government elections, meetings, politics
- **Higher education:** community college or state university system (at public schools), higher education trends
- **Race and ethnicity:** demographics, racial and ethnic groups on campus such as Movimiento Estudiantil Chicano de Aztlan (MECHA) or Black Student Union
- **Religion:** campus religious groups such as Newman Center, Hillel, Christian Campus Fellowship, Muslim Student Association, etc.(as well as religious studies departments or seminaries if you have them)
- **Politics:** city politics, elections, political science department
- **Social sciences:** including psychology, sociology, anthropology and other academic departments
- **International:** may include international students and study-abroad programs as well as academic departments in international relations, foreign languages and related fields

Lifestyle Beats

- **Housing:** on-campus dorms and apartments, off-campus housing and related issues
- **Careers and jobs:** campus career center, employment trends
- **Money:** financial aid, grants and loans, credit issues, student jobs
- **Parking and transportation:** campus parking facilities, campus shuttles and public transportation
- **Campus clubs/activities:** depending on your campus and the size of your staff, you may have several reporters assigned to related beats, such as Greek life, service groups, ethnic groups, etc.
- **Fashion:** fashion trends (as well as fashion, interior design departments if you have them)
- **Drugs and alcohol:** drinking, the bar scene, trends, drug and alcohol law enforcement

Sports and Fitness Beats

- **Intercollegiate sports:** depending on the size of your staff and the importance of sports on your campus you may have a reporter assigned to each·sport or reporters covering several sports at once
- **Extreme sports:** surfing, skateboarding, snowboarding, mountain climbing, etc.
- **Recreation:** recreational and intramural sports, gym and athletic facilities

Arts and Entertainment Beats

- **Media:** film, television, video games, campus broadcast stations (as well as journalism, film, multimedia studies and communication departments if you have them)
- **Theater and dance:** performances (as well as theater and dance departments if you have them)
- **Visual arts:** visual art (as well as art and graphic design departments if you have them)
- **Music:** music (as well as music department if you have one)

Business and Technology Beats

- **Business:** business school, employment issues
- **Technology:** technology issues as well as coverage of information technology and computer science departments
- **Engineering:** could be combined with technology or stand on its own if you have a large engineering school

Health and Science Beats

- **Health:** student health services, health issues (and allied health fields if you have them)
- **School of Medicine:** (if you have one)
- **Sex:** sex and sexuality research (including academic department in human sexuality studies if you have one), sexually transmitted diseases
- **Environment:** environmental issues as well as related academic departments such as geosciences, meteorology, environmental studies, etc.
- **Sciences:** physics, astronomy, chemistry, biology, mathematics, etc.

Covering a Beat

As you begin to cover a new beat ask yourself these questions:

1. What does this beat encompass?
2. What do I know about this beat?
3. What do I want to learn about it?
4. Who are the official sources on this beat and how can I find them?
5. What sort of unofficial sources may be helpful?
6. What has the paper written about this beat in the past?
7. Who on the newspaper staff knows something about this beat?
8. What professional journalists or journalism organizations can I tap for guidance about covering this beat?
9. What books and Web sites might be useful?
10. Who would make for interesting profiles?
11. What trends are happening on this beat?
12. What meetings or events can I attend?
13. What are four stories I can write in the next month or two?
14. What are some of the larger issues I'd like to explore?
15. What long-term project can I produce on this beat?

regular basis—daily, if possible—to check the police log and see what's happening. Even if your campus is relatively crime-free, these logs can be a gold mine of information, not just for crime stories but for trend pieces or features. Was there a drug bust in a dorm? Were police called three times last weekend to break up a rowdy party?

Student editors should think about ways to pass vital source information from one reporter to another. High staff turnover is a constant problem at college papers—even more so than in the professional world—and your paper shouldn't have to lose good sources each time a reporter graduates or leaves the staff. Some student papers have reporters post source lists on their content management system or stow them in files in the newsroom. Others require all reporters to write a beat report before they leave the publication.

At Keene State College in Keene, N.H., for example, editors at the weekly *Equinox* have reporters create "beat books." These three-ring binders contain background information about each beat, including contact information for sources and a list of stories that have been written. The books are handed off to the new staff at the end of each year.

Another way to get information on your beat is to network with professional reporters covering your beat or similar beats. Although it may be a little uncomfortable reaching out to your direct competitor, professionals at non-competing papers may be happy to share information about how to cover your beat. Join specialty groups of reporters. The Web site list at the end of this chapter includes

contact information for organizations of journalists who cover education, medicine, environment, crime and other beats. These groups often have reduced-price memberships for students and some sponsor conferences, workshops, listservs and other events or services that could help you. Getting involved in such organizations can also provide good contacts for lining up internships and jobs down the line.

Dealing with Your Public Information Office

The most obvious source of information on your campus is the school's public information office. Depending on who's in charge and the relationship you have with the staff there, this office can be a news treasure chest—or your greatest obstacle to getting information. Good public information officers (PIOs) are always on the lookout for stories, and many are willing to share them even before a news release is written or a report is issued. They can tell you about upcoming events, important visitors, demographic trends and researchers who are about to publish significant studies.

If your university's PIOs are amenable, arrange a meeting between them and key newspaper staffers—or even the whole staff—early in the year. Ask about what stories are coming down the pike and what challenges the university may be facing. Do they anticipate budget cutbacks, accreditation reviews, administrative changes, fee increases or other notable developments in the coming months? Which professors are doing ground-breaking research? What new programs are

being developed? What trends do they see in admissions or hiring? You might also ask how they want to be contacted—by phone, e-mail, cell phone or pager—on breaking stories and who in the office should be contacted for various types of stories.

While you want to have a friendly relationship with university PIOs, never forget that they're unlikely to be your best source for bad news on campus. They won't write a press release when a popular professor doesn't get tenure or when there's a rat infestation in the student apartments or when the dining hall is cited for health violations. For those stories, you need to have a strong network of other sources.

Finding Story Ideas

As noted earlier in this chapter, college campuses are breeding grounds for news. There's always something going on that's worth writing about. Your job is to find those stories. The best news tips will come from your sources, be they professors, students, coaches or public information officers. But other good stories will come from your own observations. Was your financial aid check late? Does your psychology professor make sexually inappropriate remarks in class? Are campus police cracking down on late-night parties? Are the weight machines in your university fitness center continually marked "out of order"?

Let your own basic curiosity drive you. If something gives you pause or makes you say "Hmmm, that's strange," keep snooping around. Ask some questions. You never know what you might find.

For more ideas on finding story ideas, see Tipsheet: How to Find Story Ideas.

The Tickler File

Most professional news organizations and some college papers use a tickler file to remind the staff of upcoming events, anniversaries of major campus or community incidents and other important dates. If your newsroom doesn't have one, set one up. Tickler files can be electronic or physical; an easy-to-access file drawer works well.

To start, create 43 folders, one for each day of the month and one for each month of the year. Drop in press releases, announcements, meeting agendas and other documents relating to upcoming events. If you don't have written information on the event, write up a note with the significant details. If, for example, you're waiting for a coroner's report on a suspicious death or an announcement about curriculum changes, write something up and pop it in the tickler file when you expect some new development. Someone, usually an assigning editor or general assignment reporter, should be charged with

Tipsheet: How to Find Story Ideas

1. **Look around.** Study bulletin boards, including electronic bulletin boards, and other places where public notices are posted. Is there a new club on campus? An unusual class? A protest rally coming up? Jot down the contact info and check it out.
2. **Investigate your archives.** Read back issues of your own newspaper, keeping a particular eye out for stories worth a follow-up. What's happened since an affirmative action admissions program was discontinued? How has a rape prevention policy instituted five years ago affected sexual crimes on campus? Talk to your predecessors, people who previously covered your beat, and ask about stories that warrant a second look or ones the reporter never got a chance to write.
3. **Ask questions.** Set up an informal focus group of your friends or roommates. What would they like to read in the paper? What are they concerned about, excited about, frustrated about? What do they want to know?
4. **Eavesdrop.** Listen in on conversations in the cafeteria, the bookstore, the student union and other places students gather. What are people talking about on campus?
5. **Pay attention.** Take note of announcements made in class. Your professors—or other students—may be passing on news tips.
6. **Develop sources.** See everyone you talk to—roommates, friends, professors, service workers—as a potential news source. Listen for trends, campus political developments, policy changes.
7. **Read everything.** Newspapers, magazines, newsletters, fliers, journals are all good sources of stories. Among the publications to pay particular attention to: *The Chronicle of Higher Education* (http://chronicle.com/) and the *New York Times'* quarterly "Education Life" section. They can be great for tips on trend stories that you could localize. Local newspapers are also news story bonanzas, as are other campus newspapers. As long as you don't plagiarize and you do your own reporting, there's nothing wrong with stealing story ideas. (See Newslink's links to online campus newspapers at http://newslink.org/statcamp.html)
8. **Bring research home.** Look for studies about college students that you can localize. A Google search on "study," "college students" and the current year will reveal a host of recent studies on such things as drinking habits and video game use that you could use as a launch pad for a trend story.
9. **Mine your PIO.** Read campus publications such as employee and faculty union newsletters and alumni magazines, as well as press releases issued by your university's public information office. Some PIOs also keep track of university staff and faculty in the news. A quote by a professor in a local or national newspaper or magazine may give you an idea for a deeper story on that person or her research.
10. **Open your eyes.** Look for changes—buildings being torn down, long lines, new businesses in neighborhoods near your campus. Anything fresh or different could be the beginning of a story.
11. **Peruse ads.** Read display and classified ads in your paper and in community publications. Are apartment rental prices on the rise? Are those too-good-to-be-true airfares for real? Check out unusual job opportunities—for exotic dancers, models, escort services.
12. **Do a records search.** Check legal filings and other public records on your campus and its key players. Stop by the county courthouse and see if your school or the university president has been sued.

Some questions to ask yourself: Does the racial and ethnic makeup of the faculty reflect that of the students? Is one group substantially less diverse? If there is a gap, what is your school doing to bridge it? Which ethnic/racial groups have student organizations? Which groups aren't organized? Why? Which student groups has your paper written about? Which student groups have been left out of the newspaper? Why? These are questions that may lead to stories.

Aly Colón, diversity program director for The Poynter Institute, suggests editors ask themselves these five W's of journalism from a diverse perspective:

Who: Who's missing from the story?
What: What's the context for the story?
Where: Where can we go for more information?
When: When do we use racial or ethnic identification?
Why: Why are we including or excluding certain information?

In addition to asking these questions, it can be useful to periodically evaluate your coverage. Betty Clapp, adviser to *The Cleveland Stater* at Cleveland State University, says, "Avoiding stereotyping really is based on awareness of stereotypes, so a useful exercise is to look at a story for its treatment and description of any specific groups. Does it perpetuate stereotyping? Is the description pertinent to the story? Why? Answering those questions and related ones that may develop tends to help people become more aware of stereotypes in general, and particularly in their own writing."

Covering a campus requires organization, enterprise and persistence. At times it may seem like a daunting task, particularly if your staff is small. But even just a handful of energetic, dedicated reporters, editors and photographers can be enough to take your newspaper to the next level and create an interesting, informative, even thought-provoking publication that truly covers your campus community.

To Do:

1. If your newspaper doesn't have a beat system, consider assigning reporters to particular coverage areas. If you already assign reporters to beats think about alternate ways of covering your campus, such as combining academic departments with subject areas (creating a money beat, for example, that includes personal finance, financial aid and the business school) or devising brand new beats, such as sex and relationships, drinking or other topical issues that newspapers sometimes neglect.

checking the tickler file every single day to make sure important developments and events aren't forgotten.

Covering a Diverse Community

Colleges are among the most diverse gathering places in our society. If your campus is like most, you have people from all over your state or province—and possibly from different parts of the country and the world—coming together to live and learn. In this community you most likely have people of different races and religions, different classes and political persuasions, many of whom are venturing out of their home cultures for the first time.

Diversity is part of what makes college so interesting. But it can also make covering a college campus challenging.

The best way to start familiarizing yourself with diversity issues is to get to know your campus. Your college public information office should be able to give you a detailed demographic profile of your student body and the faculty and staff who serve them.

Getting in Touch with Your Readers

■ **Robert F. Stevenson**

All week your staff works hard to create a paper for the vast campus just outside your newspaper office. You check your facts, you proofread your stories, you look for just the right photograph—and then you hope people will pick up the paper and read it.

But are you doing a good job? Do your stories interest your readers? Do your photographs capture their attention? Are your stories balanced and fair? Are you getting not just the facts, but the essence of your stories right?

It's often hard to tell. Some student newspapers don't get many letters to the editor and even when they do get a letter it can be difficult to know if the criticism is valid or just one wacky reader's opinion. Awards from state and national organizations are a great ego boost, but they don't tell you if you're truly serving your campus community.

Here are some ways to assess your newspaper and to reach out to readers:

Get to know your readers. Invite the campus to an open house to meet your staff and to see how the newspaper works. Sponsor a forum on a major issue in your community. Be sure to participate in school-sponsored student organization fairs. Maintain a portable information booth (a table with handouts, preferably manned by an editor and other staffers), and set it up around campus at various times.

Do some research. Surveying your readership is a great way to find out how you're doing and what your readers want more (and less) of. Telephone surveys are quick and inexpensive, but caller ID and answering machines have taken a serious bite out of their effectiveness. Web surveys are useful for online readers. Questionnaires included in your newspaper are inexpensive and easy; keep in mind, though, that response rates are usually low. Suggestion boxes strategically placed outside your office or in the student union give readers a way to talk back to the paper.

(See the Readership Survey at the end of this chapter. It was adapted from surveys created by *Washington Square News* at New York University, *The Spectator* at University of Wisconsin-Eau Claire and *The Broadside* at Central Oregon Community College).

Hire an ombudsman. Have one staffer serve as a liaison between the staff and the campus—a sort of middleman. This ombudsman should spot-check for accuracy and try to determine reader satisfaction with the paper. After the paper is distributed, the ombudsman can call sources mentioned in the current issue to confirm the articles' accuracy. In addition, this liaison can call students at random to determine their level of satisfaction with that issue of the newspaper. The ombudsman should report results to the editor, who can use them to plan future coverage. (For more about news ombudsmen, see Chapter 9.)

Advertise your newspaper. Keep telling your readers why they should read your paper. Put ads in your school's weekly bulletin or similar publication. Run ads in your own paper to alert readers to upcoming special projects or Web exclusives. Always have notices in the paper inviting readers' comments and questions. The *Forum* student newspaper staff at Lander University regularly posts teasers around campus—something like: "Check out who's coming to campus next week—Page 3 next *Forum*." This has proven to be an effective method to get non-readers to check the paper out.

Engage in gorilla warfare. Some newspaper staffs get downright inspired in their battle to overcome poster blindness— the condition many students develop to ignore the flood of fliers on campus. Some student newspaper staffs rent costumes, such as a gorilla or the school mascot, to hand deliver the paper. At least one college wrote the newspaper's name on hundreds of pingpong balls and dropped them in strategic places, such as a busy cafeteria. Other newspapers take the town-crier approach: a student wearing a placard advertising the newspaper rings a bell, hands out the newspaper and shouts current headlines followed by, "Read All About It!"

The goals are simple: get to know your readers and find out how satisfied they are with your newspaper. The best methods to realize your goals are probably as varied as student newspaper mission statements across the country. A combination of approaches like those just described is a good place to start. Be persistent and proactive. If your strategies work well, keep them up; if not, it's probably time to stir up the mix. The result for all this hard work, simply put, will be a better newspaper for you and your campus.

Robert F. Stevenson is director of student publications and assistant professor of journalism at Lander University. He received his Ph.D. in higher education administration from the University of South Carolina. Dr. Stevenson is a columnist for two South Carolina newspapers, the Greenville News *and the* Greenwood Index Journal.

---

2. Have reporters write beat reports (see the form at the end of this chapter for an example) that they can use to guide their reporting. Before they leave a beat ask reporters to update and file the beat reports so they can be passed down to the next reporter who will cover that beat.

3. At the beginning of your next editorial staff meeting, send the entire staff—reporters, photographers, editors and designers—out to hunt for stories. Have everyone come back in half an hour with three story ideas. Discuss the ideas as a group and decide which ones are worth pursuing.

4. If your photographers don't have beats, try giving them buildings to cover. Suggest that photographers cruise their assigned buildings every few days in search of news and feature story ideas and stand-alone photos.

5. Organize a staff workshop on covering a beat. Bring in a professional reporter to describe beat coverage or have staff members share ideas and strategies.

To Read:

Blum, Deborah and Mary Knudson, eds. *Field Guide for Science Writers*. New York: Oxford University Press, 1997.

Hancock, Elise. *Ideas into Words: Mastering the Craft of Science Writing*. Baltimore: Johns Hopkins University Press, 2003.

Schulte, Henry H. and Marcel P. Dufresne. *Getting the Story: An Advanced Reporting Guide to Beats, Records and Sources*. Needham Heights, Mass.: Macmillan Publishing, 1994.

Covering Meetings

■ **David Cuillier**

Many beats—including student government, faculty senate and city government—involve covering meetings. The following tips will help student reporters who cover meetings.

Before (Preparation)

1. **Know the meeting schedule.** Find out when regular meetings are held for the organization you are covering. Mark them on the calendar.
2. **Get the agenda.** Get a copy of the agenda, including supplementary documents that are referenced in the agenda. Read through it and identify the topics that are most likely to be of interest to readers.
3. **Promote the meeting.** Let readers have a chance of going, too. Run a brief or calendar item a few days before the meeting explaining the main subjects on the agenda that readers would care about, and the time, date and place of the meeting.
4. **Write meeting advance story.** For the advance story, focus on the most newsworthy issue. Talk to the players on all sides and get a photo. Make it a good issue piece and then mention in a box the fact that the matter will be discussed at the upcoming meeting. It gets people interested in a topic and then provides them with a way to act.

During (Coverage)

1. **Mingle.** Use the time before the meeting, during breaks and after the meeting to talk with sources and anyone else there. Introduce yourself and initiate a conversation. Sometimes they will tell you why they are there and will fill you in on what's really behind the story.
2. **Take good notes.** Get lots of quotes. Throughout the meeting, think about what you are going to focus your story on.

3. **Look for different stories.** Listen to what is being said and note potential stories. A half dozen things will be mentioned but will not be embellished. Check up on those later and follow up with stories.
4. **Zero in on your turn-around story.** Your editor is going to want you to write at least one story out of the meeting. Figure out what that will be and make sure you have all the information you need. Most likely it will be what you advanced. You want to tell readers what happened regarding the issue you raised in your advance story. In that case, you already will have a lot of the information you need.
5. **Snag people.** After the meeting snag people and ask them questions to complete the information needed to write a solid story. If someone speaks at a public hearing and you didn't get their name, track them down in the crowd.

After (Writing)

1. **Write fast.** If your deadline is the day or night of the meeting, write fast. While you are in the meeting and as you head back to the office, formulate your lede, or beginning paragraph.
2. **Don't be a stenographer.** Write the story focused on a single news angle, just like any other news story, mentioning that the matter was discussed at the meeting. Do not simply list a chronology of what happened. The news isn't the fact a meeting happened.
3. **Follow up.** Make sure to follow up on the other stories that came out of the meeting.

David Cuillier is a veteran journalist and former adviser to The Daily Evergreen *at Washington State University. This piece is adapted with permission from a tipsheet he wrote for Washington State University Student Publications.*

Selditch, Dianne, ed. *My First Year as a Journalist: Real-World Stories from America's Newspaper and Magazine Journalists.* New York: Walker and Company, 1995.

To Click:
The Chronicle of Higher Education
http://chronicle.com/

National Center for Education Statistics
http://nces.ed.gov/

Inside Higher Education
http://insidehighered.com/

Covering Crime and Justice
http://www.justicejournalism.org/crimeguide/
    chapter01/chapter01_pg03.html

Professional Organizations for Beat
    Writers:

Association of Health Care Journalists
http://www.ahcj.umn.edu/

Criminal Justice Journalists
http://www.reporters.net/cjj/

Education Writers Association
http://www.ewa.org

National Association of Science Writers
http://www.nasw.org

Religion Newswriters Foundation
http://www.religionwriters.com/

Society of American Business Writers and
    Editors
http://www.sabew.org/

Society of Environmental Journalists
http://www.sej.org/

Beat Report

Name _____

Beat _____

Sources:

Name	Title	Phone Numbers	Office	E-mail Address	Notes

Upcoming Events (meetings, conferences, performances, exhibits, etc.):

_____

_____

_____

Documents (reports, public records, publications, etc. that will help you cover your beat):

_____

_____

_____

Story Ideas:

1. _____

_____

_____

2. _____

_____

_____

3. _____

_____

_____

4. _____

_____

_____

5. _____

_____

_____

Newspaper Readership Survey

How often do you read (NAME OF NEWSPAPER)?
___ Every issue
___ Occasionally
___ Most issues
___ Never

Is the paper distributed at convenient locations?
___ Yes, I can find it if I want to
___ I'd like to see it at _____(specify location)
___ No, I never see it

Which best describes how thoroughly you read (NAME OF NEWSPAPER)?
___ Front page only
___ Read one or two sections
___ Don't read it
___ Skim entire paper and headlines
___ Read it cover to cover

How often do you read each section of (NAME OF NEWSPAPER)?

News
___ Every issue
___ Most issues
___ Occasionally
___ Never

Sports
___ Every issue
___ Most issues
___ Occasionally
___ Never

Lifestyle
___ Every issue
___ Most issues
___ Occasionally
___ Never

Arts & Entertainment
___ Every issue
___ Most issues
___ Occasionally
___ Never

Opinion
___ Every issue
___ Most issues
___ Occasionally
___ Never

How would you rate the overall quality of the newspaper?
___ Excellent
___ Fair
___ Good
___ Poor

What are you interested in reading about (check all that apply)?
___ On-campus events
___ Student government
___ Campus clubs and organizations
___ Sports
___ Administration
___ Entertainment and culture
___ Crime
___ Faculty

What would you like to see more of in (NAME OF NEWSPAPER)? (Check all that apply)
___ Information about student activities
___ Entertainment coverage
___ Photos
___ Opinion columns
___ Features and profiles
___ Student government news
___ Academic news
___ Sports coverage
___ Comics and cartoons
___ Crossword puzzles

How often do you visit the (NAME OF NEWSPAPER) Web site?
___ Several times a week
___ Monthly
___ Weekly
___ Never

What is your affiliation with the university?
___ Freshman
___ Junior
___ Graduate student
___ Staff
___ Sophomore
___ Senior
___ Faculty
___ Other (please describe) _____

Are you:
___ Male
___ Female

Where do you live?
___ Residence hall
___ Off-campus rental
___ With family
___ On-campus apartment
___ Own home

Please list any suggestions you have for improving the (NAME OF NEWSPAPER).

_____

_____

_____

Thank you for sharing your thoughts about (NAME OF NEWSPAPER).

Adapted from surveys created by the *Washington Square News*, New York University; *The Spectator*, University of Wisconsin–Eau Claire; *The Broadside*, Central Oregon Community College

Figure 4.1. A breaking news story requires reporters to think on their feet. They must collect background information, facts, reactions and statistics and be ready to write a story within minutes or hours. *The Exponent,* Purdue University

Chapter 4

Reporting

You walk into the newsroom at 10:45 a.m. and your editor hands you a flier. "Students for the Ethical Treatment of Animals is organizing a rally in front of the student union today at noon," she says. "Bring me back a story. We've already assigned a photographer; Jennifer will meet you over there."

What do you do next? Start reporting.

Reporting is the process of gathering information; of collecting facts, opinions, statistics, observations and vignettes that you can later weave into a cogent story.

How do you find that information? How do you know if it's accurate? How do you interview people? In this chapter we'll look at the ins and outs of reporting.

News Judgment

Good reporting begins with good news judgment, knowing how to recognize information that is timely, interesting and important to your readers. For a college newspaper, that means identifying stories that will have impact and meaning for students, specifically, and for the college community (staff, faculty, alumni, parents of students, neighbors) as a whole.

To have good news judgment, you need to be able to identify what's news.

All news stories have at least one of these basic elements:

Timeliness. It's happening now. With a daily paper, that may mean covering a fire or a speech or a football game today for tomorrow's paper; with a monthly, it means covering the events of this month and putting them into context for people who will read the paper next month.

Proximity. It has impact or meaning for people living in your geographic area, or, in the case of a college newspaper, people involved with your school.

Novelty. Out-of-the-ordinary events get people talking. Readers enjoy stories about the 77-year-old pursuing a bachelor's degree or the engineering student who invents a mechanical leech.

Impact. These are stories that have consequences, such as a fee hike or the adoption of a new smoking policy on campus. Newspapers help readers understand the impact news events have.

Drama. Reporters look for stories that have mystery, suspense, emotion. A story about a promising athlete recovering from a serious injury or an adopted woman who finds her birth mother has emotional appeal.

Prominence. In every community, certain people are minor celebrities because of their position or achievement. This is equally true on a college campus, where readers want to know if the president resigns or the star quarterback is arrested on drug charges.

Conflict. Readers love a good conflict, whether it's rival teams meeting on the basketball court or political factions trying to capture the leadership of student government.

Human interest. People like stories about people. It's interesting to read about the blind student who makes her way around campus with a seeing-eye dog or the English major who strips for a living.

Usefulness. Readers want to know where to buy low-cost textbooks, when to file graduation applications, how to make it through an all-night study session.

Once you understand what makes news, you can begin to make decisions about how to report it.

The Reporting Process

As you begin to report a story, ask yourself these questions:

• What is the story?
• What makes the story news?
• What do I need to know?
• Where can I find information?

To illustrate the reporting process, let's go back to the Students for the Ethical Treatment of Animals rally mentioned at the beginning of this chapter.

• **What is the story?** People are gathering on campus to protest animal research.
• **What makes the story news?** By definition, a protest involves conflict and may involve drama. The rally is also timely and geographically relevant.
• **What do I need to know?** What is Students for the Ethical Treatment of Animals? Why are people protesting? How many people will participate? What do organizers hope to achieve?
• **Where can I find information?** The best way to get information about the rally itself is to go to it. But even before it starts you should do some background research.

Resources

The reporting process is about going from ignorance to knowledge. As a reporter, you may know little about a topic when a story is assigned; by the time it's published, you will be something of an expert. A good reporter learns how to quickly gather information from various sources. These may include:

Directories. Phone books and online directories are vital tools for reporters. They help not only with phone numbers and e-mail addresses but with names and titles. (Be aware, though, that directories can be out of date or contain errors; always double-check name spellings and titles with human sources.)

Documents. Reports, lawsuits, police records and other documents provide a paper trail in reporting. Reporters can use documents to verify facts or track down new information.

Newspaper archives. Past news stories in your paper and others can provide invaluable background information.

Web sites. The Internet has revolutionized reporting. Information that used to take hours or days or weeks to find is now accessible in seconds with the click of a mouse. Networking sites like thefacebook.com and MySpace.com are particularly useful for finding students at your university. Be aware, however, that much of the information on the Web is biased, inaccurate or incomplete. (For more information about using the Internet as a research tool see Tipsheet: Evaluating Information on the Web.)

Listservs and newsgroups. E-mail discussion groups and Web-based bulletin boards can be a great way to find story ideas and sources. Just be sure to check people out before quoting them. People who present themselves anonymously may not feel bound by truth.

Human sources. Interviewing people remains a reporter's stock-in-trade. People provide the anecdotes, quotes, eyewitness accounts, opinions and perspectives that make a news story come alive.

Background Research

Let's say you have an hour to do research before attending the Students for the Ethical Treatment of Animals rally. What would you do?

A Web search is a good place to start. Let's

Developing a Reporting Plan

For every story, be it a breaking news story you report and write in two hours or a long feature you work on for weeks, you should develop a reporting plan. Such a plan will act as a roadmap for your reporting, guiding you and helping you keep your focus.

Draft your reporting plan as you begin work on a story. It may change as you find out more information.

Step One—Write a focus statement for your story.

Step Two—Write a list of questions.

Step Three—Look over your questions and figure out where you can get each piece of information.

Step Four—Make a list of individuals you want to interview and documents you want to find. Look up phone numbers and e-mail addresses for your sources.

Tipsheet: Evaluating Information on the Web

The Web is a fabulous resource for finding information. It's also a frighteningly effective vehicle for spreading misinformation, propaganda and disinformation. When considering information presented on a Web site, think critically, asking yourself the following questions:

1. Is the person or organization responsible for the contents of the page clearly identified?
2. What is the URL domain (.org, .gov, .edu, etc.)? If the domain is .gov, you know this is an official governmental organization, whereas anyone can get a .net or .com domain.
3. Does the site clearly describe its goals?
4. Can you verify the legitimacy of the organization? Is there a phone number or postal address to contact for more information? (An e-mail address is not enough.)
5. Can you tell if the page has the official approval of the organization?
6. Are the sources for any factual information clearly listed so they can be verified?
7. Does the site have many grammatical, spelling and typographical errors? (These kinds of errors don't just indicate a lack of quality; they can lead to factual errors.)
8. Is the factual information consistent with other sources?
9. Does the organization have a political or ideological bias? If so, is this bias clearly stated?
10. If the page has advertising, is it clearly differentiated from the informational content?
11. Does the organization or individual behind the site have a commercial stake in the information presented?
12. Is the topic covered in a comprehensive and balanced way? Be wary of one-sided views with critical information missing.
13. Are there dates on the page to indicate when the page was written, when it was put on the Web and when it was last revised?
14. Is there any outdated information on the site?
15. Are there many dead links? This suggests the page has not been updated recently.

---

say you go on Google and search for "Students for the Ethical Treatment of Animals" and the name of your school, then "lab animals" and your school. You find out:

- Two years ago there was a big animal rights demonstration on your campus. Five students were arrested.
- A philosophy professor on campus is a leader in the local animal rights movement.
- A number of professors have published medical research based on lab experiments with animals.

You jot down some names and facts and then go to your student newspaper archive and find the article about the students who were arrested for protesting animal research. You take note of the people quoted in the article. You also check the university directory and get phone numbers, e-mail addresses and office numbers for the professors on either side of the animal research issue.

Before going out to the rally, you go back to your original list of questions and add a few more:

- What kind of animal research is conducted on this campus?
- Why is the rally happening now?
- Is Students for the Ethical Treatment of Animals related to People for the Ethical Treatment of Animals?

- How much animal research is being done on campus?
- Are animals being mistreated? If so, how and by whom?

By now it's 11:45 a.m., time to head over to the student union. You don't know much yet, but you've got a start—you have contact information for a list of potential sources, you have a little background on the issues and you've got some ideas about what else you need to know.

The Power of Observation

On your walk to the student union, you hear drumming and chanting. "Liberate the animals! Liberate the animals!" the crowd shouts. You pull out your notebook and start to take notes. When you get to the front of the student union, you see a large crowd of people, some of them carrying signs. A young man with a bullhorn stands on the steps, addressing the crowd.

You feel a bit overwhelmed. What should you take notes on? Let your senses guide you. What do you hear? What do you see? What captures your attention?

Note the slogans on the signs. Listen to what the speaker is saying. When he utters something catchy or important, jot it down, but don't feel you have to write down every single word. Observe the crowd's reaction. Do people look bored or fired up? Do they seem angry? Try to estimate the size of the

group by counting a section of the crowd and then extrapolating. (You can also get crowd estimates from police and organizers; typically organizers overestimate and police come in with a lower count.)

Interviewing

You'll want to interview people during and after the rally. Choose a variety of sources—organizers (who may not be available until after the event is over), participants, onlookers, university officials, scientists who conduct research with animals, science students who work in labs with animals.

When doing interviews you're looking for a number of things:

- Factual information (such as when the organization was formed, why this rally is happening today, its objective)
- Reactions and opinions from a variety of perspectives (how people feel about what they've seen and heard)
- Statistics that will quantify the story (how many labs on campus do animal research? How many people attended the rally?)
- Anecdotes, or vignettes, that will help tell the story (someone drove 200 miles to come to this rally, a woman with diabetes supports animal research because it's helped pave the way for treatments)

Recording Interviews

There are two kinds of reporters in the world: those who prefer to tape-record interviews and those who prefer not to.

Nearly all reporters use an audio recorder at some time in their careers—for a Q&A, for example, or a meeting with a potentially litigious source, or any interview where the source whips out his own recorder. Political reporters typically tape interviews with politicians in case someone wants to challenge their quotes. In addition, audio recorders are becoming indispensable for the multimedia journalist who produces stories for the Web (and sometimes radio and television), as well as print.

Audio recorders are useful for:

- Getting verbatim quotes
- Picking up tone or accent
- Collecting sound and voice recordings for audio reports
- Interviewing fast talkers

However, many reporters believe audio recorders interfere with the interviewing process. For one thing, they sometimes intimidate sources. For another, reporters who rely on them often don't take good notes. And many newspaper reporters feel they don't have the time to listen to and transcribe tapes after the interview.

Tipsheet: Interviewing

Before the Interview

1. **Do as much background research as possible.** Read articles and Web sites about the topic you're covering as well as the person you are interviewing. The more you know, the more intelligent the questions you'll be able to ask.

2. **Make a list of questions.** Begin with the who, what, where, when, why and how and go from there. Think about what this source may be able to provide.

3. **Organize the questions.** Put them in a format that's easy to access and an order that makes sense. Start with easy, factual questions and build to more complex or pointed ones.

4. **Make an appointment.** Unless you're on a tight deadline, it's best not to just drop in on people. Try to find an hour when both of you will have time to devote to the interview.

5. **Dress appropriately.** Generally you want to dress as much like your source as possible. If you're interviewing the college president, wear business attire; if you're interviewing students or construction workers you should dress more informally.

6. **Be prepared.** Make sure you have a notebook, pens, a tape recorder if you use one (plus extra tapes and batteries), documents you'll be discussing and anything else you may need.

During the Interview

7. **Introduce yourself.** Always identify yourself as a reporter working on a story for publication.

8. **Build rapport.** It's good to start with a little small talk to make the source feel comfortable. Talk about the weather or current events or mutual acquaintances or remark on a picture or something in the room.

9. **Describe your story.** Explain the purpose and scope of the piece you plan to write.

10. **Write it down.** Even if you're using a tape recorder, always take notes. Don't assume you'll remember details.

11. **Ask open-ended questions.** Avoid questions that can be answered with yes, no or other one-word answers. Questions that begin with how, why or "tell me about" tend to elicit fuller answers.

12. **Show you're listening.** Nod your head or utter agreeing sounds to demonstrate you understand and are interested in what the person is saying.

13. **Make eye contact.** Even if you're frantically scribbling notes, take time to look at your source every now and then. Eye contact helps you stay focused and maintain rapport.

14. **Listen for quotable quotes.** When you hear a likely quote, take careful notes. It's OK to ask people to repeat themselves or slow down; demonstrate your commitment to quote them accurately.

15. **Follow up.** Don't feel you have to slavishly stick to the prepared questions. If your source says something unexpected or interesting, pursue a new line of questioning.

16. **Take charge.** Remember that *you* are conducting the interview. If the source strays from the topic or doesn't answer the question, it's your job to keep the person on track.

17. **Save tough questions for the end.** Build up to challenging, hard-to-ask questions. Be sure to pace the interview so that you don't run out of time before you ask the difficult questions.

18. **Wrap it up.** End each interview by asking for other things the source would like to tell you and recommendations for other good sources of information.

19. **Be appreciative.** Thank the source for taking the time to talk with you and ask permission to check back, if need be, if more questions arise. Make sure you have the source's phone numbers and e-mail address for follow-up.

After the Interview

20. **Review your notes.** Fill in missing words and spell out troublesome abbreviations while they are still fresh in your mind.

21. **Mark your notes.** Highlight key facts or quotes you may want to use in your story with a highlighter or by underlining or marking key passages with stars.

22. **Transcribe key sections.** Most reporters don't transcribe full interviews but it's good to type up significant quotes, scenes, anecdotes or details you're likely to use. This will help later when you sit down to actually write the story.

The most important thing to keep in mind when recording an interview is that recorders can fail. Batteries run out, machines break, a plane roars overhead at a key moment and your interview is lost. The solution, of course, is to take good notes whether or not you're taping. Don't rely on your recorder. In terms of note taking you should pretend it's not there. Some other tips for using an audio recorder:

1. Come prepared. Always bring extra batteries and tapes.

2. Test the recorder first. Do a trial run before meeting your source and then again in the place where you'll be doing the interview. Make sure not only that your equipment works but that background noises don't interfere.

3. Use the counter. Turn the counter to zero when you start and then write down numbers in your notes every now and then so you can find key passages easily.

4. Know the law before taping phone interviews. State laws on taping phone conversations vary. Some states require consent from all parties before a phone conversation can be taped. (For information on laws that apply to you, check out "Can We Tape? A Practical Guide to Taping Phone Calls and In-Person Conversations in the 50 States and D.C." by the Reporters Committee for Freedom of the Press, listed at the end of this chapter.)

Note Taking

Probably the best way to develop your note-taking skills is to study old-fashioned stenography. A course or book on shorthand is an excellent investment, particularly at this point in your career.

If you don't learn a formal shorthand system, you should develop your own method of speedwriting. Look for ways to shorten words—drop vowels, use symbols, abbreviate commonly used words (bc for because, w/ for with, etc.). The key is to find a system that works for you.

You also have to find a system that you can read. There's no point in taking notes quickly if you can't read your jottings a few days later when you sit down to the write your story.

When taking notes on an interview, don't feel you have to write down every single word the person says. Listen for key information or catchy quotes. When the subject says something you may want to quote, get it all down, even if it means a pause in your questions. Some reporters even ask throwaway questions to buy them time to finish writing a good quote.

E-mail Interviews

E-mail has given reporters a powerful new tool for reporting. Now you can reach people thousands of miles away in different time zones with the click of a few keys. Busy professionals often answer e-mail before they'll pick up a phone. It's fast. It's efficient. And it's also potentially dangerous.

Some of the pitfalls of e-mail interviews:

- You're never really sure who is answering your message. Is it the university president—or her secretary? The student you wrote to—or her boyfriend? Or is it the next person who got on the lab computer when your intended source forgot to log off?
- You can't ask spontaneous questions. With e-mail, it's impossible to have a real conversation with back and forth chat and follow-up questions.
- Responses can be stilted or carefully crafted. That's OK in certain circumstances, but most of the time you want quotes that are natural and unscripted.
- It's hard to read nuances. It's often difficult to tell from an e-mail if the writer is being funny or serious, sarcastic or sincere. You don't have tone of voice, facial expressions and gestures to help you interpret the words.
- Your e-mail messages can be forwarded. You may not want one source to pass on your comments and questions to another person.

Despite these drawbacks, e-mail does have its place in the reporter's toolbox. Here are some guidelines to follow:

1. Use e-mail for making contact with people and setting up interviews.
2. Try to conduct interviews by phone or in person. Do primary interviews by e-mail only as a last resort.
3. Use e-mail to ask quick follow-up questions or to check information.
4. Make sure you know the e-mail source's name. Don't use interviews from an anonymous source.
5. Be professional in your messages. Keep in mind that anything you write may be forwarded to other people. When using e-mail, try to verify that the information comes from the intended source. If any information provided via e-mail sounds fishy, check it out.

Math for Journalists

Statistics, percentages and other numbers add specificity and context to stories. But many journalists—professionals as well as students—get uncomfortable when they have to explain concepts in numbers instead of words. Here's a primer on some of the basic math journalists have to deal with.

Percentages

Percentages are useful for comparing two or more numbers without regard to their differing size. For example, you can look at the raw numbers of African-American, white and Asian students at your university but it's more telling to compare the percentages of each racial group.

To understand how percents work, it helps to look at the root of the word. "Per" means "out of" and "cent" means "one hundred." So percent after a number means that many out of 100.

To calculate X as a percentage of Y: Divide X by Y and multiply the result by 100.

Example: Of the 25,000 students who attend your university, 5,000 live on campus. The percentage of students who live on campus is:

(5,000 divided by 25,000) x 100
= 0.2 x 100
= 20 percent

If X is larger than Y, the result is a percentage greater than 100.

To calculate the percentage change from X to Y, calculate the difference and divide it by X. Then multiply by 100.

Example: Your university's budget was $12 million last year and $15 million this year. The percentage change is:

[(15 - 12) divided by 12] x 100
= [3 divided by 12] x 100
= .25 x 100
= 25 percent

Therefore, the budget is 25 percent higher this year.

To change a decimal to a percent, move the decimal point two places to the right.

Example: .75 = 75 percent

To change a percent to a decimal, move the decimal point two places to the left.

Example: 75 percent = .75

Keep in mind that a 100-percent increase is a doubling, a 200-percent increase is a tripling, and so forth.

Example: Your university police department charged 15 students with drug viola-

---

■ Checklist

Reporting for Accuracy

The process to achieve accuracy ends with editing and proofreading, but it starts with reporting. To report for accuracy, ask yourself:

1. **Did you use primary sources?** You should base most of your reporting on primary sources—official documents; reports; and interviews with eyewitnesses, leaders and spokespersons for groups, or people who have direct knowledge of a situation or event. Secondary sources, such as other news articles and people who don't have direct knowledge of the topic, should be used for background research.
2. **Did you double-check all names?** Ask each person you interview to spell their name, even if it's a common one. John can be Jon and Jane can be Jayne.
3. **Did you double-check phone numbers, addresses and Web addresses?** Don't just review the number, dial it. Same goes for Web site addresses; look up the URL.
4. **Did you double-check dates and times?** Make sure all dates and times, especially for upcoming events, are correct. You don't want to tell people the lecture starts at noon when it really begins at 11 a.m.
5. **Did you use credible sources?** Check out the people you talk to. If a source gives you suspect information, confirm it with another source.
6. **Did you double-check math and numbers?** Every number in a story—whether you got it from a source or calculated it yourself—should be verified.
7. **Do you have varying versions of events?** If one person says something and another source contradicts it, go back to the first source. If both sources stand by their statements, look for additional sources. Or include both accounts with proper attribution and note the discrepancy.
8. **Did you check the documents?** If the university president says your school passed its accreditation review, ask to see the accreditation documents. If an alleged crime victim says she reported a crime to the police, look for the police report. Whenever a document is available, seek it out.

Tips from a Pro

■ **Mike Donoghue**

The police beat at most professional newspapers is normally considered the most stressful assignment. It probably is no different at a college or university. You are dealing with people—police, college officials, classmates, victims, etc.—who are under stress.

You, too, are under stress to produce a story, often with a short deadline.

School officials love to talk about a major grant won by the college or a winning season for a university team. Student leaders will tell you how hard they are working for students. When it comes to bad news, however, everybody runs for cover. It is often your job to overcome the stone wall that is erected.

People have a right to know about crime and how safe a campus is for students, faculty, staff and visitors. Informed people make informed decisions about their personal safety habits. Knowledge is the basis for making those informed decisions. The presence of the media at a crime scene or major incident plays an important and necessary role in meeting its responsibility to educate the public.

It is also the responsibility of the media to tell the public about the performance of authorities and how they reacted to a situation.

The following are a few basic tips for dealing with law enforcement and campus officials:

1. **Explain deadlines to campus law enforcement personnel.** They need to know why you need the information now, in two hours or in two days. Deadlines are different for daily and weekly campus newspapers and for the college radio or television station.

2. **All comments made to you as a reporter should be considered "on the record."** If somebody tries to use "off the record," "between you and me," or "for deep background," make sure you are in agreement as to what these phrases mean. People have different definitions.

   For example, if a security guard tells you, "Off the record, there was a major theft of computers from the lab," it might mean: "Don't use this until I tell you officially." It might also mean, "Chase this story—it's true, but I'm not authorized to tell you." Alternatively, the tipster might let you use it but not want you to make any reference to an anonymous campus police officer as the source. Some police/security departments are so small that leaks can easily be traced.

3. **If you are at a public institution, know your state's (or province's) freedom of information laws backwards and forwards.** Some groups, like the Society of Professional Journalists and state press associations, have wallet-sized copies of the law. If you are at a private institution, appeal to the institution to do the right thing by voluntarily disclosing campus crime information.

4. **Always be polite in seeking information.** Use a written request under a state open records law only as a last resort. If you are too formal, the custodian of the record might make you jump through every hoop required by the law.

5. **Make copies of any documents that might be available, especially in sensitive cases.** You might not think something is important when you read it, but when you write your story it might become a key point.

6. **Check the numbers.** Some colleges and universities provide the full police log. Many private institutions, however, provide only a breakdown of what they think is important. Some major incidents are deleted because college administrators believe they put the school in a negative light. If you get a police log, try to check the case numbers assigned to each complaint. Complaints or cases are normally assigned numbers in numerical order. If one is missing from the log or list you are given, don't be afraid to ask about it. Don't easily accept an excuse that the record is not available or is locked up. Records can usually be "found" when necessary.

7. **Get out of the newspaper office or radio/TV station and go down to the campus police station.** Don't expect campus police to make news judgments for you. Some campus police telephone lines are tape-recorded.

---

tions last year and 45 students with drug violations this year. You can express this increase two ways:

Drug violations tripled in the past year.
Drug violations increased 200 percent from last year to this year.

Ratios and Rates

A ratio describes the number of times larger one number is than another.

To calculate the ratio of X to Y, divide X by Y.

Example: Your university has 12,000 students and 600 faculty. The student-faculty ratio is:

12,000 divided by 600
= 20 to 1

A rate describes a number in terms of how it fits into a larger population, usually expressed per hundred, per thousand, per hundred thousand, etc.

To calculate the rate of X cases in a population of Y, divide X by Y and multiply by a basis number (such as 1,000).

Example: Your campus has a population of 25,000 and there were three sexual assaults last year. The sexual assault rate was:

3 per 25,000
= 3 divided by 25,000
= 0.000012

Then multiply by the number to express it in various ways:

0.000012 x 1,000 = 0.012 per 1,000
0.000012 x 10,000 = 0.12 per 10,000
0.000012 x 100,000 = 1.2 per 100,000

Averages

An average is a way to summarize a set of numbers with a single number. This is useful for stories that deal with professors' salaries, grade-point averages, the costs of a college education at different schools, etc.

There are three types of averages: the mean, the median and the mode.

- The mean is the sum of all numbers divided by the number of numbers in the set.
- The median is the one in the middle.
- The mode is the most common answer.

Somebody who might want to give you a tip is less likely to do so if the line is recorded. You will often learn the most simply by hanging around the police office. (And don't be afraid to bring an extra soda or coffee to share when you stop by!)

8. **Ask the right questions.** If you contact the campus police office every day and ask, "Is anything happening?" it is too easy for them to simply say, "No." Instead, ask an open-ended question like: "What's the most important thing (or three most important) things the department has done in the last 24 hours?"

9. **Quote people by name.** Don't attribute everything to "Police said." Names make news. You like to see your byline, don't you? Well, some cops like to see their names in print.

10. **In a tragedy, never ask a victim's family, "How do you feel?"** Learn something positive about the victim before you approach family or friends. The family will respect you more if you are able to say up front that you knew the victim was "a history major and a real leader for the field hockey team."

11. **Look to other sources, including public records.** One private college president once said that two on-campus rapes were confidential and could not be discussed. Yet, down the street at the courthouse the case was spelled out in public court records, including the names of the victims and witnesses.

12. **Try to develop a relationship with the local police before you have to do it in the heat of battle.** That way you are likely to get information the college is not inclined to release. The local police department will usually either be handling the case, assisting the college police, or at least have the information, composite photograph or other material that will be helpful to you. Neighboring departments might also have the information. Don't be afraid to play to their sense of justice. "The paper wants to make sure the person responsible is caught. We'll run the composite or any information." Unfortunately, some colleges and universities have a "circle the wagons" mentality. They don't realize that when they try to hide

things, journalists by nature tend to dig deeper, wondering what else is hidden.

13. **Don't be afraid to turn to the local media to help you dig out the story.** If you are stonewalled by the college or university, the school may be less likely to offer a "no comment" to the local daily newspaper when one of its reporters calls about a rape, major theft or serious assault on campus. The local reporter might also be able to help you with possible sources to check. In return, you can be a valuable campus resource for the local newspaper or electronic media outlet. It's a two-way street.

14. **If you are denied access to records, don't be afraid to write about it.** You can also share the story of the denial with the local news media, which may have an interest in the story. It might be interesting to see if local reporters are denied the same information.

15. **Don't compromise your position as an ethical, independent observer.** Even if the police lie to you, don't think it is acceptable to lie to them.

16. **Join up.** Consider having your media outlet support one or more of the following: Student Press Law Center, Society of Professional Journalists or the Reporters Committee for Freedom of the Press. They can provide needed resources and help if you run into roadblocks.

Mike Donoghue is an award-winning journalist with The Burlington (Vt.) Free Press. *He has worked as a reporter for more than 30 years, much of it as a police/court reporter. He is also an adjunct professor in the journalism department at St. Michael's College and has been a co-adviser to its award-winning student newspaper,* The Defender.

This piece, under the title, "Tips from the Front Line: A Veteran Police Reporter Shares Some Tricks of the Trade," is reprinted with permission from Covering Campus Crime: A Handbook for Journalists, *a publication of the Student Press Law Center, Arlington, Va. The handbook is available for download from the SPLC's Web site at http://www.splc.org/pdf/ccc3.pdf.*

The most common way of calculating an average is to find the mean, or arithmetic average.

To calculate the mean of X numbers, add up the numbers and divide by X.

Example: Full professors in one department at your university are paid $76,000; $68,000; $83,000; $152,000 and $65,000 a year. What is their average salary?

(76,000 + 68,000 + 83,000 + 152,000 + 65,000) divided by 5 = an average salary of $88,800.

The problem with the mean is that it can be misleading. In the example above, one high-paid professor skews the whole equation. All but one of the professors are making $83,000 or less but the mean average is $88,000.

A median is often used to average dollar amounts to avoid distortion caused by a few extreme values. The median is the middle number in a series.

To calculate the median of several numbers, arrange them from smallest to largest and choose the middle number.

Example: Using the example of professors' salaries above, the median is $76,000.

If you have to find the median of an even number of numbers, it's the mean of the two middle numbers. In the example above, if you had another professor making $72,000 you would find the mean of $72,000 and $76,000 by adding the numbers and dividing by 2.

(72,000 + 76,000) divided by 2 = 74,000.

The median would be $74,000.

The third kind of average is a mode, the number that appears most often. This is rarely used. But let's say you're trying to figure out the most common price students are paying for a particular textbook. You interview a dozen students and you find:

Jan paid $49.99.
Alex, Grace, Mark, Stephen and Rodrigo paid $59.99.
Esperanza paid $51.
Joyce and Trevor paid $61.
Tom, Carla and Yasmin paid $55.99.

The most common price paid for the book was $59.99.

Accuracy

Being a reporter is an enormous responsibility. When people read an article in the newspaper, they expect it to be true. If you get the facts wrong you won't just embarrass yourself, you'll let down your whole paper—and you may even leave yourself open to a lawsuit (more about that in Chapter 13). So the No. 1 rule of journalism is Get It Right.

Factual accuracy means checking and rechecking every statement, fact and detail and also making sure the overall account—the way the details are assembled—is true. Professional reporters work painstakingly to achieve accuracy and you should, too. The fact that you work for a college newspaper, that you're still learning, doesn't excuse sloppy reporting.

This is easy to say but hard to do. Virtually every reporter, student and professional can remember (with a grimace) a time they got a fact wrong. Maybe it was a quote they misheard or a number they miscopied or a name they misspelled.

Remember that most errors are preventable. It's just a question of taking the time to check your facts.

To Do:

1. Make a reporting plan for the next story you're assigned. Write the focus statement and questions. Then think about who or what could answer those questions and make a list of sources.
2. Create a reporting sourcebook or database for your newspaper. Have students share lists of useful sources, including reports, documents and helpful people. Put it in a form and place—a binder in a corner of the newsroom, an electronic database accessible from the Web—that will be available to your entire staff.
3. Organize a staff discussion about interviewing. Discuss challenges and solutions. Encourage green reporters to share their fears about interviewing and have others share what they've learned. Invite skilled reporters—professionals or veterans on your staff—to share how they get reluctant sources to talk.

To Read:

Adams, Sally. *Interviewing for Journalists.* New York: Routledge, 2001.

Blum, Walter and C. Theo Yerian. *Personal Shorthand for the Journalist.* Portland, Ore.: ERA Learning, 1980.

Biagi, Shirley. *Interviews that Work: A Practical Guide for Journalists.* Belmont, Calif.: Wadsworth, 1992.

Brady, John Joseph. *The Craft of Interviewing.* New York: Vintage Books, 1977.

Gibbs, Cheryl and Tom Warhover. *Getting the Whole Story.* New York: Guilford Press, 2002.

Mencher, Melvin. *News Reporting and Writing, 10th ed.* Boston: McGraw-Hill, 2005.

Rich, Carole and Chris Harper. *Writing and Reporting News: A Coaching Method, 5th ed.* Belmont, Calif.: Wadsworth, 2006.

Scanlan, Christopher. *Reporting and Writing: Basics for the 21st Century.* New York: Oxford University Press, 2000.

Schwartz, Jerry. *The Associated Press Reporting Handbook.* New York: McGraw-Hill, 2002.

To Click:

The Facebook:
An online directory that helps college students connect through social networks at their schools. It's also an invaluable reporting resource because you can look up students who come from a particular place or are in a particular major.
http://facebook.com/

The Art of the Interview: Neal Conan, Poynter Online, July 2002
http://poynter.org/content/content_view.asp?id=9572

The Art of Interviewing: Gregory Favre, Poynter Online, October 2001
http://poynter.org/content/content_view.asp?id=5165

The Bare Facts of Interviewing: Jim Alexander, Poynter Online, March 2004
http://www.poynter.org/content/content_view.asp?id=60317

Shut up and Listen: Getting the Most from Your Interviews: Steve Buttry, No Train, No Gain Web site
http://www.notrain-nogain.org/train/res/reparc/interv.asp

Guidelines for Interviewing Confidential Sources: Who, When, and Why?: Al Tompkins, Poynter Online, March 2000
http://www.poynter.org/content/content_view.asp?id=4361

Guidelines for Interviewing Juveniles: Al Tompkins, Poynter Online, May 1999
http://poynter.org/content/content_view.asp?id=4571

To Tape or Note to Tape (This article contains a link to a fascinating feedback board on the pros and cons of taping interviews): Chip Scanlan, Poynter Online, December 2002
http://www.poynter.org/column.asp?id=52&aid=15200

Can We Tape? A Practical Guide to Taping Phone Calls and In-Person Conversations in the 50 States and D.C.: Reporters Committee for Freedom of the Press
http://www.rcfp.org/taping/

Figure 5.1. On September 11, 2001, student newspapers around the country were put to the test. Their goal: to deliver complete, accurate and balanced coverage that would put the attacks on the United States into perspective for their readers. *The Ball State Daily News*, Ball State University

Newswriting

"Student dies after 5-story fall."

Who died? Where did it happen? When did it happen? Why did the student fall?

These are some of the questions that would go through a typical reader's mind after reading the headline that appeared in the *Washington Square News*, New York University's daily student newspaper, on October 20, 2003.

A reporter's job is to answer these questions clearly and quickly. Here's how Kate Meyer, the reporter, wrote the story:

Police are investigating the death of an NYU student who fell from a University Place apartment building Saturday night.

Michelle Gluckman, a 19-year-old in the General Studies Program, fell at about 10 p.m. from a sixth-story window to the enclosed courtyard on the second floor of a non-NYU apartment building at 1 University Place, police said. She was taken to St. Vincent's Hospital where she lay in critical condition until she died seven hours later.

The details surrounding the death remain unclear, but the police said Gluckman likely jumped and was not pushed. "There's no criminality involved," said Sgt. John Grimpel, a police spokesman.

Gluckman's death is the second at NYU in nine days and the third this semester. A College of Arts and Science freshman jumped to his death from the 10th floor of Bobst Library on Oct. 10, and a CAS junior leapt from the same floor of the library Sept. 12.

Notice how in four paragraphs—just a little over 150 words—the writer has answered the basic questions and even put the story into the context of the previous suicides. Interested readers can continue reading for more details; others can move on in the paper, having gotten the gist of the story.

Clear, succinct, informative prose—that's what newswriting is all about.

The Basic News Story

The goal of newswriting is to convey a lot of information efficiently. Journalists do this by using a spare, clean, direct writing style and organizing stories so that readers can get the main points quickly.

Though there are many ways to write a news article, the basic news story generally follows a simple formula, known as the inverted pyramid. In this technique the writer presents information in descending order of importance. The most important facts are presented first in the lede (or lead)—the opening paragraph. Succeeding paragraphs provide added details (Figure 5.2).

The who, what, where, when, why and how—known as the five W's and an H of journalism—are generally answered in the first two or three paragraphs.

An inverted pyramid story usually starts like this:

1. A lede that hooks the reader and captures the essence of the story.
2. A second paragraph that amplifies, or backs up, the lede. This paragraph often explains the impact of the story and answers the who, what, where, when, why and how questions not addressed in the lede.

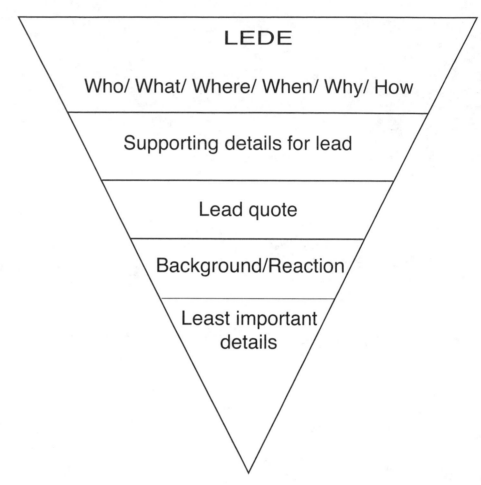

The Inverted Pyramid

LEDE
Who/ What/ Where/ When/ Why/ How

Supporting details for lead

Lead quote

Background/Reaction

Least important details

Figure 5.2. The inverted pyramid is the traditional form for a news story, with a lede (or lead) that summarizes the news, followed by less important details in descending order of importance.

3. A lead quote that augments the lede. It's usually the strongest quote of the story and adds a human dimension.
4. A nut graph, a paragraph or two that provides context and tells readers why they should care.

The rest of the story typically includes reaction and background information in descending order of importance.

Ledes

The lede of a story is crucial.

"Three seconds and the reader decides to read or turn to the next story," Donald M. Murray writes in his book *Writing for Your Readers: Notes on the Writer's Craft from the Boston Globe.* "That's all the time you have to catch a reader's glance and hold it; all the time you have to entice and inform."

The goals of every lede are to:

- Report the essential details of the story
- Lure the reader into the story
- Make the reader want to read more

Ledes are generally divided into two categories: hard-news ledes and feature ledes. (Lead is sometimes spelled lede, harkening back to the days when editors wanted to distinguish the beginning of the story from the lead type used in printing.)

Hard-news Ledes

A hard-news lede, also known as a summary lede or direct lede, delivers the news immediately:

The Student Center was evacuated for about an hour Wednesday as a result of a phoned-in bomb threat. It was the second threat made on the building in less than a month.

—*The Temple News,* Temple University

Steps to Writing a Story

1. Review your notes. Mark key passages you plan to use—statistics, sources, quotes.
2. Talk through the story. If possible, discuss the story with an editor, fellow reporter or friend. Talking will often help you understand what's most important or most interesting about the story.
3. Decide what's most important. Think about what's most current, what's most interesting, what has the greatest impact.
4. Write a focus statement. Ask yourself: What is the story about? How will it affect readers?
5. Write an outline. It needn't be formal, but sketch out a roadmap for the story, including facts, quotes, anecdotes and observations you want to include.
6. Write a draft. Write it quickly, without worrying too much about style. You can revise and polish later.
7. Craft the lede. Make sure the opening is short and punchy, that it captures the essence of the story and makes readers want to read more.
8. Revise. Read the story aloud to see how it flows. Then go back and rewrite.
9. Check your facts. That includes names and titles, all numbers, addresses, phone numbers, etc.
10. Turn it in. Let the editor know you'll be available to do additional reporting and revising.

Former Northwestern linebacker Braden Jones, who left the university in March after being charged with assaulting and trying to rob a taxi driver, will return to NU as a student and football player this week, he said Monday.

—*The Daily Northwestern*,
Northwestern University

Hard-news ledes are generally short—one sentence or two at the most—and include the most important details. Writers typically try to limit hard-news leads to 30 words or fewer so they'll be easy to read.

Feature Ledes

A feature lede, also known as a soft lede or delayed lede, takes more of a storytelling approach. It may start with an anecdote or a scene that draws a picture for the reader like these:

When friends of 2003 College alumnus Arshad Hasan notified him that he was pictured on the cover of this year's commencement brochure, he was initially flattered. But upon closer examination, Hasan and his friends realized that one detail from his costume was missing—the rainbow tassel that had hung beside the standard black tassel from his cap.

Hasan distinctly remembered having the rainbow tassel—distributed by the Lesbian Gay Bisexual Transgender Center to be worn during graduation ceremonies—as part of his academic regalia. He also knew that it was distinct enough that it could not simply be covered up due to the angle of the photograph.

But while University officials in charge of commencement materials have admitted since then that the photograph was edited, they have also said that slight alteration to published images is standard procedure.

—*The Daily Pennsylvanian*, University of Pennsylvania

Kevin Costello should have spent last Friday doing what every college freshman does during his or her first couple of weeks at their new campus and home—settling into dorm life, getting to know his classmates and looking forward to the semester ahead.

Instead, Costello's family and friends remembered the 17-year-old in a private memorial along the coast of Monterey Bay, after he died Aug. 31 from serious injuries sustained in an accidental fall in the Marin Headlands.

—*Golden Gate [X]press*, San Francisco State University

Feature ledes may be several paragraphs long. Because readers don't always know from the start where the story is heading, writers need to provide a nut graph to guide them. A nut graph, or focus graph, explains the point of the story and why readers should care. It should come early in the story, usually in the third to fifth paragraph.

Here's an example of a soft lede and a nut graph from *The Arkansas Traveler* at the University of Arkansas:

When Charles Martin left the UA (University of Arkansas) in 1941 to fly C-87s across the infamous Himalayan passage to China called "The Hump," he was a senior and "president of everything," he said, chuckling as he looked through his UA Razorback yearbook.

Now, while working through UA correspondence courses, he suffers occasional "senior moments" of another type.

"It's so much more difficult now," he said. "I don't know if you know what a senior moment is, but sometimes I have senior moments and it makes taking examinations a lot harder."

Martin, his hair grayed and his 6-foot-2-inch frame bent by arthritis, will walk with the class of 2005 and earn a Bachelor of Arts in Journalism, the degree he started in 1937.

The fourth paragraph, the nut graph, explains why Charles Martin is newsworthy.

Another type of soft lede, sometimes known as a "scene setter," evokes a vivid image.

It is mid-July, and piles of papers are scattered across the floor and tables of Assistant Dean of Freshman Lesley Nye Barth's Hurlbut Hall apartment. As she sorts through the collection of papers, her cat wanders into the room, stepping on and destroying a few carefully ordered stacks—groups of four roommates that she had spent hours assembling as she culled 550 or so housing applications for the perfect match. The cat's romp sends her back to step one, and she gathers the papers to rematch the students.

Such is the life of the three assistant deans of freshman (ADFs), Lesley Nye Barth, James N. Mancall, and Sue Brown, who spend nearly two-and-a-half months hand-picking rooming groups and then assigning these groups to create entryways.

It's a process that takes hundreds of hours and turns the summer—when most administrators take a relaxing break from the frenetic pace of the school year—into some of the busiest months for the Freshman Deans Office (FDO).

—*The Harvard Crimson*, Harvard University

Another popular technique is to use an anecdotal lede, one that employs an anecdote or vignette to illustrate the main point of the story.

Anecdotal ledes work particularly well for trend and issue stories because they bring broad topics or problems down to a personal level. Such ledes must be followed by a nut graph that puts the anecdote into context.

Indiana Daily Student reporter Gavin Lesnick used this approach in 2005 for a story on how Indiana University was taking in student refugees after Hurricane Katrina closed several Gulf Coast universities:

John Spotts strolled down Bourbon Street last Friday night, about to begin his freshman year at the University of New Orleans. The next morning, Spotts awakened to a city evacuating ahead of Hurricane Katrina and a college education put on hold.

"It actually happened really quickly," said Spotts, a Brownsburg, Ind., native. "Friday night I was walking around the city and Saturday I woke up and evacuated. I drove to Houston and I realized I wasn't going to be back in New Orleans for awhile."

Spotts is one of a growing number of students who are transferring to IU from universities forced to close in Katrina's wake. Colleges in Louisiana, Mississippi and Alabama have been shut down for an undetermined time. IU has received calls from at least 25 to 30 families and 10 to 15 students have already begun enrolling, said Registrar Roland Coté.

The third paragraph in this story is a classic nut graph. It explains how John Spotts is part of a trend and why the story is timely and important.

Other Elements of a News Story

Once you've crafted a lead, you need to think about what else goes into your story. Most news stories should include some, if not all, of the following elements:

- Numbers—Statistics, dimensions, percentages, population figures quantify and give context to a story. How many people does this affect? How big is this new building?
- History/background—Historical details put a story into context. What happened in the past? How long has this been going on? What do readers need to know about the past to understand what's happening now?
- Financial figures—How much will this cost? What are the financial implications of this policy or program?
- Reaction—How are different types of people reacting to this news? Be sure to include a variety of perspectives—students, faculty, staff; opponents and proponents; winners and losers. In many stories, it's also important to tap people of different races, ethnicities, religions, genders and socioeconomic groups.

- Chronology—In a story with several developments, it may help to lay out a sequence of events. What happened first? Then what happened? What is expected to happen next?
- Description—What do the places, people and things you're writing about look like? Use your senses—sight, taste, touch, smell, hearing—to help you describe what you're reporting on.

In deciding how to order these elements, ask yourself which are the most interesting or most important for the reader to know. Put those elements up high. Then place the less important, less interesting (but still relevant) details lower in the story.

Attribution

In academic writing, scholars generally use footnotes to show where they got their information. In newswriting, journalists use attribution.

All quotations, opinions and statements of fact (unless they are commonly known) should be attributed. Here are some examples:

Factual attribution: The crash occurred at 5:29 p.m., according to the National Transportation Safety Board.

Direct quote: "This is an important time for our campus," said Darlene Smith, vice president for student affairs.

Indirect quote/paraphrase: Assistant Coach Jason Peters said the quarterback will not be allowed to play for the team until the case is resolved.

Quotes

Quotations from sources add human voices to a newspaper story. Quotes capture emotion, offer varying perspectives and add authority to your stories.

But not just any quotes will do. Just as strong quotes can enliven a story, dull quotes can bog it down.

So, what's a good quote? It's vivid, colorful or personal. It expresses a strong opinion (the source's, not necessarily yours). It conveys drama.

When deciding what to quote, listen to the words. Look for quotes that are colorful or original, funny or poignant. The best rule on quoting: If the source says it better than you can, use the quote. If you can say it better—more clearly, more powerfully, more succinctly—paraphrase.

The first quotation in a story is sometimes called the lead quote. The lead quote is usually the strongest quote you have and often sums up the theme or main points of the story or adds a note of emotion, humor or irony.

This story by Elizabeth Cook for *The Minnesota Daily* at the University of Minnesota

Tipsheet: Newswriting

1. **Write tight.** Use short sentences, short paragraphs. A good rule on sentences: If you can't say it in one breath, break it into two sentences.
2. **Leave unnecessary details out of the lede.** Street addresses, times, even unfamiliar names, should go lower in the story.
   Examples:
   Poor: Janet Wong, a 22-year-old engineering major who lives at 22 Mockingbird Lane, was hit by a car while crossing Park Street.
   Better: A 22-year-old engineering major was hit by a car while crossing Park Street.
3. **Avoid passive verbs.** Use active verb construction, where the subject is doing something rather than having something done to him, her or it.
   Examples:
   Poor: Last week's allegation of rape on campus was retracted Monday, said a university police spokesman.
   Better: A woman who claimed last week she had been raped retracted the story Monday, said a university police spokesman.
4. **Translate jargon.** Interpret bureaucratic, legal, scientific or technical language for readers.
5. **Steer clear of clichés.** Avoid tired, overused phrases. Strive for original language.
6. **Omit unnecessary words.** After writing a story, read through it and see how many words you can take out.
7. **Vary sentence lengths.** Stories become dull when all the sentences are the same length.
8. **Back up your lede and nut graph.** Make sure you provide adequate evidence—quotes, facts, statistics—to prove what you say in the beginning of your story.
9. **Read your story out loud.** Listen for word repetition, overly long sentences, awkward phrasing.

Self-Editing

When writing a news story, ask yourself these questions:

1. Does the lede capture the essence of the story?
2. Is it 30 words or less? If not, can you tighten it?
3. Does the lede entice readers to read more?
4. Is the main idea of the story explained clearly in the lede or a nut graph?
5. Is the story concise? Can you remove any unnecessary words?
6. Do the first few paragraphs of the story answer the who, what, where, when, why and how questions?
7. Are the paragraphs short?
8. Is the writing objective, free of editorializing?
9. Does the story have quotes? Are they properly attributed?
10. Are all the facts right? Are they properly attributed?
11. Are the tenses consistent?
12. Is the story free of spelling, punctuation, grammar problems?
13. Does the story follow the newspaper's style?
14. Are all names in the story spelled right?
15. Are all phone numbers correct? (Check by dialing.)
16. Are all dates and addresses correct?
17. Are all Web site addresses correct? (Check by going to the Web site.)

demonstrates the power of a strong lead quote:

> A man convicted of killing a University student in 1997 was executed Thursday.
>
> David Martinez was executed in Huntsville, Texas, for the July 1997 murder of University student Kiersa Paul.
>
> "Only the sky and the green grass goes on forever, and today is a good day to die," Martinez said as his last statement before the lethal injection began.

Some guidelines for using quotes:

- Punctuate quotes properly. Open the quote with open quotation marks and close with close quotation marks. Commas and periods always go inside the quotation marks. A question mark goes within the quotation marks if it's part of the quoted material. Otherwise, it goes outside the quotation marks.

  Example: She said, "Do you really think that's funny?"

- Attribute. Identify the speaker, not just by name but by title or the role the person plays in the story. Put attribution high in the quote, usually after the first sentence.

  Example: "We want this team to be the strongest it can be," said Roger Johnson, coach of the women's basketball team. "We're not going to let a few losses get us down."

- Make a transition between speakers. Each time you quote a new source you should

start a new paragraph. A good way to transition between speakers is by introducing the speaker first and then running the quote like this:

> Junior Sarah Anderson said the college atmosphere helps students hook up without worrying about consequences.
>
> "College students don't feel a societal pressure to commit, which makes a hooking-up lifestyle easier," Anderson said. "It's a fun age to just be able to go out and have fun."
>
> —*The Daily Northwestern,*
> Northwestern University

- Only use quotes you've heard. Don't lift quotes from other news reports; do your own reporting. If you must use a quote from another newspaper, say where you got it.

  Example: "Torture is never acceptable, nor do we hand over people to countries that do torture," President Bush said in an interview with *The New York Times.*

- Clean up quotes—a little. Journalists frequently disagree about how much to correct quotes. Most agree writers should eliminate ums and ers and many believe poor grammar should be corrected. If you do make slight change, use an ellipsis (. . .) to represent deleted material and put any additional words in brackets [ ]. And make absolutely sure you don't change the sense of a quote. If a quote needs too much correcting, it's best not to use it at all.

- Use said. Don't feel you have to come up with synonyms for "said" in attributing quotes. Verbs like stated, remarked, opined, avowed and declared usually sound stilted or overly formal. Readers generally don't notice repeated use of said.

- Keep quotes tight. Don't feel you have to quote long passages from an interview. Look for short, snappy quotes that express the point succinctly.

- Save a catchy quote for the ending. A quote often makes a nice kicker, an ending that finishes a story with a climax, surprise, or punch line.

To Do:

1. Look over the ledes in your paper. Are they brief and concise? Do they entice readers into the story? Do they make readers want to learn more? Do the ledes tend to be similar or do they take a variety of approaches?

2. Plan a lede-writing workshop to help your reporters write better ledes. Invite a professional journalist, journalism instructor or one of your staff's best writers to lead it or just have a group discussion about the ledes in your paper.

3. Set up a buddy system for reporters. Have two reporters talk through stories and read each other's work before turning copy in to their editors.

4. If other media (college newspapers or professional papers, including the *Chronicle of Higher Education*) cover events and issues you cover, compare the stories. Look at the ledes—which were better and why? What details did each story stress? Are the stories equally fair and balanced?

5. Draft a focus statement for every story you write. This will help you organize your stories and write leads and nut graphs.

To Read:

Baker, Bob. *Newsthinking: The Secret of Making Your Facts Fall Into Place.* Boston: Allyn & Bacon, 2001.

Cappon, Rene J. *The Associated Press Guide to News Writing.* Forest City, Calif.: IDG Books Worldwide, 2000.

Chance, Jean and William McKeen, eds. *Literary Journalism: A Reader.* Belmont, Calif.: Wadsworth, 2000.

Fink, Conrad C. *Writing to Inform and Engage: The Essential Guide to Beginning News and Magazine Writing.* Boulder, Colo.: Westview Press, 2003.

Fox, Walter. *Writing the News: A Guide for Print Journalists, 3rd ed.* Ames: Iowa State University Press, 2001.

Franklin, Jon. *Writing for Story: Craft Secrets of Dramatic Nonfiction*. New York: Plume, 1994.

Goldstein, Norm, ed. *The Associated Press Stylebook and Briefing on Media Law*. Cambridge, Mass.: Perseus Publishing, 2002.

Hicks, Wynford with Sally Adams and Harriet Gilbert. *Writing for Journalists*. New York: Routledge, 1999.

Jackson, Dennis and John Sweeney, eds. *The Journalist's Craft: A Guide to Writing Better Stories*. New York: Allworth Press, 2002.

Kessler, Lauren and Duncan McDonald. *When Words Collide: A Media Writer's Guide to Grammar and Style*. Belmont, Calif.: Wadsworth Publishing, 1999.

Klement, Alice and Carolyn Matalene, eds. *Telling Stories/Taking Risks: Journalism Writing at the Century's Edge*. Belmont, Calif.: Wadsworth, 1998.

Knight, Robert M. *A Journalistic Approach to Good Writing: The Craft of Clarity*. Ames, Iowa: Iowa State University Press, 2003.

LaRocque, Paula. *The Book on Writing: The Ultimate Guide to Writing Well*. Oak Park, Ill.: Marion Street Press, 2003.

Murray, Donald M. *Writing for Your Readers: Notes on the Writer's Craft from the Boston Globe, 2nd ed*. Guilford, Conn.: Globe Pequot Press, 1992.

Woods, Keith, Christopher Scanlan, Karen Brown, Don Fry and Roy Peter Clark, eds. *Best Newspaper Writing*. St. Petersburg, Fla.: Poynter Institute and Chicago: Bonus Books. Published annually since 1979.

Zinsser, William. *On Writing Well, 25th Anniversary Edition: The Classic Guide to Writing Nonfiction*. New York: Harper Resource, 2001.

To Click:

Bob Baker's Newsthinking
www.newsthinking.com

Poynter Online's "Ask Dr. Ink"
http://poynteronline.org/column.asp?id=1

Poynter Online's "Chip on Your Shoulder"
   Chip Scanlan's column
http://poynteronline.org/column.asp?id=52

Poynter Online's "Fifty Writing Tools"
http://poynter.org/content/content_view.asp?id=61811

The Power of Words: Weekly lessons on the craft of newspaper writing. The Power of Words has been publishing writing tips by the staff of *The Providence Journal* almost every week since August 1997.
http://www.projo.com/words/past.htm

MS&U
The State News

¡Salsa!

Sounds and styles from Latin America carry over into Lansing's Metro Bowl where Salsa sways a diverse crowd

By Megan Frye
The State News

It's a well-known fact that the Caribbean clock is not in sync with our tickers in the United States.

Things happen when they happen in this free-spirited lifestyle. The stress-free Caribbean clock carries over to Lansing on Saturday nights.

Saturday night is, and has been for the past two years, salsa night at the Metro Bowl Entertainment & Sports Complex, 5141 S. Martin Luther King Jr. Blvd. in Lansing.

The building houses a bowling alley and multiple bars. Salsa nights are held in a relaxing lounge area with a bar and a dance floor and ample seating.

By 11 p.m., about 50 people are congregated in the lounge, catching up with old friends and making new ones. The music is on, the lights are low and there's a multicolored strobe light hanging from the ceiling. Scents of women's perfume and burning tobacco fill the room, adding a haze to the atmosphere.

Saturday night at the Metro Bowl is the ideal time to witness amazing salsa dancers in action. Many of them have been dancing their entire lives and the ages in the lounge range from 18 to late 60s and early 70s.

Couples hit the dance floor for an intense and exciting dancefest to songs often lasting between six and 10 minutes. On a good night, an average of 50 men and women of all ages, ethnicities and dancing abilities show up to the warm lounge to have the time of their lives.

please see **SALSA**, page 2B

▲ Rosa Quinones dances with Marino Martec on Saturday night at the Metro Bowl Entertainment and Sports Complex. The pair came from Grand Rapids for the Latin dancing hosted at the Lansing club.

◄ Dancers fill the floor Saturday night at the Metro Bowl Entertainment and Sports Complex, 5141 S Martin Luther King Jr. Blvd in Lansing.

Photos by Megan Spelman
THE STATE NEWS

1·2·3·salsa

Salsa is danced in eight beats, with stress on the even beats. On the even beats, dancers shift their weight, and on the odd beats, they break (split their feet apart). The leader usually starts with the right foot and, after four beats, repeats the steps with the left. Here are the basic salsa steps (advanced salsa dancers can embellish them):

① Shift weight to right foot on first beat

② Move left foot forward on second beat

③ Shift weight back onto right foot on third beat

④ Move left foot back next to right foot on fourth beat

Repeat the first four steps, this time starting on the left foot

Source: http://www.geocities.com/Broadway/Orchestra/3202/salsa_patterns.htm

Nick Mrozowski/The State News

Figure 6.1. Lifestyle pages should capture the passions of your readers and bring graphics, photos and text together into an enticing package. *The State News,* Michigan State University

The Lifestyle Pages

Perhaps more than any other section, the lifestyle pages in a student newspaper should be relevant, edgy, fresh. Don't simply look to the big daily newspaper in town for ideas; you don't want stories about home decorating or how to plan for retirement.

Your lifestyle coverage should capture the obsessions, frustrations, gripes and passions of your student population. For possible models, look to your favorite magazines or alternative weeklies. Better yet, look and listen around you. You should be writing about the things people talk about in dorm rooms and cafeterias, at parties and in the laundry room.

Lifestyle Coverage

Lifestyle, or feature, stories may be light, frothy pieces about fads and fashions or serious and insightful ones about such weighty issues as date rape, binge drinking or suicide. The best newspapers make room for both.

The State News at Michigan State University, for example, produces a daily "MS&U" page with a mix of lifestyle and entertainment coverage.

On Tuesdays the paper runs "Faces & Places," a weekly section devoted to in-depth feature stories and photos (Figure 6.2). "The section tries to capture the character of MSU and its community," says Perry Parks, editorial adviser to the newspaper. "The students try to do stories that branch out, ones that don't quite fit into the other features sections."

Lifestyle pages shouldn't limit themselves to straight text stories. "A relevant, hip college features section must include alternative storytelling: lists, Q&As, first-person squibs, '5 minutes with' shorts, the list goes on," says Alicia Roberts, features editor for *The State* in Columbia, S.C., who worked on *The Flyer News* at the University of Dayton. "Think of your favorite magazine; it usually has a handful of meaty stories and a raft of short, easily digestible items. Features sections should be planned the same way."

Types of Lifestyle Stories

Whether they run in a designated lifestyle section or on the front page, feature stories usually fall into one of several categories:

Profiles. Feature stories about a particular person.

Trend stories. Stories that capture a trend, such as an increase in foreign students, or a fad, like Texas Hold'em or lip piercing.

Service features. How-to, where-to-go or what-to-do stories that provide a service to your readers.

First-person accounts. Stories in which the writer shares his or her own experiences.

Features linked to a news event are called news features. Other timely pieces may hang on a holiday, season or cultural happening. Stories without a time peg are known as evergreens because they can run any time. A good features editor always has a few evergreen stories on tap in case another story falls through.

Profiles

Profiles are a great way to humanize your coverage and bring people to your pages. Some newspapers have a regular spot for pro-

---

INSANE IN THE BRAIN: Cypress Hill commits with 'Till Death Do Us Part' release. **page 4B**

Section **B**

Faces & Places
The State News

TUESDAY
April 27, 2004

"I wish I could do it again... I hope the same thing continues to happen at MSU and every other college campus that does animal research."
— Rodney Coronado, convicted ecoterrorist

Convicted eco-terrorist Rodney Coronado is arrested in March for interfering with a mountain lion hunt in Arizona.   Francisco Medina/Tucson Citizen

RODNEY CORONADO
Then: In the early 1990s, the militant Animal Liberation Front launched an offensive against several fur farms and animal researchers during "Operation Bite Back." In 1992, Coronado took part in a raid of MSU research facilities that destroyed more than 30 years of research and caused more than $125,000 in damage.
He was later sentenced to 57 months in prison for his involvement in the raid.
Now: Since he was released from his probation terms in 2002, Coronado has returned to the circuit, making speeches and encouraging others to join the movement. He said his history gives him a platform for serving as a voice of the revolution.
Impact: He isn't interested in going back on the front lines. Coronado said, "I am not going to be burning anything down. Those days are over."

ACTIVISTS UNCAGED

Convicted terrorist warns 'U' could still be a target 12 years after attack rocked campus

STORY BY STEVE EDER

Notorious eco-warrior Rodney Coronado is warning animal researchers at MSU and elsewhere that they are being watched and targeted by the radical environmental movement.
But don't expect Coronado to be the one lighting the fire.
Rather, the 37-year-old who spent 57 months in prison for firebombing MSU research laboratories is traveling the country and inciting a new generation of militant environmentalists to carry the torch.
"Our direct action is more necessary now more than ever," Coronado said during a phone interview last week from his home in Tucson, Ariz. "It is, more than ever, up to citizens to hold corporations and individuals accountable for their environmental crimes."
Coronado, a longtime leader of the underground Animal Liberation Front, has been connected to numerous raids against animal research centers, some of which occurred about a dozen years ago. In the early 1990s, ecoterrorists invaded several fur farms during "Operation Bite Back," an offensive aimed at bringing mink research to a halt.
On Feb. 28, 1992, Coronado and the Animal Liberation Front struck MSU, destroying research and causing more than $125,000 in damage.
The aggressors stormed the office of now-retired animal science professor Richard Aulerich, erasing more than 30 years of exploration into nutrition and the natural decline of mink populations. The bombing also claimed 10 years of work by then-assistant professor Karen Chou, who was studying ways to use fewer animals in experiments.
They also ransacked an MSU mink research farm

please see **ATTACK** page 3B

KAREN CHOU
Then: When ecoterrorists bombed Anthony Hall in 1992, Chou lost 10 years of research on ways to use fewer animals in experiments. Then an animal science professor, Chou vowed to press on and continue her work.
Now: Chou is an assistant professor of toxicology, studying how environmental contaminants impact human health.
Impact: The attack forced Chou to consider what breeds environmental radicals, and she began to evaluate her own research techniques. "I believe in the value of life," she said. "I don't ever design a study without first thinking how many animals I need and what's the value of the study."
Chou says the best way for environmentalists to make a statement is to begin communicating with researchers.

Gina Friga/The State News

Eric Morath Faces & Places editor ● phone (517) 355-8252 ● fax (517) 353-2599 ● e-mail morather@msu.edu

Figure 6.2. The weekly "Faces and Places" section in *The State News* offers in-depth coverage of the people and places that make Michigan State University unique. *The State News,* Michigan State University.

files. *The Otter Realm* at California State University, Monterey Bay, for example, has used its back page for "Artist Spotlight," a full-page profile of a student in the arts. One semester, the page focused on visual artists and included photographs of their art pieces; the scope was later expanded to include student musicians, dancers, actors and other artists.

Other newspapers regularly profile interesting professors or staff members.

Profiles needn't be told in straight prose. Q&As and list formats also work well. *The Auburn Plainsman* at Auburn University has run a regular feature called "Joe/Jane Random," a Q&A with a random student on campus. Questions include: What's your favorite place in the world? What's the best advice you've ever received? What was your most embarrassing moment? What's the easiest class you've taken?

The Simpsonian at Simpson College in Indianola, Iowa, runs a weekly feature called "The FlipSide," a "Dewar's Profile"-style piece on a student, faculty or staff member that lists the subject's favorite movie, food, drink, motto, etc. "These stories are very well-received by our readers," says Brian Steffen, faculty adviser to the newspaper.

Trend Stories

Are toga parties back in vogue? Are more students studying Italian than ever before? Are ballet slippers or flip-flops or belly button rings or charm bracelets all the rage? Trend stories capture fads, fashions and, well, trends.

The best way to spot a trend is to look and listen around you. What are people wearing, doing, talking about? What's hip? What's new? What's different?

When a hookah bar opened in the college town of Chico, Calif., Ashley Nelson, staff writer for *The Orion* at the California State University campus there, wrote a story on hookah smoking for the features section. It began:

> When you hear students talking about a load of shisha, they're not talking dirty, they're talking hookah.
>
> Taking a hit of the 'hubbly-bubbly' has become one of the latest crazes around college campuses, and Chico is no exception.
>
> With the smokin' opening of Café Nile at 243 W. Ninth St., students can sit down, relax and buy a load off the latest hookah lounge in town.

Nelson did her research. The story went on to include the history of hookahs (Middle Eastern water pipes), comments from one of the café's owners and even health information about the risks of hookah smoking.

Colorful illustrations and interesting graphic packaging made the story appealing.

When writing a trend story, try to track down statistics that capture the phenomenon. If, for example, you're writing a story about the knitting craze, it would be impossible to find out how many people on your campus knit. However, you can find out how many new knitting supply stores have opened in your community in recent years and get measures of how those stores are doing. A shopkeeper may tell you that business has doubled in the past year or a knitting instructor may say she's had to add five new weekly classes to keep up with the demand.

And with the Internet it's easy to find publications, associations and trade groups associated with virtually any hobby, business or health condition you can think of. Such groups can often provide just the statistics you seek.

Service Features

Where can you take a date for dinner for under twenty bucks? How should you prepare for a semester abroad? How do you get into the most elite sororities and fraternities? What are some ways to reduce stress around final exams?

Service features offer expert advice and useful tips on meeting the challenges of life. As with trend stories, the key to a good service feature is research. If you're doing a story about reducing stress, don't just ask five random students how they cope with tension.

Talk to experts. Interview a psychology professor who has written a book on stress. Look for research studies on stress reduction. Sit in on a meditation or yoga class on campus, and follow up by interviewing the teacher and some of the students. The more thorough your research, the more useful your story will be.

First-person Accounts

Unlike news stories, features occasionally use first person. When should you use this more personal writing style? When you've got a unique perspective on the story.

If you overcame your fear of water by taking a whitewater rafting trip or you had a near-death experience with anorexia, you've got a story to share. Tell it. Often, though, first-person writing is simply a crutch. Think about whether you have something extra to offer the reader. If you don't, stick to third person.

Finding an Angle

College newspapers often write about the plagues of young adulthood—drug addiction, credit card debt, eating disorders, abortion. These are interesting and important topics for college students and absolutely appropriate fodder for a college newspaper.

However, these stories can often sound like generic term papers on social problems. The trick is to find a fresh angle.

Recent statistics or research studies often provide such an angle. News developments are even better. When a 21-year-old student

Tips from the Pros

■ **Debby Herbenick and Jennifer Bass**

Want to write a sex column but don't know where to start? Running out of ideas for topics? Wondering where to get quality information? The Kinsey Institute Sexuality Information Service for Students (KISISS), which publishes the syndicated sex Q&A column *Kinsey Confidential*, offers these tips on writing sex and relationships columns.

1. **DO be clear about your goal for the column.** Is it to provide information? Advice? Entertainment? Or some combination of these?

2. **DO search for accurate, research-based information.** Thanks to the Internet, it's possible to search online in a range of professional, scholarly journals. You can find these through your campus library, Ovid, Ebsco or http://scholar.google.com.

3. **DO use clear language and specify behaviors.** For example, 'having sex' may not mean the same thing to all of your readers.

4. **DON'T assume the gender or sexual orientation of readers.** For example, if a woman writes in asking how to perform oral sex on her partner, don't presume that her partner is a man.

5. **DO ask professionals with expertise in public health, medicine or psychology to review your column.** Sexual health is an important area of life that many students struggle with, and accurate information can be tough to come by.

6. **DON'T sacrifice accurate information for a laugh.** Respect the fact that your newspaper's column may be some students' only source of sex education.

7. **DON'T use the column for the sake of self-exposure.** Yours is a forum for ideas and information, not exhibitionism.

8. **DO refer to resources for additional information.** A Web site with reference links is a good addition to any column. For suggested references, see the list at the end of this column.

9. **DO strive for a balance between accurate information and interesting writing.** Accurate information is only useful if students actually *read* the column.

10. **DO have fun with the column!** Sexuality is often portrayed exclusively through a lens of disease and difficulty. Let's not forget how pleasurable sexuality can be.

Sex Information Sites

Society for Human Sexuality
http://www.sexuality.org/

Kinsey Institute Sexuality Information Service for Students
http://www.indiana.edu~kisiss

The Kinsey Institute for Research in Sex, Gender, and Reproduction
http://www.indiana.edu/~kinsey/

The Center for Sex Research at California State University Northridge
http://www.csun.edu/~sr2022/

Society for the Scientific Study of Sexuality
http://www.sexscience.org/

Alan Guttmacher Institute
http://www.agi-usa.org/

Planned Parenthood Federation of America
http://www.plannedparenthood.org/

American Association of Sex Educators, Counselors and Therapists
http://www.aasect.org

Sexuality Information and Education Council of the United States
http://www.siecus.org

Debby Herbenick is a researcher and the coordinator of The Kinsey Institute Sexuality Information Service for Students. Jennifer Bass is the head of information services at The Kinsey Institute for Research in Sex Gender and Reproduction at Indiana University.

---

at California State University, Chico died in a fraternity hazing incident in 2005, student newspapers (as well as professional papers) around the country wrote about hazing in their communities. A rash of suicides at New York University prompted student papers to explore the issue of student suicide.

If there's no news to peg a feature to, prowl the Web looking for organizations, news stories and published research that may help you find a fresh angle. Look for experts on your campus by asking the public affairs office, checking your school's online database of experts or talking to professors in related departments. With each potential source, look for something new. Is there a new treatment for this condition? Is a professor doing research on this topic? Are police seeing an increase or decrease in reports of this type of crime?

Sex and Relationships Columns

It's hard to say if Carrie Bradshaw, the fictional columnist of "Sex and the City," spawned them, but sex columns have become a staple of 21st century college newspapers. From "Between the Sheets" in *The Tufts Daily* to "Sex on Tuesday" in the University of California, Berkeley's *Daily Californian,* these columns have raised eyebrows around the country.

In a number of cases, they've also raised the hackles of campus officials. In 2003, officials at Wagner College in Staten Island pulled copies of *The Wagnerian* and threatened to fire the adviser after the biweekly paper published a graphic sex column. In 2005, the editor of *The Campus Communicator* at Craven Community College in North Carolina cancelled the paper's sex column,

"Between the Sheets," after getting complaints from readers and administrators.

One defense for writing a sex and relationships column is to make it educational. That means doing real research—scouting for studies, reading books on sexuality, interviewing experts (scientific researchers and therapists, not just the Casanova down the hall). A number of universities have sexuality research centers on campus. (See the resources list at the end of Tips From the Pros.)

To Do:

1. Organize a features brainstorming session for your lifestyle staff (if you work for a small paper without a dedicated features staff, put together a group of reporters, editors and designers or even invite the whole staff). Start with a particular ques-

Confessions of a Sex Columnist

I've been stopped in the street, pointed at, whispered about, hit on and hollered at. In the small, middle-of-nowhere town of Chico, Calif., with just over 70,000 people and a university where everyone knows your name and 15,000 students binge with pride, even the average student can find it hard to go unnoticed.

I volunteered to write a weekly sex column for the school's award-winning newspaper, *The Orion.* I crossed my fingers, hoping the community would enjoy reading about all the times I uncrossed my legs.

Every Wednesday, I taught 20-somethings how it was, how it could be, how it is and of course, how it should be. Every day, as I strolled through campus, almost everyone passing by knew my sexual resume. I revealed things I hadn't even told my best friends about. Oscar-worthy fake orgasms, threesomes, dentist chairs, home videos, vibrators, oral sex and back doors—nothing was too hot for me to handle.

Gaining celebrity status in such a small town was quite an adventure. Within the first 10 weeks I managed to make a name for myself as "the sex girl." And once I realized that my audience reached far beyond the town of Chico, that's when it really climaxed. Imagine your parents knowing all your sexual experiences—in print. Weird.

It's funny how it happened. I wasn't a writer and I didn't study journalism; I was a graphic design major.

I was the art director of *The Orion* and just happened to be around when the editorial staff was throwing around the idea of adding a sex column. With the recent prevalence of sex columns in college newspapers throughout the nation, it sounded like a great idea.

So one night in September 2003, I fell asleep an average college student and woke up a "sexpert."

Some moments were a little creepy, like going to a party and finding my picture cut out of the newspaper and hung on the refrigerator. Or when the person next to me in class would be reading my column and look up at me, then back down at the picture and up again, realizing that there I was, in the flesh, while reading about my anal sex preferences.

■ Jessie Gardner

Jessie Gardner was the sex columnist for The Orion, the weekly newspaper at California State University, Chico, from September 2003 to May 2004. During her four years with The Orion she also served as designer and art director. She graduated in 2004 with a degree in communication design. She now lives in Reno, Nev., where she works as a designer for Primo Advertising.

But it was the e-mails that shocked me the most. One person blamed me for AIDS and cultural decay, while others actually thought I would call and have sex with a complete stranger because they sent me their number. Just because I wrote a sex column didn't mean I was easy.

A few of my ex-boyfriends got mad after they read the column and found out I didn't mean it when I said, "I love you, too." And some got back in touch with me after they learned how I felt about sex with an ex.

I wasn't sure how being the sex columnist would affect my sex life, but it made it better. I didn't even know it could get any better. My text messages got steamier and I found new ways to make sex fun outside of the bedroom. Even though my parents were mortified, other women were resentful and ex-boyfriends sent me hate mail, it felt so good to be naked—stripped of society's baggage and free to own my sexuality and to share it with anyone who wanted to read about it.

In college, there's a lot to deal with. School, stress, work, roommates, relationships and, yes, sex. There was a lot of it going on where I went to school, and not many sexually active college students are willing to be open about it, so why not write a sex column, address the issue and encourage a healthy sexual lifestyle?

---

tion like: "What's hard about being a student?" or "What are the best things about this school?" or "What's frustrating about going to school here?"

2. Come up with a theme for a standing feature or column for your lifestyle section. It could be a student-artist-of-the-week or professor-of-the-week profile or some kind of tips list (such as a weekly 10 best—the 10 best places to kiss on campus, the 10 best classes, the 10 best places for a first date, etc.)

3. Designate at least one designer to focus on your lifestyle section. Make sure that person comes to meetings, including lifestyle staff brainstorming sessions and editorial budget meetings.

4. Look for service feature ideas and try to assign one for each lifestyle page.

To Read:

Blundell, William E. *The Art and Craft of Feature Writing.* New York: Penguin, 1988.

Franklin, Jon. *Writing for Story, Craft Secrets of Dramatic Non-Fiction by a Two-Time Pulitzer Prize Winner.* New York: Penguin, 1986.

Friedlander, Edward Jay and John Lee. *Feature Writing for Newspapers and Magazines: The Pursuit of Excellence, 4th ed.* New York: Longman, 2000.

Johnson, Carla. *21st Century Feature Writing.* Boston: Pearson Education, Inc., 2005.

To Click:

American Association of Sunday and Features Editors
http://www.aasfe.org/

Association of Food Journalists
http://www.afjonline.com/

Society of American Travel Writers
http://www.satw.org

Question & Answer

What did you get out of your college newspaper experience?

Working on my college paper helped me develop a voice and work quickly on deadline. By editing other people's stories, I learned to see the holes in my own. Writers often get wrapped up in the details and forget to give the reader a straightforward, one-sentence summary of what the story is about (often called the "nut graph," or it could be considered your thesis statement). I make sure I always put this three or four paragraphs into my story so the reader is comfortable and isn't still asking "What's this story about?" on the jump page.

What do you know now that you wish you had known when you were on your college newspaper?

That paid circulation is much harder to achieve than a free newspaper passed out to students! Also, that if you want a job in this industry, you need to hammer the cops and do breaking news stories to be taken seriously by employers. Features can be a great outlet, but no rookie college grad is going to land a general-assignment lifestyle or entertainment position. You have to pay your dues.

What can student newspapers do to make their features and lifestyle stories more relevant and interesting to readers?

Pull them to the front page. If you think features should only be confined to the features page, you're only writing fluff. Feature writing gives stories room to breathe. They're the crucial articles that uncover trends that don't happen overnight, that won't be in a breaking news article, but tell us something important about the world we live in. Think of features like enterprise articles, or news articles written in a narrative style. Don't pigeonhole them as fashion articles, celebrity news and quirky profiles.

A strong feature would be about students

■ Josie Roberts

Josie Roberts started making newspapers in second grade, when she created the Peters Creek Press on primitive fax paper and tucked it behind all her neighbors' mailbox flags. She's never stopped reporting. At the University of Virginia, she served as life editor (2000-2001) and assistant managing editor (2002) of The Cavalier Daily. After an internship with National Public Radio in Washington, D.C., she landed her first paid job in Niagara Falls, NY with the Greater Niagara Newspaper chain. She currently reports for the Pittsburgh Tribune-Review.

using Ritalin to stay up late and study for exams—why is this happening, where do they get the prescription, what are the dangers, how prevalent is it? Just because there's a news angle doesn't mean it can't be approached as a feature. This would be one to plant as the centerpiece on the front page.

What kinds of stories would you want to see in a student newspaper lifestyle/features section?

I think the features should mine the pulse of the campus. In 10 years, if someone picks up an old issue of the newspaper, it will be less important who won the student council election and more important that you catalogued the trends on campus, the attitudes of the students, the political swayings, the unique quirks that made that year so distinct. It's like a cultural study. I always say that you should look at the lifestyle pages as entries to a time capsule.

What advice do you have about finding subjects for and writing personality profiles?

Talk to your friends—you're surrounded by interesting people on campus. *The Washington Post* once did a story where the reporter hammered six nails into a phone book and profiled the people where the nails stopped. It was fascinating and proved that everyone has a story.

Don't overquote. Use details. Make the person's character come out.

Any tips for finding trend stories?

Look around you. When you have an idea, write it down right then. Otherwise, you will forget it. And trust your instinct. If you think something is interesting, pitch it to the editor. If it caught your eye, it probably will catch others' too.

We once did a "reporters' challenge" where four teams (two reporters and a photographer each) met at 9 a.m. at a central location, ventured north, south, east and west, and had to a have a story and photos in by 9 p.m. We were forced to find stories in everyday situations and found some of our strongest features by just talking to a bakery owner out in the countryside and interviewing people passing through our town at a rest stop.

Any other advice for college newspaper reporters or editors?

Get an internship at a *daily* paper.

Get a second internship in another medium like radio, television or the Internet. Media is becoming mass media and the next generation of journalists will have to do it all.

Finally, read, read, read. Read *The New York Times*. Read *The Washington Post*. Read *Smithsonian* magazine. Read *People*. Read everything.

Figure 7.1. Large photos and information boxes in the sports section sometimes tell the story better than long text articles can. *The Missourian,* University of Missouri

Sports editor: **Mark F. Barnett** | tel. 882-5729 | e-mail barnettm@missouri.edu

PLAY

The sporting life, both in the stands and in the air.

NEWSUNDAY MISSOURIAN · September 19, 2004

With a 7-0 win against Arizona, the Cardinals clinch a playoff spot. **MAJOR LEAGUE BASEBALL, PAGE 4B**

A friendship between two Missouri volleyball players from China has spanned six years and many miles. **PLAYERS, PAGE 5B**

Skydiving isn't just for the deranged. B.J. Wolters shares tips for beginners. **GEARHEADS, PAGE 16B**

MISSOURI 48, BALL STATE 0

BACK ON THEIR FEET

Tigers' crushing win sets stage for Big 12 play

Gary Pinkel knew his team needed to improve after a disappointing game at Troy.

"I think there's an expectation level out there, and there should be," Pinkel said. "I told our football team after the game a week ago is that we let a lot of people down, and there's an expectation level out there. Missouri fans expect us to have a very good football team."

On Saturday at Memorial Stadium, the Tigers treated the 57,279 fans in attendance to a 48-0 win against Ball State, the biggest shutout since they defeated Kansas in 1986.

"I thought it was more of a complete game," Pinkel said. "Obviously, it feels a little bit better, get some of that bad taste out of our mouth from a week ago. Offensively, defensively, kicking-wise, it was probably our best team performance."

Pinkel and the Tigers have a little time to enjoy this one. They have a bye before beginning the crucial section of their schedule, Big 12 Conference play.

"Now it's Big 12 time, and we've got to become a better football team," Pinkel said. "That's the message I've sent to my team. I think we're a lot better than what we have shown, but we have got to become a better team."

The Tigers open Big 12 play Oct. 2 when they host Colorado, which has won five straight games against Missouri.

Now the expectations get heavier.

— S. Scott Rosenberg

MORE INSIDE

Missouri's defense keeps getting stronger, holding Ball State to 142 total yards of offense. **Page 10B**

Highs and lows: Thomson Omboga cranked up the speed, but false starts hurt Missouri in the fourth quarter. **Page 10B**

The Tigers prevented Ball State from gaining ground in the second quarter. **Page 10B**

Players of the game. **Page 8B**

Reserve running back Tyrone Roberson runs Ball State's Chris Allen over Saturday. Due to the large margin of victory, most of MU's back-ups played in the fourth quarter.
SHAUNA BITTLE/MISSOURIAN

5 KEYS ANSWERED

1 STARTING QUICKLY: The Tigers came out slowly, going three plays and out on their first possession but soon had their offense working methodically. They outgained the Cardinals 111-56 in the first quarter but scored three points. They scored on the first play of the second quarter, though.

2 SUSTAINING THE QUICK START: The Tigers played their best second quarter of the season, scoring 28 points and turning the game into a rout. Quarterback Brad Smith ran for 50 yards and passed for 98 in the quarter. The Tigers scored 14 points in 17 seconds late in the quarter.

3 STRENGTHENING THE DEFENSE: Excluding the effort of Adell Givens, the Cardinals struggled to produce. The Tigers became the third team this season to hold the Cardinals to less than 220 yards, allowing 142. The Tigers had three sacks.

4 TURNING AROUND TURNOVERS: The Tigers finished with a plus-two turnover ratio, but more important, they did not commit a turnover, the first time this year that has happened.

5 ELIMINATING MISTAKES: Although they did well for most of the day, the Tigers committed some offsides penalties, six for 44 yards. The penalties didn't stop any drives, though. Still, the Tigers committed several penalties on punt returns, which negated long returns from wide receiver Thomson Omboga.

— Missourian staff

Chapter 7

Sportswriting

Whether it's fall football games that bring thousands of shivering, beer-swilling fans to the stands every weekend or boisterous pick-up soccer games on the quad, sports are a vital part of college life, and the sports pages are an integral part of any college paper.

Good sports stories not only inform and entertain, they help build a sense of community on campus. Here's where your readers can follow the ups and downs of your school's teams, learn about the people inside the uniforms and get an understanding of the role athletics play on your campus.

In the professional world, sports sections are among the best read—and often among the best written—pages of the newspaper. Readership studies show that 50 percent to 70 percent of newspaper readers turn to the sports sections. This can be equally true—or even more so—at the college level, where team loyalty can get downright obsessive.

If you're passionate about sports, being a sportswriter can be one of the most fun and most creative jobs on the newspaper. "It allows you a lot of latitude," says Tyler Kepner, a former sports writer, sports editor and editor in chief for *The Vanderbilt Hustler* who went on to cover the Yankees for *The New York Times*. "You can express yourself a lot more than you can in other sections of the paper while still abiding by the rules of journalism."

But the sports section needn't be the "toy department," as some have called it. College sports is big business and there are myriad opportunities for hard-hitting investigative stories. Why is your school spending millions on a new stadium when classes are being cut? What's the graduation rate for your basketball players? How does your football coach's salary compare to that of your most popular English professor? To what lengths are your college's recruiters going to lure star athletes?

In this chapter we'll look at the ins and outs of sports coverage, from reporting on tonight's basketball game to interviewing the next stars of the NBA, NFL and MLB.

The Role of the Sportswriter
In the *Associated Press Sports Writing Handbook*, Steve Wilstein, a national AP sports writer and columnist, writes, "The sports writer's challenge is to describe events with elegance and passion and wit, to make readers share their laughter or tears or rage, to entertain and inform, to break the news that no one else knows or describe a game that everyone has seen, to impart a feeling for what it was like to be there in the stands or on the field or in the locker room, to give the event meaning and put it in perspective."

Sports writing is about sports, yes, but it's also about good reporting and good writing, about observing and describing, about seeing what's really going on and transmitting that information to the reader.

One of the best ways to understand how sportswriters work is to watch the pros sitting next to you in the press box, advises Mike Rosenberg, a sports writer and columnist for the *Detroit Free Press*. "Figure out which ones do the best job, figure out what makes them the best, and if possible, ask them what you could do better." Such infor-

mal friendships with professional sportswriters can also lead to internships and jobs later on.

After you've written your story, see how the professional reporters covered the same event. Did they lead with a similar anecdote? How did they describe that key play? What structural devices did they use? Which statistics did they include? Take note of their use of quotes and description.

Most sports stories fall into one of these categories: advances, game stories, profiles, trend stories, sports news stories and sports columns. Let's take a look at each type of story.

Advances
A sports advance is a preview story that gives readers insights and information about an upcoming game. Such stories typically include background on the rivalry between the teams and quotes from coaches and key players about what they expect.

In an advance story, it's vital to find a fresh angle. You don't want to simply report that your team is playing the Tigers on Saturday. If your coach or one of your players used to be associated with the competing team, that's your angle. Or focus on the long-simmering rivalry between the two schools, including the last-minute upset the last time they played. Or get players to talk about their concerns about facing the best team in the division.

And don't just stick to your usual sources. Try interviewing coaches and players from

opposing schools who can offer a different perspective.

Game Stories
Game stories—accounts of a particular game or a series of games—are the bread and butter of most sports sections. Written on a tight deadline, particularly for a daily newspaper or Web site, they're essentially breaking news stories.

"You should treat a game story like a news story with the same who-what-where-when-why questions," advises Rosenberg, who worked at the University of Michigan *Daily* as a sportswriter, sports editor, editor in chief and humor columnist between 1992 and 1996. "Why was it important? Why did the team you cover win or lose? If the team lost because of rebounding, feel free to write the whole story about that."

While you want to incorporate details from important moments in the game, Rosenberg adds, "Don't write too much play-by-play. Nobody wants to read about who scored to tie the game in the first half, unless it was a spectacular play. Three or four specific plays are often enough."

For each game story, think about what your readers want to know:

- What made the team (or, in individual events, the athlete) win?
- How did the star athletes perform?
- How did an individual athlete's efforts affect the outcome?

- Were any of the players injured and if so, how did those injuries affect the game?
- Did weather or other environmental factors, such as the condition of the facilities, affect the game?
- How does this game affect the teams' standings and future prospects?
- How did the fans respond?

A game story should include a summary of the game, significant details, key statistics and quotes from players and coaches that offer analysis about what happened. Game stories are often written in inverted pyramid structure, like news stories (as described in Chapter 5), although reporters may use a feature lede rather than a summary news lede.

For daily reports you generally want to open the story with the element that made the difference: Why did the victorious team win? How did a key player save the game? "A game almost always turns on something," says Mark Fainaru-Wada, an investigative sports reporter for the *San Francisco Chronicle* who worked for *The Daily Northwestern* when he was a student at Northwestern University. "You want to be looking for a single play or a period in time or something that dramatically shifts the game."

Here are some examples:

For Travis Mayle, game-winning kicks are becoming just as routine as putting on his uniform every Saturday. Mayle's third field goal of the game—a 33-yard field goal with 13 seconds to play—gave Kent State (2-1, 1-0 Mid-American Conference) the 16-13 win over Youngstown State (2-1) Saturday at Dix Stadium.
—Rob Meyer, *The Daily Pennsylvanian*, University of Pennsylvania

Trailing for the majority of the second half and tying the game on 14 different occasions in the final 20 minutes, it looked as if the UCLA women's basketball team would succumb to Washington and drop just their third game of the season at home.

But the leadership and maturation of the Bruins peered through Thursday night at Pauley Pavilion. Never was it more evident than in the game's final three minutes as UCLA went on a 10-2 run and coerced the Huskies into committing three turnovers, leading to a crucial 86-81 conference victory over Washington (9-13, 5-7 Pac-10.)
—Bryan Chu, *The Daily Bruin*, University of California, Los Angeles

It could have been Jason Dourisseau's final game as a Nebraska Cornhusker. That's why the senior guard did every-

thing in his power to make sure that didn't happen.

With a game-high 20 points on 8 of 13 shooting and six rebounds, Dourisseau helped the Huskers pull off a 71-64 win over Missouri on Thursday night in the first round of the Big 12 Conference Tournament in Dallas.
—Robin Washut, *Daily Nebraskan*, University of Nebraska

Scoring and Notetaking

To help keep track of each play, Fainaru-Wada recommends sportswriters come up with an effective notetaking and scoring system. "It's useful to keep a running log of what's going on," he says. "You want to come up with some sort of formula that works for you and that's easily readable."

When he covers a baseball game, for example, Fainaru-Wada uses a scorecard but he also keeps a log in his notebook as each player comes to bat. He marks every pitch and notes details about the expression on the player's face or movements made by the coach. At the back of his notebook he writes random notes, ideas for the angle he may take with his story or impressions he wants to include.

"It's kind of a juggling act," Fainaru-Wada admits, commenting that he frequently makes notations in his laptop computer as well as his notebook and scorecard when covering a game. "Most of the stuff I won't use but it helps keep me really focused on the game."

Profiles

A profile is a portrait of a particular player, coach, trainer or athletics official. Alumni are also good subjects, particularly if they are still working in the sports arena. One of Tyler Kepner's most memorable profiles for *The Vanderbilt Hustler* focused on Joey Cora, a Vanderbilt alum who was then playing for the Chicago White Sox. "It was all about his college days. He talked about his coach and how he was great in math," Kepner says. "He hadn't really talked about those times for years."

Players and coaches who have overcome obstacles are also good profile subjects, as are those from sporting families. Look for key moments, like when one of your players faces his brother on the basketball court or when a player returns to the game after weeks or months of being out with an injury.

Bruce Tran of *The Daily Bruin* at UCLA won a national award from the Society of Professional Journalists in 2004 for his profile of a football player who was injured in a motorcycle accident. Here's how it began:

For several seconds, Keith Carter could have cared less about the National Football League.

Instead of dreams about the NFL draft and lucrative contracts, Carter's thoughts turned to his family, his friends and his life. Despite side-splitting pain, the UCLA tight end couldn't help but wonder about his coaches and teammates.

Even as he was being lifted into the ambulance, even after he had come so close to losing his life, and even as his mangled motorcycle lay on the ground just yards away, he muttered to the paramedics, "You guys have no idea how bad my coaches are going to kill me for this."

And in that instant, everything about Keith Carter changed. His thoughts no longer centered on professional football.

They focused on simply making it back to the Rose Bowl in a UCLA uniform.

When you're reporting for a profile, try to interview the source off the field or the court. The best profile interviews are conducted in people's homes, where you can see how they live and gain insights about their personal lives. Ask about their goals, their motivations, their strengths and insecurities. Find out when they started playing and what obstacles they faced. Ask about the person's childhood and how it influenced their commitment to the game.

Good profiles have multiple sources. Coaches, fellow players, roommates, family members, lovers and friends can all offer insights into what makes the person tick. And don't forget to watch your subject in action—at practices, at games, even in the classroom.

Sports Features

Feature stories capture a trend or a slice of life about a sport or a team. When writing feature stories about a team, look for winning or losing streaks, how a team works together, tensions that lead to divisiveness. You can also do features on recruiting, tryouts, training regimens, coaching philosophies or how a particular news event—such as the resignation of a coach or a series of player injuries—affects the team.

The pressures and demands on college athletes can also make for good sports feature stories. Robert Samuels wrote an insightful piece for *The Daily Northwestern* in 2003 about African-American athletes on the mostly white campus and the stereotyping they face. Joe Watson blew the lid off college football recruiting in a piece for *The State Press* at Arizona State University.

Sports News Stories

When a coach resigns, is hired or fired, that's news. When a melee breaks out after a basketball game, that's news. When an athlete is charged with sexually assaulting another student, that's news.

Many of the stories on sports pages around the country are news stories. Such stories follow the structure of standard news stories and should respect the same rules of balance, objectivity and fairness. Often big sports news stories will start on the front page and jump inside.

Sports Columns

Columns can personalize your sports pages, and really good ones can build a loyal fan base. But that doesn't mean you should hand out regular columns to every aspiring columnist who steps into your newsroom.

Column writing is hard work. And it demands three qualities that most people don't have: an inspired understanding of the sport being covered, an engaging writing style and the creativity to come up with a new angle for each column.

Many wannabe columnists have great ideas for two or three columns and then they run dry. Before assigning someone a regular column ask for a few sample columns and a detailed description of how they plan to approach the column. Make sure the person knows the sport. And ask what they plan to offer readers. Columns can't just report on games or team changes; they must give readers added value.

Covering Sports for a Non-daily

Game stories are fine if you're working for a daily paper. But what if your newspaper comes out weekly or even biweekly? A game story a week or two after the event can be about as enticing as the turkey sandwich you left in your backpack last week. Don't despair. There are two approaches you can take.

One is to can post game stories between editions on your newspaper's Web site. Brief reports on games with photos or photo galleries will give fans the information they need and keep your Web site fresh. *The State News,* Michigan State's five-day-a-week newspaper, for example, posts "Web updates" on games throughout the weekend.

The other option, if you don't have the staff to post breaking stories on your site, is to take the *Sports Illustrated* approach: Use great writing and analysis to keep game stories fresh. "If you're writing for a non-daily paper, you're not writing game stories, you're using the game to tell a broader story about the team or a certain player," says Fainaru-Wada of the *San Francisco Chronicle.* "If a guy is emerging as a star on the team or having troubles, you're going to use that game to tell part of your story." Details from games can also help with trend stories or mood pieces on the team.

Nils Rosdahl, a former sports editor who advises *The Sentinel* at Idaho Valley College in Coeur d'Alene, recommends students working on non-dailies open game stories with a look-ahead lede. "Write about what's coming up, what do you expect of your team's next opponent, what's the team doing to prepare? Then you can do a roundup of games since the last issue and talk about what worked and what didn't."

Beyond Team Sports

What if you don't have a championship football or basketball team on campus? What if only 25 fans—most of them parents, girlfriends and roommates of the players— show up for a typical game? What if the biggest sport on campus is ultimate Frisbee? Then you write about ultimate Frisbee. Fill your sports pages with news about the sports that people are talking about—the new women's rugby club on campus, how the gym just got three new elliptical trainers, the cool sailing class that has a waiting list each spring.

At North Idaho College's *The Sentinel,* some of the most popular sports stories are features about non-team pursuits, many of which occur off campus. The paper frequently writes features and columns on hunting and fishing, whitewater rafting and frisbee golf. "We find these stories lend themselves to some of the best photos in the paper," adviser Rosdahl says. "We always have full color on the back and we often reserve the back page for these kinds of stories."

Special Sections

One of the best ways to whet your readers' interest in a new sports season is to produce a special preview section (Figure 7.2). Such special sections help to build reader loyalty; your paper gets to be seen as the authority on your team.

You can also create special sections for championship events or "the big game" with your school's arch rival.

Components of a typical preview section include:

- A game schedule
- A team roster
- Player profiles
- Team and player statistics
- Bios on coaches
- History timelines

Web Coverage

The potential content for sports coverage is virtually limitless. Most college sports editors find they have more information than they can possibly put in two or three pages of a newspaper. So more and more, savvy sports editors are looking to the Web to enhance their sports coverage.

The Daily Pennsylvanian has a Web page for each team—from men's squash and basketball to women's fencing and tennis—with standings, statistics and stories from that season (Figure 7.3). *The Daily Orange* at Syracuse University hosts forums on its major sports, basketball and football, where readers can comment on games, coaches, how the team is performing.

Non-daily papers can take advantage of the Web's immediacy by posting game stories or even just game scores online between editions. Slideshows and galleries of game photos are also popular features on many student newspaper Web sites.

Avoiding Bias

If you're covering sports, you're probably a sports fan and if you're writing for your college newspaper, you're probably a fan of your school's team. **Don't let it show**.

"The trickiest part of sportswriting is not showing that you're rooting for the team you're covering," says Lee Jenkins, a former *Vanderbilt Hustler* sportswriter and editor who went on to become a sportswriter for *The New York Times.* "You have to learn not to cheer in the press box, even if you want to. Your stories should cover the team through the eyes of someone interested in the team but not rooting for that team. You have to take the bias out."

That means not wearing a college sweatshirt or hat to games, not raising your fist when your team scores a touchdown, not using "we" when writing about the team. "Every sports writer was a fan at one time," Jenkins says. "You have to learn to restrain that part of you."

To Do:

1. Invite a sportswriter or sports editor from your local professional paper to speak to your sports staff.

2. Think about ways to use your Web site to enhance your sports coverage. Consider posting slide shows and Web updates or creating team pages fans can use to get complete, up-to-the-minute coverage.

3. If you don't already have one, consider creating a preview section for the biggest sport or sports on campus. Include profiles of athletes, Q&As with a coach, game schedules, history timelines and other elements that will be useful and interesting to readers.

4. Try to go beyond day-to-day sports coverage by planning a special project or feature. Study National Collegiate Athletic Association statistics and reports or look for interesting trends worth exploring.

Figure. 7.2. Sports preview sections help whet fans' appetites for a new season or a big game. 7-11 *Ball State Daily News*, Ball State University

To Read:

Fensch, Thomas. *The Sports Writing Handbook, 2nd ed.* Hillsdale, N.J.: Lawrence Erlbaum & Associates, 1995.

Fink, Conrad C. *Sportwriting: The Lively Game.* Ames, Iowa: Iowa State Press, 2001.

Swan, Jennifer. *Sports Style Guide & Reference Manual: The Complete Reference for Sports Editors, Writers, and Broadcasters.* Worcester, Mass.: Triumph Books, 1996.

Wilstein, Steve. *Associated Press Sports Writing Handbook.* New York: McGraw-Hill, 2001.

To Click:

National Collegiate Athletic Association
http://www2.ncaa.org

College Front Page: This site, created "by student journalists, for student journalists," offers PDFs of college newspapers' sports section fronts, as well as front pages.
http://collegefrontpage.com/

Sportspages.com
http://www.Sportspages.com

The Journalist's Toolbox/Sports
http://www.journaliststoolbox.com/sports/
    onlineindex.html

Associated Press Sports Editors
http://apse.dallasnews.com

College Football History
http://www.collegefootballhistory.com/

The Chronicle of Higher Education, Athletics Section: *The Chronicle of Higher Education* runs articles and special reports on college and university sports.
http://chronicle.com/athletics/

Association for Women in Sports Media
http://www.awsmonline.org/

The Freedom Forum-NCAA Sports Journalism Scholarship Program:
The Freedom Forum, through NCAA, sponsors eight scholarships to college juniors who want to pursue sports journalism.
http://www.ncaa.org/leadership_advisory_
    board/programs.html

The Sports Institute: The Sports Institute at Boston University's College of Communication offers an intensive four-week summer study program on the sports industry.
http://www.bu.edu/com/sports_institute/

Question & Answer

What do you think college papers should do with their sports sections? What can college papers do to compete with professional papers on sports coverage?

Don't believe that just because you're a college paper, you should accept the professional paper in your city breaking the significant news. You're the one on campus. You're the one in class with the student-athletes. And as a journalist, you should want to break news. There are disadvantages here: Coaches and administrators often purposely leak information to the professional paper's beat writer because they're perceived to have more power. But that can be overcome to some extent with diligence.

Also, a college paper typically will have more space to devote to that university's athletics, so use that to your advantage.

What tips do you have for college journalists on covering sports?

Remember to tell a story. At major colleges, everyone is already going to know how each important point was scored by the time they read the article recapping the event. And at smaller colleges, which don't receive the same scrutiny, or possibly the same interest level from fans, no one wants to read a recitation of how every point was scored.

Also, don't discount the importance of being a reporter, even if you're on the sports staff. In nearly every story, there ought to be a nut graph, summarizing what happened and why it's important. And there are plenty of issues in sports. Good sports reporters ought to be able to produce issues pieces— known as enterprise stories—and features to complement game coverage.

Do you have any specific suggestions for covering games?

Use the advantages you have over professional sports writers—including time. Even during games that begin in the afternoon, I'm frequently on deadline. While I try to spend as much time interviewing after the game, I often must return to my laptop sooner than I would like to begin writing so that I make deadline. College journalists, just like those working for *Sports Illustrated* and magazines that cover sporting events, can spend extra time speaking with the athletes and coaches, getting stories and details about what transpired. Also, don't squander that extra time by heading to the newspaper office to write up the story late on the night it's due. Start early.

■ **Adam Rubin**

Adam Rubin started covering sports for The Daily Pennsylvanian *in 1991, his freshman year at the University of Pennsylvania. He served as sports editor in 1994. After graduating from Penn in 1995, he did a one-year internship with* The Birmingham (Ala.) News, *where he covered the U.S. men's Olympic soccer team and then worked in the news department for about six months. He worked as a sportswriter at the Shreveport, (La.)* Times *before returning to a full-time position in the sports department in Birmingham. In 2000, the* New York Daily News *hired him as a general-assignment sports writer; he took over the Mets beat in 2003.*

How about going beyond game coverage?

Again, use the built-in advantages you have. Sometimes it's difficult for a professional journalist—perhaps a guy in his 40s or 50s—to get an athlete to feel comfortable speaking with him, because he comes from a different background and has different interests and an age gap to overcome. You and the athlete you're covering have so much in common, being fellow students, taking similar classes, living in the same dorms, etc. The best interviews come when you're having a conversation with the person you're interviewing, not from a dry Q&A session.

Any thoughts on finding feature ideas?

You glean feature ideas by simply having conversations with the people you cover, being visible and maximizing the amount of time you spend with them.

Features don't only cover the on-field exploits of the best athlete on the team. It's finding out about their personalities and interesting things that have occurred in their lives. You get that by spending time with them and making them feel comfortable, with a pad or tape recorder away.

What advice do you have for sports writers and editors at schools with not-very-competitive or no sports teams?

Whether you're at a university where the athletics teams draw little interest, or covering what's perceived as a minor beat at a major Division I college (I initially covered men's tennis and women's fencing), you do yourself a tremendous disservice by worrying about the actual interest. You need to treat your beat like it's important. The athletes and coaches will notice the interest you're taking and reward you by opening up. Plus, sometimes off-the-radar teams are the best to cover. It's very hard on a major professional beat to write a

feature about an athlete that hasn't already been told. You're telling stories for the first time. And often these people will have fascinating backgrounds if you dig deep enough to uncover them. Also, you're probably underestimating the actual readership, especially with most newspapers now on the Internet. Parents and other relatives read the stories, as do fraternity brothers, sorority sisters and other friends of the athletes, plus opposing coaches.

What were your most memorable moments as a college journalist?

From a journalism perspective, the most exciting moment was the night before Penn was to name its new athletics director, Steve Bilsky. As sports editor, I found out Bilsky would be arriving on an Amtrak train from Washington the night before the news conference. We dispatched a reporter and photographer to meet him at the 30th Street Station. As he's riding the escalator up from the tracks, we're shooting pictures of him arriving in Philly. He also consented to a brief interview. His first words were, "Boy, you guys are good."

From a sports perspective, it was a thrill to cover Penn's trip to the NCAA basketball tournament and clinching the Ivy League football title at rival Princeton. While you're supposed to be dispassionate as a journalist, you're still a student at the university and (quietly) revel in the success.

How can college papers make better use of their Web sites in covering sports?

College papers, whether they publish Monday-Friday or weekly, may want to post a short recap quickly after weekend sporting events—like after a Saturday football game—on their Web sites to address the competition from professional papers if it exists, or merely to increase hits on the site.

Consider creating pages on your Web site for each team, with links to the most recent stories, roster, schedule, statistics, etc. With technology these days, you can also put up audio or video of interviews, etc.

How did your experience on the college paper prepare you for your professional career? What do you wish you had known about sports writing then that you know now?

I would not be a sports writer today without *The Daily Pennsylvanian*. I was enrolled in Wharton, the business school at Penn. But I enjoyed so much working for the *DP*—first because of my affinity for sports, then because of my affinity for journalism—that I decided to seek internships with newspapers rather than in business. By the time I graduated, it was a natural choice to enter journalism.

There are so many things you learn about sportswriting after college that it's difficult to cite just one. One warning, though, would be that journalism in competitive markets can be all-consuming. As a baseball beat writer, I'm typically on the road 170 days a year.

Figure. 7.3. *The Daily Pennsylvanian has a section on its Web site for every major sport.* Dailypennsylvanian.com, University of Pennsylvania

the lowdown

on the web:
www.statenews.com/lowdown

MS&U entertainment • The State News

grand ole **LANSING**

Why does such a large and unique mix of country exist in a Midwest, capital city?

2B

Animal science senior Curtis Shoup sits and plays the banjo. Shoup is an avid listener of country music, which is on the rise in the East Lansing area.

Julie Dewey/The State News

march 4-march 10: get out. get down.

happenings
get out and do something.
Go online for a list of upcoming events.

www.statenews.com

tada!
jot down your inner emo.
Make your very own fabulous, fabric-covered angst receptacle — adorned with buttons.
page 6B

film
screen king
'Rings' star moves on to new project with Friday's release of 'Hidalgo.'
page 4B

Elysia A. Smith MS&U editor ● **phone** (517)355-8252 ● **fax** (517)353-2599 ● **e-mail** msandu@statenews.com

Figure 8.1. The arts and entertainment section of a student newspaper should be an indispensable guide to what is happening on and near the campus. *The State News,* Michigan State University

Chapter 8

Arts and Entertainment Writing

I t's Friday afternoon and a bunch of friends are sitting in a dorm room planning for the weekend. What's playing at the multiplex? Is that student production of "Midsummer Night's Dream" worth seeing? What band is performing at the student union tonight?

If your arts and entertainment section is any good, the savvy students will depend on your paper to find out what's hot and what's not.

College students are among the biggest consumers of pop culture. While everyone else is raising kids, going to work and getting up early in the morning, students are out late, soaking up the local culture. So arts and entertainment coverage should be a major component of any student newspaper.

While you want to be an authoritative source of information, don't make the mistake of trying to imitate the daily newspaper—or even the funky alternative weekly—in town. Instead, set your own course.

"Student newspapers should offer up-close reporting on college life and culture," advises Peter S. Scholtes, a staff writer for *City Pages* of Minneapolis, who got his start at the *Minnesota Daily* at the University of Minnesota. "Most of the time, student papers focus on the same things other papers focus on when it comes to arts and entertainment. Young journalists want to be like older professionals and don't realize that their greatest resource is being themselves—young and surrounded by student life."

Arts writing should be evocative and distinctive, like this piece on the band the Cramps Sean McCourt wrote for *Golden Gate [X]press*, the weekly newspaper at San Francisco State University:

If the creatures, monsters, demons and derelicts that haunted many of the classic B-movie horror films of the 1950s came to life, invaded the Memphis recording studio of Sun Records, and partied with Carl Perkins, Elvis Presley, Johnny Cash and Jerry Lee Lewis, the end result of those sessions might have sounded something like the Cramps.

For nearly three decades now, the Cramps have been unleashing their fiendishly twisted and mutated style of rock 'n' roll on an unsuspecting world—surviving revolving door line-up changes, disastrous record label deals, and a myriad of obstacles that would have caused any lesser group of musical monsters to drive a stake through their own hearts. But through it all, the mainstay devilish duo of Lux Interior on vocals and Poison Ivy on guitar have proved that staying sick (and true to their ideals) pays off in the long run.

Chances are, you wouldn't find that in a mainstream daily newspaper.

Entertainment coverage should be diverse. It's fine if the music reviewer is a Shania Twain fanatic, but the A&E editor should make sure the section covers more than country music. Your A&E pages should have a mix of music, dance, film, theater and

Tips from a Pro

■ **Roger Ebert**

Before becoming a celebrated film critic, Roger Ebert was a columnist and editor for The Daily Illini *at the University of Illinois. Ebert has written for the Chicago Sun Times since 1967 and is well known for his TV work opposite critic-colleague Gene Siskel on "Siskel and Ebert" (they were formerly hosts of PBS's "At the Movies"). In 1975, he became the first film critic to win a Pulitzer Prize. He is the author of several books on the cinema, including* A Kiss Is Still A Kiss *(1984), and screenplays, most notably Russ Meyer's cult classic,* Beyond The Valley of the Dolls *(1970).*

You were editor of *The Daily Illini*. What memories do you have of working on the college paper? How did your experiences as a student journalist influence your career?
I published and edited a weekly alternative paper as a freshman, then went over to the DI as a columnist and became news editor before I was editor. It was, and is, a real daily newspaper, independent of the university, and the best education was working with a union printing shop, which of necessity made deadlines real.

What can college papers do to make their arts and entertainment coverage interesting and relevant to their readers? What can they do to set their coverage apart from professional papers?
Find and develop colorful, quirky first-person essayists, and the taste of the majority of the students be damned.

What advice do you have for young arts and entertainment writers? What tips do you have on writing reviews?
Always write in the first person. Be closely in touch with what you really felt, even more than what you really thought. Experiment with form.

What can student reviewers do to research and become more knowledgeable about the films they review?
Simple. See lots of movies, read about them, talk about them, study them, teach them.

Any other tips, advice, words of wisdom for young journalists?
1. The muse visits during the act of composition, not before.
2. No article will ever be finished unless it is started.
3. If you procrastinate, play with deadlines and delay doing assignments, get out of the business. You're not enjoying it.

visual arts and cover many different genres within each category.

Arts and entertainment sections primarily run five types of stories:

- Previews
- Reviews
- Columns
- Feature stories
- News stories

Since we've covered features and news stories in other chapters, we'll stick here to previews, reviews and columns.

Previews
Previews, or advances, are stories that tell about upcoming performances and exhibits. These are often the most useful stories be-

cause they help readers plan what they want to see. An A&E section with strong previews becomes an essential guide to culture in your community.

Advances may be written as briefs or as longer feature stories. You can take a general approach or focus on a specific aspect of the artist or performance. For example, if a student group is staging a play on campus, you may write a story that takes readers behind the scenes of a rehearsal or one that focuses on the hopes and aspirations of the director. For a preview of an art show, you may decide to bring readers to the artist's studio or interview the curator about what the work represents. If an out-of-town band is coming to town, try to interview members a week or two before by phone to give readers a sense of what's in store.

When writing a preview, be sure to include practical information for the reader, such as dates, times and location of performances or exhibits; phone number for the venue; and, if appropriate, ticket prices. This information may be written in italics at the end of the story or, better yet, included in an information box packaged with the story and photo.

Reviews

Nearly every writer who has sat through an embarrassingly bad film or been transported by a glorious musical performance has fantasized about becoming a critic. What could be more fun than sharing your fervent opinions with thousands of readers dying to know what you think?

But reviewing isn't simply about dumping your opinions, says Harry Kloman, a film critic who advises *The Pitt News* at the University of Pittsburgh. "To be a real critic, and a good critic, you need to have three things: First, you need to have the ability to write well. Second, you need to have the ability to report. And third, you need to have the ability to think."

A review is a critical analysis of a performance, exhibit or other artistic work. Most reviews include five basic elements:

- A catchy opening that draws readers into the piece
- Identifying information, including the name of the work, the primary artists involved, where and when it can be seen
- A concise summary of the content of the work
- A critical assessment of the work, including its strengths and weaknesses and whether the audience would appreciate it
- Background and history, such as other creative works by this artist and how this work compares with others in the genre.

"Do your homework," advises Scholtes. "Learn how to use libraries and book stores and Google and Lexis-Nexis so that you really know where a piece of art or music or film is coming from, and you aren't just using press releases."

In his book *Five Stars! How to Become a Film Critic, the World's Greatest Job,* Christopher Null, editor in chief of Filmcritic.com, offers one simple rule to writing a good review: BE HONEST.

"That's it!" writes Null, who worked on *The Daily Texan* when he was a student at the University of Texas at Austin. "Whether you are writing your first review or your 3,000th review, if you aren't honest with yourself, with the film, and with your readers, your review is useless. You can 'be nice' about your criticism or you can get really de-

■ Checklist
Entertainment Review

When writing a review, ask yourself these questions:

1. Do you clearly identify the performance, CD, film, exhibit, etc. being reviewed?
2. Does the review include relevant information (perhaps in an accompanying information box) about times, dates, locations of performances or showings, prices, etc.?
3. Does the review clearly identify the genre (such as classical, hip-hop, reggae, country-Western for music; comedy, drama or thriller for film; modern, ballet, flamenco for dance, etc.) and describe how this work fits in with other pieces in this genre?
4. Do you explain how the performance, film or other work being reviewed achieves its intent? Does the work make you laugh, cry, think the way you're supposed to? Why is it effective or not effective?
5. If there's a story, do you give enough of a synopsis to help the reader understand the work without giving away the whole plot?
6. Do you offer a critique of the work, detailing what was effective, what wasn't and why? Do you back up your criticism with telling examples?
7. If relevant, do you critique individual performances, explaining what worked, what didn't and why?
8. Do you include background information or history about the artists involved? Is this the first time this actor has performed at this theater? Is this band homegrown or visiting from afar?
9. Do you include audience reaction if that's relevant?
10. Do you give readers a sense of whether they would enjoy this work or performance?

tailed with your complaints, but all of this is meaningless if you don't tell the truth and provide an analysis that comes from your heart."

That said, you may want to use tact when criticizing student artists. It's one thing to slam the latest Jim Jarmusch movie or Linkin Park CD; it's another to skewer a student actor or musician who has screwed up his courage to get on stage. That doesn't mean you should give a glowing review to a dull, lifeless performance. But save the big guns for someone making the big bucks.

The First-person Dilemma

To write in first person or not to write in first person; that is the question for every critic. And even professional reviewers can't agree on the answer. Some see first-person writing as arrogant, unprofessional or just plain lame. "The use of 'I' is a crutch for a young critic," says Kloman, the Pittsburgh critic and *Pitt News* adviser. "You should do more than just *discourage* it. You should *banish* it."

Others say first person adds personality and intimacy to a review. Pulitzer Prize-winning critic Roger Ebert of the *Chicago Sun Times,* for example, advises reviewers, even students, to *always* use first person.

Perhaps the best advice is to write what feels natural to you. Each reviewer has to find his or her own style, a persona in print.

Columns

Just like columns in your sports section, A&E columns provide unique perspectives that add personality to your paper. Some newspapers have columnists who regularly cover film, music or another artistic arena.

Columnists should have a deep understanding of the art they cover. You needn't be a film major to cover film, but you better know your Spike Lee from your Spike Jonze.

To Do:
1. Invite a professional critic to give a lecture on reviewing to your A&E writers or to your entire staff.
2. Invite professors from your theater, film, music, television, dance or art departments to participate in a panel discussion or a series of workshops for your staff on arts coverage.
3. Contact the visual and performing arts groups and classes on campus to find out when they are having exhibits and performances.
4. Assign a reporter and photographer to follow one production from beginning to end. Ask if you can sit in on tryouts, rehearsals, set and costume design sessions. The reporter and photographer's collaboration could become a series, a long feature or multimedia piece on the making of the production.

Tips From a Pro

■ **Sean McCourt**

When I was working on my student newspapers, co-workers sometimes would come up to me and ask, "How in the world did you ever get to interview (insert band name here)?!"

It doesn't take a miracle, or having some shady connection in the music business, to set up interviews with bands—even famous ones. But it does take a little effort, patience and passion on your part. Here are some tips for making it as a music writer:

1. **Take advantage of time spent on your student newspaper.** You will probably have more freedom to do what you really want to do now, when your editors and co-workers are fellow students, than when you're working at your first job. Don't put off trying to set up the interview with the band or musician you have always dreamed of. It may take a while for you to establish yourself after you graduate, and if you follow rock 'n' roll, you know there is a distinct possibility that the performers you most want to interview will have broken up (or even be dead) by the time you're a pro.

2. **Make contacts.** Come up with a list of local clubs, venues and promoters, and call or e-mail all of them. Tell them who you are and ask to get on their mailing lists and to receive their press releases. Chances are that your readers are their target customers, and they should be happy to work with you.

3. **Maintain a professional attitude.** Don't expect to immediately get in to every concert for free or expect special treatment. Professional relationships in the music business can take as long to cement as romantic ones do.

4. **Reach out to local bands and record labels.** They are more likely to get excited about coverage and can be a great source for other contacts as well—not to mention the fact that many independent bands playing in smoky dive bars are just as good as, if not better than, the ones getting all the radio airplay or MTV coverage.

5. **Spend a night out on the town.** Try to make it out to as many concerts and shows as your schedule and budget allow. You'll get a much better sense of the pulse of the local music scene and hopefully, enjoy yourself while doing it.

6. **Make it happen.** When you see that a band or musician you want to interview is coming to your town, get in touch with your contact at that particular venue, and ask for the band's contact information. The act's manager or record label will arrange to set up the interview and provide you with a press kit, advance CDs, etc. Most of the time you will do the interview over the phone—that way the article can run in advance of the group's local appearance. With local bands, it is more likely that you'll be able to do the interview in person, which can give you a better feel for the people involved.

7. **Be persistent.** If you can't get an interview the first time, try again. It took me three years to get an interview with Mike Ness of Social Distortion, but it was well worth the effort.

8. **Remember to relax.** Don't get intimidated by a big interview. It can be hard at first, but if you are comfortable and at ease, your subject will most likely be as well.

9. **Do your research.** Even if you think you know all there is to know about the history of the band or musician you are going to interview, take the time to really get to know them. Listen to as much of their music as possible, read old interviews, look them up on the Internet, etc.

10. **Think your questions through, and write them down.** Don't throw together 10 random questions right before the interview. Try to think of as many different queries as possible. Try for something a little meatier than the standard "what are your influences?" or asking for drunken tour stories (although they can occasionally be entertaining).

11. **Use a tape recorder when conducting an interview.** But take written notes as well. You never know if the tape will break, the batteries will run out, or the recorder will suddenly seem to be possessed. If you at least have some basic notes, you can usually salvage the interview—not to mention face your editor when he or she asks what happened to the great story you promised the week before.

12. **Avoid using clichés.** It can be tempting, especially if your deadline is looming, and we are all guilty of it as beginners, but try to work around them. In this business, it's all about setting yourself apart from others. If you sound just like everybody else, you won't make a name for yourself.

13. **Most of all, have fun!** That's why we're doing it, right? If you're passionate about something, it shows—especially in your writing.

Sean McCourt is a freelance writer who specializes in music. While attending San Francisco State University, he worked on the Golden Gate [X]press *newspaper as a staff writer and arts and entertainment editor. During his time on* [X]press *(and at his junior college newspaper) he interviewed both local bands and world-famous musicians, including members of Nirvana, the Pixies, Social Distortion, X and the Cramps. He has written for the* San Francisco Bay Guardian, Sierra Magazine, 7x7 Magazine, *and* Rockabilly Magazine.

To Read:

Corrigan, Timothy. *A Short Guide to Writing About Film, 5th ed.* Upper Saddle River, N.J.: Longman, 2003.

McCoy, W.U. *Performing and Visual Arts: Writing and Reviewing.* New York: University Press of America, 1992.

Null, Christopher. *Five Stars! How to Become a Film Critic, the World's Greatest Job.* San Francisco: Sutro Press, 2005.

Titchener, Campbell B. *Reviewing the Arts, 3rd ed.* Mahwah, N.J.: Lawrence Erlbaum Associations, Inc., 2005.

To Click:

American Theatre Critics Association
http://www.americantheatrecritics.org/

Association of Music Writers and Photographers
http://www.amwp.org/

Blogcritics.org
http://blogcritics.org/

Broadcast Film Critics Association
http://www.bfca.org

Dance Critics Association
http://www.dancecritics.org/

FilmCritic.com
http://filmcritic.com/

Music Critics Association of North America
http://www.mcana.org/

New York Film Critics Circle
http://www.nyfcc.com/

Online Film Critics Society
http://ofcs.rottentomatoes.com/

Screen Actors Guild
SAG represents nearly 120,000 actors in film, television, industrials, commercials and music videos. As a member of the press you can get names of talent agents of most actors.
http://www.sag.org

Question & Answer

When did you decide you wanted to be a TV critic?

Pretty much my senior year of high school. I was the first entertainment editor of my high school's newspaper and I decided I preferred TV over film as a medium.

What intrigued you about writing about TV?

I'm very drawn to character-driven storytelling and in TV writers have 22 episodes to tell a story, which allows for a lot more nuance and realistic development than one can get in a two-hour movie.

Were you a TV junkie as a kid?

Not really. I liked TV, but we never had cable growing up and my parents did limit my TV viewing time. TV was not a babysitter for me.

What experiences at *The Daily Orange* helped shape you as a writer and a critic?

Hmmm, all of them. *The Daily Orange* was like an incubator for real-world journalism. I learned about internal politics at a newspaper and dealing with writers who can't meet a deadline. I learned to manage difficult personalities, encourage younger writers and balance work at the paper with school work. They're all useful skills that translate into real post-collegiate life.

What advice do you have for students who want to cover arts and entertainment?

Just do it. By that I mean, don't be afraid to approach the student newspaper and its editors with your ideas. My first year at Syracuse University in 1989, I wrote up a preview of the fall 1989 TV season and walked it up to *The Daily Orange*, figuring they'd never run it.

Little did I know campus papers are constantly starved for copy. They ran that story and every other movie/TV review I wrote during the next four years.

■ Rob Owen

As a student at Syracuse University, Rob Owen dreamed about becoming a full-time television critic. In his freshman year he started writing about TV and movies for The Daily Orange, the campus newspaper, and went on to become the paper's lifestyle editor. After graduating in 1993, he went to work for the Richmond Times-Dispatch as a feature writer and co-creator of a teen section called inSync. He got his first TV critic job at the Times Union in Albany, N.Y. in 1996 and in June 1998 got his dream job—full-time TV editor at the Pittsburgh Post-Gazette. In 1997 he published the book Gen X TV: The Brady Bunch to Melrose Place, an account of the TV programs members of the Generation X age group grew up watching, the shows they watch now and the programs that depict their lives.

Specifically, it's great to cultivate a network of sources, whatever beat you take on. If it's the movie beat, try to get passes to press screenings of movies before they open. If it's the music beat, call the record companies and get on their mailing lists. Don't expect things to come to you, you have to go after what you want.

How can student journalists and critics get film, music and other entertainment industry people to take them seriously?

By acting professionally and by not being a flake. If you ask for an interview and they grant it, send them a clip. If you ask for a CD to review and you review it, send them a clip. Do not request a pass to a movie just because you want to see the movie.

Learn to work with the publicity folks. That doesn't mean you do what they tell you or take every pitch they send your way, but building a rapport and relationships will definitely help you get taken more seriously.

How can college papers provide a fresh angle on entertainment coverage when there's so much coverage in professional newspapers?

College newspapers are at ground level of youth culture, which is what seeps into the

pop culture, so college papers can be at the forefront of covering what bubbles up from youth culture, particularly when it comes to music.

What kind of research is involved in entertainment criticism? What can student critics do to be more authoritative and knowledgeable in their criticism?

Read, read, read. Read as much criticism as you can. Not to copy it, but to get examples of different styles of critical voice. It also does not hurt to have a broad liberal arts base, particularly when it comes to movie/TV criticism (wish I had more of that). Take courses in the subject area that's your beat and become an expert in that area. Talk to the critic on your beat at the local paper to get his/her advice.

Any other words of wisdom for entertainment or lifestyle writers and editors?

Be organized! Your life will be much easier if you plan ahead. That said, also be prepared to rip up a page to make it more timely. That will happen in the real world.

COMING UP
Columnist Aaron Lalic discusses what the university can do to compete with other campuses for new students.

OPINION
THE SHORTHORN

ABOUT OPINION
Brock Rutter, editor
opinion-editor.shorthorn@uta.edu
Opinion is published Wednesday and Friday

Friday, September 14, 2001

Page 3

EDITORIAL/OUR VIEW

Cutting Class

The UT System should have canceled classes Tuesday so the community could recover

EDITORIAL ROUND-UP

The issue:
The UT System should have given students Tuesday off.

We suggest:
UT System officials exercise more consideration in the future.

The UT System did its students and employees a disservice by not cancelling classes Tuesday in the wake of the day's disaster. The decision was unproductive, unprecedented and disrespectful to students and employees who were fearful for loved ones' lives.

Whatever UT System administrators hoped to accomplish not canceling classes was surely not accomplished. Many students simply were too shocked or too transfixed by the news to come to class at all. Others who did go to class, did so with the burden of the day's news weighing heavily on them, diminishing their ability to pay attention. Still others went to class to find that the day's lecture had been turned into a discussion of the horrible events — something better done in the company of friends and loved ones. Whether or not any progress was made in any specific classes, almost without exception, the material covered will have to be re-covered because of absences.

Tragedies of this magnitude are fortunately few and far between. Perhaps the only two tragedies on par with this in any living person's memory are President John F. Kennedy's assassination and the Japanese attack on Pearl Harbor in 1941. Tuesday's tragedy, involving more deaths than either of the two — and civilian deaths at that — is arguably the worst of the three. In the previous cases, nearly everything in the United States shut down.

New York is a big city — some say a business capital of the world. As a consequence, many at UTA and through the UT System have friends, family and loved ones there. For some, the first reaction to Tuesday's news was to telephone or e-mail acquaintances living there to be sure they were safe. That is more important than class. Anecdotal stories from students who were berated for being late or missing class because they were trying to contact loved ones are particularly disturbing.

Let us hope we will not live to see another such tragedy. However, if we are unfortunate enough that that should happen, let us hope the UT System will have learned a message in human nature and good taste and give us all, students and employees, the day off.

GUEST COLUMN

A New Patriotism

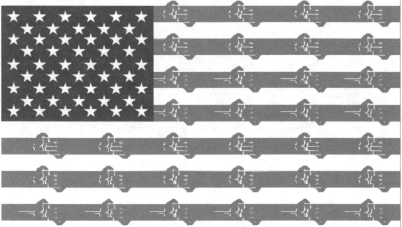

The Shorthorn: Jeff Shaw

Terrorist attacks spur a forgotten sense of American pride

Joel Fish is a journalism senior. He can be reached at opinion-editor.shorthorn@uta.edu

Buried under the piles of rubble and depressing emotion in the aftermath of the worst terrorist attack ever on American soil is a glimmer of something wonderful.

Let me demonstrate what I mean:

Several months ago a friend of mine reacted to an American flag draped on the wall of my new apartment. He laughed, asking irreverently if I was "patriotic or something?"

My answer, obvious as it seemed to me, was a confused and fervent "Yes." He chuckled and shook his head.

Tuesday evening, as I watched the White House press conference addressing the horrors in New York City and Washington, D.C., my friend phoned me to talk about the incident. His tone couldn't have been more different than it had been just several months before. Like most Americans, he felt violated and fearful. But most of all, he felt patriotic.

America has indeed gained something wonderful from this disaster. People are singing the national anthem and, miraculously, they really mean the words they sing. I can't help but wonder if I've ever experienced that before.

With media speculation teeming about who is to blame, and Osama bin Laden on the chopping block, Americans want to know who should be hunted down and punished. Their shared anger, honed like a razor, has brought them back to an "us versus them" usually reserved only for wartime.

Let's not admonish this attitude. There are bad guys and good guys, and I won't insult readers by categorizing those responsible for the attack. It's been a long time since America has faced such a personal threat, and Americans can't forget that the horrors of past wars still exist.

In closing, allow me to shock you with this statement: The terrorists involved in this attack have inadvertently given all surviving Americans a gift worth more than all of the gold and jewels in the world.

A long-needed new patriotism has materialized, just in time for the new century.

The Sleeping Giant

Terrorist attacks can't threaten America's existence.

While Tuesday's terrorist attacks on Washington, D.C., and New York were terrifying indeed, in the long run they will not serve the interests of those who carried them out. America, while shocked, is not in mortal danger but only has been awakened.

Wars of terror and attrition can sometimes be successful for a smaller party if it has limited goals, which a more powerful party can satisfy without making concessions that will threaten its very existence. In such cases, the strength of the smaller party is its superior resolve and determination, with which it gradually wears down the will of the stronger power.

Take the examples of the French in Algeria or Vietnam and the Soviet Union in Afghanistan. In all three cases, one party in the conflict was faced with what it saw as a fight for its existence, whereas the stronger party was fighting merely to maintain a superior position of wealth and influence. France's existence never was threatened by the loss of any of its colonies, nor was the Soviet Union threatened by a change of government in Afghanistan. In all three cases, the human and material cost of keeping people down eventually trumped limited advantages gained through occupation.

Brock Rutter is a history senior. He can be reached at opinion-editor.shorthorn@uta.edu

But such strategies do not work when a nation's existence is threatened. Look at Israel today or Britain during the Blitz of World War II. Nearly since its inception, Israel has been the subject of almost continuous terrorist attacks. Israel has proven time and again that its army can defeat any military combination its neighbors can field, yet still terrorist groups seek to wear down the state's will to exist. Similarly, the Germans in World War II calculated (probably erroneously) that they did not have the might to assault Britain head-on in the months after Dunkirk. Instead of attacking military targets, they sought to erode the public's will to fight by bombing British cities.

The campaign against Britain did not work, and Israel still exists despite 50 years of attrition attacks. When a nation's very existence is at stake, there is simply no point at which its people will throw up their hands and say, "It's not worth it." And in such a case, the greater power will win.

On the contrary, when terror is brought to civilians, the population is galvanized. Doves and pacifists are silenced, and the nation under attack finds a new unity. Resolve is mixed with indignity that an enemy would have the audacity to slaughter noncombatants, and the nation under attack finds a focus previously lacking.

Such is the nature of the campaign against the United States. Regardless of who is to blame, the world is awash in the rhetoric of those who call for its destruction, and any moral high ground the attackers claim to have is lost with the lives of innocents. There is no limited concession America is being asked to make that would satisfy the anti-American activists of the world.

In all likelihood, even if Americans gave up their Middle East interests or any other limited goal, extremists still would hate them.

These countries despise America's capitalism, individuality, disciplined political scene, wealth and freedoms that allegedly breed immorality. In short, some groups hate everything America holds dear and, as such, threaten Americans' right to exist. Without a feasible exit, America, or any nation, will fight to the death.

THE SHORTHORN
Since 1919

EDITOR-IN-CHIEF
Jason Hoskins

E-MAIL
editor.shorthorn@uta.edu

The Shorthorn is the official student newspaper of the University of Texas at Arlington and is published four times weekly during fall and spring semesters, and twice weekly during the summer sessions. Unsigned editorials are the opinion of THE SHORTHORN EDITORIAL BOARD and do not necessarily reflect the opinions of individual student writers or editors. Shorthorn advisers or university administration. LETTERS should be limited to 300 words. They may be edited for space, spelling, grammar and malicious or libelous statements. Letters must be the original work of the writer and must be signed. For identification purposes, letters also must include the writer's full name, address and telephone number, although the address and telephone number will not be published. Students should include their classification, major and their student ID number, which is for identification purposes. The student ID number will not be published. Signed columns and letters to the editor reflect the opinion of the writer and serve as an open forum for the expression of facts or opinions of interest to The Shorthorn's readers.

Figure 9.1. Opinion pages provide newspaper staff members and readers alike a place to vent. *The Shorthorn,* University of Texas at Arlington

Chapter 9

Opinion Pages

When *The Baylor Lariat* at Baylor University wrote an editorial in support of gay marriage, the piece didn't exactly play well on the campus of the largest Baptist university in the world. Within days of publishing the editorial, the Waco, Texas college paper was lambasted by faculty and administrators on the school's student publications board, as well as the university president, who said espousing a view "so out of touch with traditional Christian teachings is not only unwelcome, it comes dangerously close to violating university policy."

If you think opinion pages have to be stodgy and dull, think again.

The editorials, cartoons and columns that grace opinion pages can be among the most popular and well-read features of a student newspaper. A good opinion section is a virtual town square for your college community, a place where students, faculty, staff and community members can debate the issues of the day. But this is also the place where student newspapers are most likely to stir up trouble. Because they are so, well, opinionated, opinion pages can be lightning rods for controversy.

Clearly the line between what is provocative and what is simply offensive is narrow—and sometimes ill-defined. What passes for edgy on one campus may be considered insulting on another. In this chapter we'll look at how to create a stimulating, provocative opinion section—and how to deal with the flak that sometimes goes along with that.

The Opinion Section

The classic opinion section comes in two parts—the editorial page and the op-ed (opposite-editorial), or commentary, page. In professional newspapers, the opinion page and op-ed pages are generally on facing pages, often the last two facing pages in the main news or local news section. With less space, college newspapers often combine editorial and op-ed sections into a single page.

The editorial page (Figure 9.2) usually includes:

- A masthead—names of the publisher and the principal editors
- Editorials—opinion pieces that comment on the news and reflect the views of the paper's editorial board
- Editorial cartoons—humorous sketches that comment on news and politics
- Letters to the editor—responses from readers

Let's take a closer look at each of these elements.

The Masthead

At professional papers, the masthead usually names the publisher and top editors, such as the executive editor, managing editor and editorial page editor, and the editorial board. Many student papers, especially those with a small staff, include the names of all editors or even all staffers in their mastheads. Some papers include e-mail addresses for each staff member to increase accessibility.

Editorials

Professional papers generally have dedicated editorial writers whose job is to do research,

form opinions and write cogent editorials on the issues of the day. These people are often senior staffers who came up through the ranks as reporters or editors. Typically they meet as a group on a regular basis to decide what issues they want to weigh in on and what stance the newspaper will take. "At its most basic, the editorial board is a debating club of sorts," Al Lanier, an editorial writer for the *Chicago Tribune*, wrote in a column explaining the process to readers. "We meet three times a week to talk about world events, large and small."

Student newspapers usually have an opinion editor and many have columnists, but few have dedicated editorial writers. Depending on the publication, editorials may be written by the editor in chief or individual editors or reporters. Typically, these are unsigned. It's important to keep in mind that unsigned editorials represent the institutional voice of the paper and the opinions expressed should speak for the editorial board, not just the individual writer.

Editorial Cartoons

Want to get readers to your opinion section? Find a great cartoonist.

Like professional papers, student newspapers use editorial cartoons to comment on the news in a graphic and often humorous way (Figure 9.3).

While editorial cartoons can bring fans to your paper, they can also win you some foes. But that's not necessarily a bad thing, says Dan Carino, whose cartoons for *The Daily Aztec* at San Diego State University were syndicated through KRT Campus and U-Wire for several years. Carino has won numerous national awards, including the prestigious John Locher Memorial Award from the Association of American Editorial Cartoonists.

He's also stirred up a heap of trouble.

On one occasion, students seized thousands of copies of *The Daily Aztec*, demanding apologies from the paper for publishing two racially charged cartoons. One depicted then-Iraqi President Saddam Hussein and Palestinian leader Yasser Arafat as camels with President Bush in the middle, thinking, "Definitely time for a regime change." The other cartoon showed an overweight man labeled "China" speaking in broken English in reaction to the North Korea nuclear weapons program.

In another incident, students and faculty at Indiana University in Bloomington demanded the resignation of the *Indiana Daily Student* editorial staff for running a syndicated Carino cartoon concerning affirmative action.

Despite the flak, Carino, who graduated from San Diego State University in 2003, says

he appreciates the liberty he had as a student. "I believe that there's more freedom in student newspapers and that's something that an aspiring cartoonist should use to his/her advantage," he says. "The nature of political cartoons is to take issues and push them to the extreme, hoping to draw readers into a debate."

Letters to the Editor

Printing letters to the editor is one of the best ways a newspaper can show it's listening to its readers. Your paper should clearly state its letters policy on the editorial page, giving guidelines on length and acceptable language and explaining your right to edit.

Many college newspaper editors complain they don't get enough letters to the editor. If readers aren't coming to you, consider reaching out to them. "You have to go out and sell the idea of writing a letter to the editor to people who don't normally write letters," advises Denny Wilkins, who teaches opinion writing at St. Bonaventure University in St. Bonaventure, N.Y.

A former editorial page editor for *The Recorder* in Greenfield, Mass., Wilkins recommends opinion page editors actively seek out letters by telling everyone they meet—faculty, staff, students—about the letters section and the role it serves. "You should put up posters and fliers; market the page as a place where students can write to tell you what they think about what you think. Go on the campus radio station or TV station and say, 'We want letters to the editor.'"

Wilkins also suggests putting a prompt line on your editorial page each week asking readers to respond in 75 words or less to questions like: What do you think of the new sculpture in front of the student union? Does the school spend too much money on athletics? How is the new registration system working?

Another sure way to get more letters, Wilkins says, is to provide "provocative, evocative content that people will respond to. Write editorials that piss people off."

The Op-ed Page

The op-ed page is a spot for columnists and community members to share their views. Unlike editorials, which reflect the views of the editorial board, pieces that appear on the op-ed page represent the opinions of individual authors.

To make your op-ed page inclusive and lively, solicit contributions from around the campus. If there's a controversial issue on campus—a labor contract dispute, a new smoking ban, a scandal in the administration—solicit opinions from faculty, staff and students who have a stake in the matter. Be sure to seek divergent views.

The Editorial Page

Masthead
A list of the editorial board members, usually the editor in chief, editorial page editor and other representatives of the newspaper staff appointed by the top editors.

Editorial
An opinion piece that comments on the news and reflects the views of the paper's editorial board.

Editorial policy
An explanation of whose views are expressed in editorials and columns and restrictions on opinion section content.

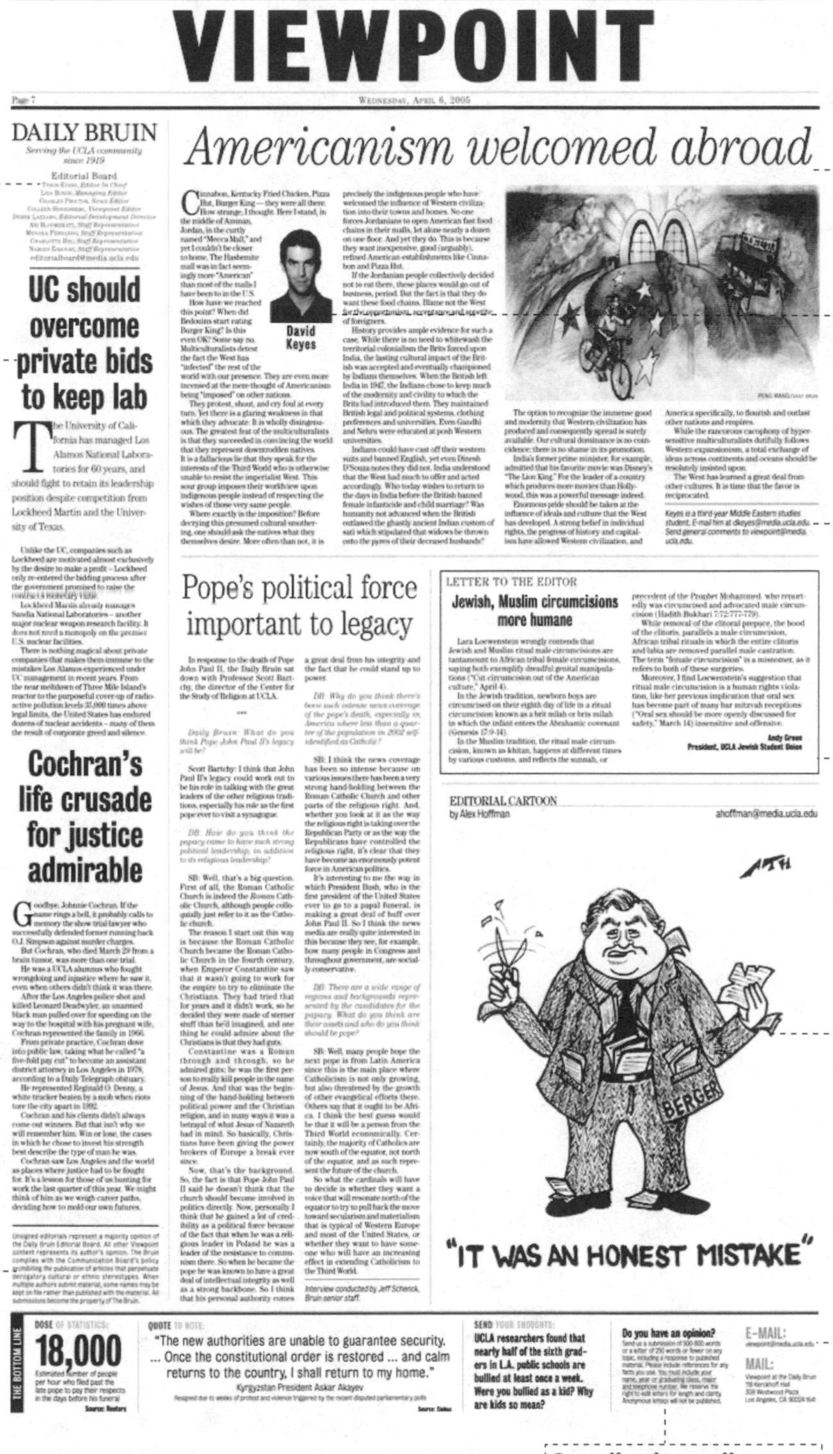

VIEWPOINT

Page 7 — Wednesday, April 6, 2005

DAILY BRUIN

Serving the UCLA community since 1919

Editorial Board

UC should overcome private bids to keep lab

Cochran's life crusade for justice admirable

Americanism welcomed abroad

David Keyes

Pope's political force important to legacy

LETTER TO THE EDITOR

Jewish, Muslim circumcisions more humane

EDITORIAL CARTOON

by Alex Hoffman

"IT WAS AN HONEST MISTAKE"

THE BOTTOM LINE

DOSE OF STATISTICS:

18,000

QUOTE TO NOTE:

"The new authorities are unable to guarantee security. ... Once the constitutional order is restored ... and calm returns to the country, I shall return to my home."

Kyrgyzstan President Askar Akayev

SEND YOUR THOUGHTS:

UCLA researchers found that nearly half of the sixth graders in L.A. public schools are bullied at least once a week. Were you bullied as a kid? Why are kids so mean?

Do you have an opinion?

E-MAIL:

MAIL:

Column
A personal opinion piece by a staff columnist, staff writer or other contributor. Some newspapers label columns as "staff column" and "guest column."

Column logo
A label for a column that includes the writer's name and head shot. Also known as column sig.

Columnist bio
A brief biographical note about the columnist that may include the writer's major, year in school and position on the newspaper staff or job title if it's a faculty or staff person. It may also include the writer's e-mail address.

Letters to the editor
Letters from readers.

Editorial cartoon
A humorous sketch that comments on news or politics.

Contact box
Information on how readers can contact the newspaper opinion section, including mailing and e-mail addresses.

Contribution policy
An explanation of how readers can contribute columns or letters to the opinion section.

Figure. 9.2. The Editorial Page. *The Daily Bruin*, University of California, Los Angeles, Graphic by Eugenia Chien

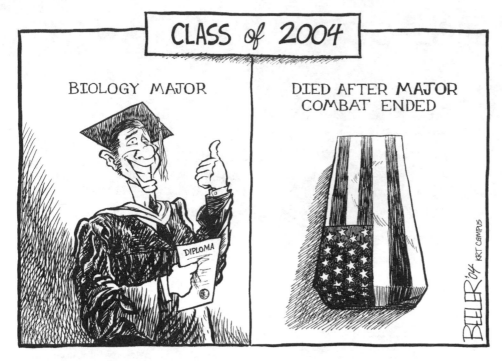

CLASS of 2004

BIOLOGY MAJOR

DIED AFTER MAJOR
COMBAT ENDED

DIPLOMA

BEELER '04 KRT CAMPUS

Figure. 9.3. Editorial cartoons present opinions in a graphic, often humorous way. Reprinted with permission from Nate Beeler

The Editorial Process

Editorials are designed to do more than simply report. Their role is to explain, persuade, warn, criticize, entertain, praise or lead. Some editorials may call for action on a local issue, such as the resignation of an embattled campus official or the overturning of an unpopular policy. Others, like *The Baylor Lariat's* piece on gay marriage, take a stance on an issue of national or international importance.

Many student newspapers have an editorial board that discusses the editorials for each issue. The editorial board may be made up of all the editors of the paper or some subgroup of editors. At the *Iowa State Daily* at Iowa State University, for example, the editorial board is comprised of the opinion editor, the editor, the managing editor and two or three others chosen by the opinion editor through an application process.

"They meet, bring topics to discuss, discuss them, vote on the editorial stance, assign someone in the majority to write the editorial," says Mark Witherspoon, adviser to the paper. "Then that person goes and researches further, but also uses the debate to frame the editorial argument."

While most professional papers have one person, usually the publisher or the editorial page editor, guide the direction of the editorial page, many student editorial boards decide positions by taking a vote of the board. This can be difficult, particularly on divisive issues, and you may want to leave final decisions to the opinion editor or editor in chief. Whatever your approach, make sure you have written guidelines in place on how decisions will be made. Such a policy can help prevent conflicts later on.

Finding Editorial Subjects

Typically the lead editorial for each edition focuses on an issue that's been covered in the news pages of your paper. If your school's governing board recently approved a hefty tuition increase or the college president has just resigned or a fraternity was recently disciplined for hazing, your editorial board will most likely want to comment on it.

But what do you write on those slow news days? Jill "J.R." Labbe, deputy editorial page editor for the *Fort Worth Star-Telegram*, says the best way to find ideas is to look at and listen to the campus around you. "The place you get editorial ideas is the same exact place you get story ideas," she says. "You should be writing about what people care about. Listen to what people are talking about in the cafeteria or in the laundromat or in the bar after class."

Robert Bohler, director of student publications at Texas Christian University where he advises *The Daily Skiff*, recommends students focus on local news. "Nearly anybody can offer up a solution, informed or otherwise, on the strife in East Timor or some other exotic locale, but there are a lot of writers who can do it better than can most college students. What those other writers can't cover or offer opinions on is what's happening locally. If the college newspaper thinks enough of local issues to write stories about them, then those issues have enough impact to warrant thoughtful commentary. It's the next logical step in the citizen's thought process."

Writing an Editorial

Writing an opinion piece, be it an editorial or a column, doesn't mean you can simply spout off at the mouth on the topic of your choice. Opinion writing requires solid reporting. "Most college opinion pages are heavy on the opinion but light on the facts and sources that add any credibility to them," says the *Fort Worth Star-Telegram*'s Labbe.

"You must do your homework. It's easy to have an opinion; it takes hard work to have a reasoned opinion. A plausible argument depends on evidence that is accurate, pertinent to the main assertion and sufficient to support. And there's only one way to gather evidence. You must be a good reporter before you can be a good opinion writer."

Before you sit down to write an editorial, gather your facts. First, read whatever news articles you can find on your subject from your newspaper and others. Next, seek out reports, studies, lawsuits and other documents that will inform your decision. Then pick up the phone and do some original reporting. "I don't know any editorial writers who don't do their own reporting," says Harry Austin, editorial page editor for the *Chattanooga Times Free Press*.

Once you've collected the facts, it's time to write. Editorials usually follow this general format:

- Introduction
- Reaction or stance
- Discussion and details
- Conclusion

■ Checklist
The Editorial

When writing or editing an editorial, ask yourself:

1. Does the editorial have one primary message?
2. Does it sufficiently support the argument it's trying to make?
3. Are the facts accurate?
4. Does the editorial give the reader adequate background and context?
5. Does the editorial make a clear statement about what could or should happen next?

Tips From a Pro
■ Jill "J.R." Labbe

The letters to the editor feature in your newspaper gives your readers one of the few chances they have to speak their minds in public. Letters also help create interest in your editorial pages and, theoretically anyway, should increase readership.

That said, handling letters to the editor can be one of the bigger pains in the butt that an editorial page editor—or, in most of your cases, the editor in chief—has to deal with. If you're doing it right, that is. Because if all you are doing with the letters you receive is slapping on a headline and sticking them in the paper, you are asking for trouble.

You take responsibility for what you publish, and that includes the letters. If they are factually incorrect, or if they contain potentially libelous statements, you're putting yourself and your newspaper in a position to be sued.

That is why a written letters to the editor policy is not just suggested; it should be mandatory. You need to set the ground rules for how letters will be handled, and you need to stick to them. Outline for your readers a suggested length, and tell potential letter writers that you reserve the right to edit their submissions for taste, grammar, libel, length, etc.

Editing letters takes time and a delicate touch. Sometimes, however, no matter how delicate that touch, no matter how hard you tried to maintain a writer's voice and salient point while cutting out the superfluous, you will be accused of violating a writer's First Amendment right of free speech by editing the letter or, even worse, by not running it at all.

Such calls provide you with the wonderful opportunity to gently deliver a constitutional lesson. Only the government can violate someone's free speech right. Last time I checked, I don't work for the government. The letter writer may call it censorship; I call it editing.

If that isn't good enough for your upset contributor, you can even cite a court case. In *Miami Herald* vs. Tornillo, the Supreme Court ruled there is no legal right of access to a paper's letters to the editor column.

All that said, know that some readers will react—some of them vigorously—if you shorten, alter or refuse to print their letters.

Verify, verify, verify. Require name and address and a telephone number at which the letter can be verified. You don't want to get burned by someone writing a letter and then signing someone else's name. Trust me, it happens. I know from experience.

It is the policy at my newspaper not to accept anonymous letters. Some newspapers publish a letter and withhold the author's name upon request. This is dicey territory. Our feeling at the *Star-Telegram* is that credibility comes with signing one's name. It allows the reader to judge for himself or herself the veracity of what the writer is saying.

All of our reporters and columnists have to sign their work; we rarely allow an anonymous source to be quoted in news reports. We think readers have a right to know who's expressing an opinion in the letters feature.

It can also trigger interesting responses. At my former paper we ran a letter to the editor singing the praises of a certain elected politician. It wasn't until we got a response that we found out that the original letter writer was the politician's mother. Had we known, we probably wouldn't have run that first letter—it's only news when your mother says you're a turd, not when she says you're marvelous.

A common complaint among college newspaper editors is that you don't get letters. So, what can you do to spark interest?

1. The most obvious thing is to put something in the rest of the paper that's worth commenting about. I have to tell you, I've seen some pretty dull front pages from college newspapers. Dry stories, boring art. Come on, people. You're in college! You should be shaking things up!

2. Make it easy for your readers to respond to stories they see in your paper. Add a letters link at the end of every online story. Add an e-mail address at the end of printed stories and columns where readers can e-mail responses.

3. Include a box with one of your editorials that says, "Now it's your turn to weigh in on this topic. Send us your letters." Include the mail address and how to respond online.

Jill "J.R." Labbe is the deputy editorial page editor for the Fort Worth Star-Telegram. *When hired in 1992, she became the first female editorial writer in the newspaper's history. Labbe is on the board of the National Conference of Editorial Writers.*

Bear in mind that unlike news stories, editorials are supposed to state an opinion. A good editorial synthesizes the news for your readers, puts the issue in context and tells them what to think about it.

But be wary of letting your fervor or rage for your topic carry you away. "Don't mistake hyperbole for persuasion," Labbe says. "Yes, editorials and columns should be strongly worded, but if you are trying to persuade someone to at minimum consider your viewpoint, you can't make that happen if you take their heads off with a blowtorch."

Wilkins offers this simple advice on writing opinion pieces:

1. Make one point.
2. Support it.
3. Shut up.

A good editorial, he says, is written with equal parts of passion and logic. "You have to be pissed about something to get the passion you need to drive you through," he says. "But at some point you have to let your outrage and passion slide into the construction of a credible argument to support your point."

The Ombudsman
If you've got a provocative opinion section, chances are you'll hear from your readers. And they're not all going to be sending flowers and words of praise. One way to deal with the inevitable criticism is to hire a news ombudsman, or reader's advocate.

Beginning in the late 1960s, a number of professional newspapers created positions for news ombudsmen—sometimes called reader representatives or public editors—to monitor their coverage for fairness and accuracy and to respond to readers' complaints. (Ombudsman is a Swedish word meaning "representative of the people.") Today, more than two dozen newspapers in the United States and Canada have such positions, including *The Washington Post, The Toronto Star,* the *Detroit Free Press* and the *Philadelphia Inquirer. The New York Times* hired its first public editor in 2003 after reporter Jayson Blair was fired for plagiarizing and fabricating stories.

The Organization of Newspaper Ombudsmen, formed in 1980, defines a news ombudsman as someone who "receives and investigates complaints from newspaper readers or listeners or viewers of radio and television stations about accuracy, fairness, balance and good taste in news coverage. He or she recommends appropriate remedies or responses to correct or clarify news reports."

The organization offers these reasons for having an ombudsman:

- To improve the quality of news reporting by monitoring accuracy, fairness and balance
- To help his or her news provider to become more accessible and accountable to readers or audience members and, thus, to become more credible
- To increase the awareness of its news professionals about the public's concerns
- To save time for publishers and senior editors, or broadcasters and news directors, by channeling complaints and other inquiries to one responsible individual
- To resolve some complaints that might otherwise be sent to attorneys and become costly lawsuits

Michael Arrieta-Walden, public editor for *The Oregonian* in Portland, Ore., says, "I see my role as fostering the conversation between the newspaper and the readers. I encourage that conversation by serving as a contact for the public, and get that feedback to the appropriate staff. I also evaluate and comment on that feedback as well as the performance of the newspaper, with the interests of readers in mind."

Arrieta-Walden says student newspapers could benefit from having a news ombudsman. "I think the position strengthens the newspaper and its journalism. I also think that, given a college campus, the discussions and debate about the journalism would be especially lively and interesting."

The Daily Illini at the University of Illinois at Urbana-Champaign; *The Washington Square News* at New York University; *The Diamondback* at the University of Maryland, College Park; *The Cavalier Daily* at University of Virginia; *The Daily Northwestern* at Northwestern University; and *The Pride* at California State University, San Marcos are among the college papers that have had an ombudsman in recent years.

Andy Guess established an ombudsman at *The Cornell Daily Sun* when he was editor in chief. The paper had been embroiled in a number of controversies, and, he said, "We had to do something to attempt to reinforce

the trust we hope readers put in our paper. We felt that the best way to do this was through an independent voice rather than having us defend our own editorial decisions. Readers can trust that an independent source does not have any stake in these decisions."

Under Guess' tenure, *Daily Sun* ombudsman Jason Perlmutter wrote a biweekly column in the opinion section called "The Public Editor." In it, he freely commented on the paper, criticizing stories he thought were boring and offering suggestions for enlivening the coverage.

Newspapers generally take one of two routes to select an ombudsman. Either they choose a reporter or editor who has been on the paper, remove him from the editorial staff and hire him solely as ombudsman, or they select someone with knowledge or interest in journalism who is not involved at all with the paper. In any case, the ombudsman should not be part of the regular editorial staff.

Guess has one final word of caution: "Before you decide to add an ombudsman, realize that there will be inevitable clashes and resentment from the editors and staff. And make sure the ombudsman knows that too!"

To Do:

1. Analyze the editorials that have run in the past few issues of your paper. Are they well researched? Do they help readers understand the issues explored? How could they be better?
2. If your newspaper needs a strong cartoonist, start hunting for one. Put up fliers around campus, especially around the art or graphic design departments. Sponsor a competition for the best editorial cartoon and offer the winner or winners a regular spot on your editorial page. If you can't find a cartoonist, consider buying cartoons from a syndication service such as KRT Campus.
3. To beef up your opinion section, solicit submissions from leaders of campus groups, faculty members, administrators and other prominent people on campus. When you have a major issue brewing, invite the players to submit commentaries.
4. Consider hiring an ombudsman. Invite former staffers and outsiders to apply. Have each write a sample column or two.

To Read:

Casey, Maura and Michael Zuzel. *Beyond Argument: A Handbook for Editorial Writers.* Harrisburg, Pa.: National Conference of Editorial Writers, 2001. *Can be ordered from http://www.ncew.org/foundation/beyond_argument.htm*

Fink, Conrad C. *Writing Opinion for Impact.* Ames, Iowa: Blackwell Publishing, 2004.

Rystrom, Kenneth. *The Why, Who and How of the Editorial Page.* State College, Pa.: Strata Publishing, Inc., 2004.

William David Sloan and Laird B. Anderson. *Pulitzer Prize Editorials: America's Best Editorial Writing, 1917-1993, 3rd ed.* Ames, Iowa: Blackwell Publishing, 2003.

Vahl, Rod and H.L. Hall. *Effective Editorial Writing, 4th ed.* Iowa City, Iowa: Quill and Scroll Foundation, 2000.

To Click:

National Conference of Editorial Writers
http://www.ncew.org/

Association of American Editorial Cartoonists
http://info.detnews.com/aaec/

Association of Canadian Editorial Cartoonists
http://www.canadiancartoonists.com

Organization of News Ombudsmen
http://www.newsombudsmen.org/

Explanatory Notes
Many professional newspapers run explanatory notes about their opinion pages on their Web sites. Among them:

The Chicago Tribune Guide to the Opinion Pages
http://www.chicagotribune.com/news/opinion/chi-001231opinionpagesindex.special

The Seattle Times Guide to Editorial and Opinion Pages
http://www.seattletimescompany.com/editorial/index.htm

Question & Answer

What do you see as the role of opinion pages in a student newspaper?

I think the role of the opinion section in a student newspaper is the same as for professional newspapers: to promote debate on issues affecting the community and be a venue where differing perspectives can be offered. They certainly shouldn't be a pulpit for specific people or institutions, but every reasonable person should, in theory, be able to have their side of the debate aired. Op-ed pages, while running biased, unbalanced content, should strive to be fair and balanced as the sum of their parts. However, I don't have that big of a problem with the newspaper taking an ideological stance on the op-ed pages if its community has another newspaper with a different ideology. The more perspectives on issues the merrier.

When did you start drawing cartoons? Which professional cartoonists have inspired you?

I started drawing editorial cartoons my sophomore year in high school in Columbus, Ohio. I was initially very influenced by Jeff MacNelly, Mike Luckovich and Jim Borgman, but after a year or so I was introduced to Pat Oliphant's work, and he has since been my biggest influence. In middle school I drew comic books, so comic artists have played a huge role in what I think makes for dynamic, dramatic art. Of course, comic strips also played a big role, and Bill Watterson, Bill Amend, Berke Breathed, Charles Schulz and Winsor McKay have been the big ones for me.

Where do you get ideas for editorial cartoons?

I get my ideas living out the day: talking to people, reading newspapers, watching TV, surfing the Internet. The other night I was struggling to think up a cartoon when a confluence of ideas fused together to form a seed of one. I was sitting on the couch watching TV after just having read a couple of newspaper front pages online when it happened. A segment on the Masters golf tournament came on. There was an image of Phil Mickelson putting on the green with a sand

■ Nate Beeler

Nate Beeler has been drawing editorial cartoons since he was a sophomore in high school. During his college years at American University, his cartoons ran every week in the student newspaper, The Eagle. He graduated with a degree in journalism in December 2002. As a student, Beeler received the Charles M. Schulz Award for best college cartoonist from the Scripps-Howard Foundation and the John Locher Award for best college editorial cartoonist from the Association of American Editorial Cartoonists. He also won first place in the national Society of Professional Journalists' Mark of Excellence Awards. He was the first cartoonist ever to win these three major awards in the same year.

Beeler's cartoons are syndicated by Knight Ridder/Tribune Information Services to nearly 300 campus publications nationwide. His cartoons have appeared in The Arizona Republic, The Providence Journal, USA Today and The Northern Virginia Journal. In 2005, he was hired as a cartoonist for The Washington Examiner.

trap behind him, and I thought to myself, "Sand wedge." From there, I thought, "Wedge issue." Combine them together: "Sand wedge issue." In golf, that brings to mind someone having trouble getting out of a sand trap. In terms of "wedge issue," Iraq immediately popped into mind. So, I drew George Bush shoulder deep in a sand trap (labeled "Iraq") whacking away at a ball but only digging a deeper hole for himself. To add a further layer to the cartoon, I had him facing the wrong way with the hole marker behind him in the distance, and two other guys are waiting by it and saying, "George! The hole's over here!" I tried to be clever with it, but the most important thing, to me, is that it says what I think and makes a valid editorial statement about a newsworthy situation.

What do you do when you don't have an idea?

When I don't have an idea, I keep trying. There's always a new idea out there floating in the ether, and you just have to work hard to catch one.

What makes a successful cartoon?

I think a successful cartoon is one that makes readers want to talk about the topic. If it makes them grin or laugh, that's a bonus. Humor is a device that can be used to help get your point across. It's not the end; it's the means. An editorial cartoon must have a point, because if it didn't, it should be on the comics pages. My most successful cartoons

have done this, I hope. One way you can tell they're successful is if people want to share them with their friends or family by cutting them out or talking about them. Even having people write letters to the editor about a cartoon shows that it was successful.

What do you see as the role of an editorial cartoonist on a student paper? Is it any different in the professional world?

The role of an editorial cartoonist on a student paper is the same as one on a professional one: Draw something that says how you feel about an issue that's important to you and your neighbors in the campus, city, state, nation or world community. Help lead the public debate.

What advice do you have for up-and-coming editorial cartoonists?

Aspiring editorial cartoonists need to remember first and foremost that they are journalists. Their cartoons can skewer people, but they need to be fair and balanced in their research for the cartoons. Reading different newspapers and books is a must. Also, the power of cartooning is derived from its visual nature. Therefore, cartoonists should strive to draw dynamic-looking cartoons. A good idea can be ruined by a poorly drawn cartoon, just as a bad idea can turn an artistic masterpiece into junk.

THE DAILY ORANGE

THIS IS AN **EXTRA EDITION** OF THE D.O.   **DO** SYRACUSE UNIVERSITY'S STUDENT NEWSPAPER   MARCH 25, 2005 **FRIDAY**

STUDENT CHARGED WITH MURDER

THE ACCUSED BRIAN T. SHAW
Police charged Shaw, a 23-year-old Syracuse University senior, with second-degree murder in the death of Chiarra Seals, the mother of his 4-year-old daughter. He will be arraigned in Syracuse City Court Friday morning.

THE VICTIM CHIARRA SEALS
Seals, 23, lived on the North Side of Syracuse with her two children. Police found her body in a suitcase behind a garage at 112 Avondale Place, a residence near Westcott Street.

THE REACTION ON CAMPUS
Chancellor Nancy Cantor offers sympathy and counseling to the university community. Shaw's fraternity brothers commend him as "a great friend and brother to all of us."

Senior allegedly kills mother of his daughter

BY STEVEN KOVACH
NEWS EDITOR

Syracuse police charged Brian T. Shaw, 23, a Syracuse University senior enrolled through University College, with second-degree murder Thursday in connection with the death of Chiarra Seals, 23, the mother of his 4-year-old daughter.

Syracuse police were called to Seals' home at 160 Jasper St. after a neighbor noticed a suspicious vehicle parked in the driveway, said Syracuse Deputy Police Chief Gary Miguel. Police entered the home and found Seals' 17-month-old and 4-year-old children alone in the house, Miguel said.

The 4-year-old girl told police her "daddy," whom she referred to as Brian, had come to the house and had a physical fight with Seals in Seals' bedroom, Miguel said. The 4-year-old said that the man later exited the bedroom carrying Seals in a bed sheet, Miguel said.

Thomas Seals offers a different account of the early events that led to police arrival on the scene.

Thomas Seals, who is Chiarra Seals' great-uncle and the Syracuse common councilor for the university and downtown area, said he was leaving his home Wednesday night around 7:30 p.m. when he received a phone call from Chiarra Seals' aunt saying she was missing.

A tenant who lives in the apartment upstairs from Chiarra Seals came home to find the rear door leading to a common hallway open, which Thomas Seals said the tenant found unusual. He said the door appeared to be forced open and that the tenant called the building's

SEE **ARREST** PAGE 3

POLICE LINE DO NOT CROSS

Mark DiOrio / Photo Editor

Brian Shaw allegedly brought the body of Chiarra Seals to his home, 545 Columbus Ave. (above), before stuffing the body in a suitcase and leaving it behind a garage at 112 Avondale Place.

Allegations shock SU community

Cantor, fraternity react to charges in written statements

BY MEREDITH BOWEN
AND HEATHER COLLURA
ASST. NEWS EDITORS

As news of Syracuse University senior Brian T. Shaw's arrest on a charge of second-degree murder spread through the community Thursday, Chancellor Nancy Cantor sent an e-mail to students, faculty, staff and local alumni to address the tragedy and offer counseling to those who need it.

"As of now, our comprehension of this unspeakable tragedy is incomplete," Cantor wrote in the e-mail. "Neither our heads nor our hearts permit us to fully understand all that has happened and why."

"The children and the family of the deceased are in our thoughts, as are those on campus who know Brian Shaw," said SU spokesman Kevin Morrow.

He said the university is cooperating fully with the Syracuse police and the Onondaga County District Attorney's office.

The university places students charged with violent crimes on interim suspension pending resolution by the criminal justice system, Morrow said. The university has yet to receive a report from police on Shaw's arrest, Morrow said, but expects one soon. When the university receives the report Shaw will be placed on interim suspension, he said.

Shaw is a member of the SU cheerleading team and a brother in the Sigma Phi Epsilon fraternity. He attended Henninger High School in Syracuse. The victim, Chiarra Seals, attended Corcoran, another city high school. The two had a four-year-old daughter together. Seals had a 17-month-old son with another man.

"Brian T. Shaw has been a great friend and brother to all of us at Sigma Phi Epsilon," the Syracuse chapter of the fraternity said in a written statement. "We are deeply shocked and saddened by this inci-

SEE **REACTION** PAGE 2

Great-uncle remembers life of Chiarra Seals

BY HEATHER COLLURA
ASST. NEWS EDITOR

Thomas Seals, the Syracuse Common Councilor for the Syracuse University and downtown areas, described his great-niece as a free spirit.

"She always had a smile on her face," the 64-year-old said.

Chiarra Seals was found dead Thursday morning in a suitcase behind a garage on Avondale Place. Brian T. Shaw, an SU senior and father of her 4-year-old daughter, allegedly killed her Wednesday evening, according to Syracuse Police.

Thomas Seals and his great-niece had been estranged for over a year, at which time she seemed to be doing well, he said. He added, however, that he doesn't like to pry into the lives of his nieces and nephews.

"There is a deep reservoir of faith that keeps you stable when something drastic happens in your life," Thomas Seals said. "There is nothing you can do; you can't bring her back."

Chiarra Seals was raised by her grandmother after her mother abandoned her as a baby and her father moved to Seattle, Thomas Seals said.

His great-niece was close to his daughter because the two girls attended Corcoran High School together, Thomas Seals said.

The last time he spoke with Chiarra Seals she was working as a nurse's aid at St. Camillus Health & Rehabilitation Center in Syracuse, he said.

SEE **VICTIM** PAGE 3

Thomas Seals

BODY FOUND NEAR CAMPUS
The victim lived on the North Side; her body was found near Westcott

Victim's residence
160 Jasper St.

290

690

Erie Blvd.

92

81

E. Adams St.

Shaw's residence
545 Columbus Ave.

THORNDEN PARK

Body found
112 Avondale Place

SYRACUSE UNIVERSITY

Chapter 10

Editing

An editor—be it a section editor, managing editor, or editor in chief— does far more than simply edit words.

A good editor needs skills in diplomacy and leadership, in organization and managing people, in boosting battered egos and smoothing ruffled feathers. You've got to be able to inspire your staff to produce prize-worthy stories while making sure the pages you're responsible for get to the printer on time. One minute you're planning photos, graphics and text for a big package and the next you're on the phone with an irate reader.

In the professional world, learning this wide array of skills often happens gradually. Typically, a reporter interested in editing starts by helping out with an occasional night or weekend shift on the desk. With that experience she may be promoted to assistant desk editor, then city editor and then managing editor. This move up the ladder usually takes years.

But at a campus newspaper, a reporter may find herself in an editing position—even a top management job—after only a few months or a year on the staff.

"At a student newspaper, you go from being a peer and a colleague and a friend to a being a boss," says Ralph Braseth, director of student media at the University of Mississippi. "It's a difficult transition. You can lose friends, you can lose respect. It's a dangerous job to take, especially if you're not prepared for it."

Being responsible for other people and their work can be an overwhelming experience. In this chapter we'll discuss what it takes to be a good editor and provide tips and strategies for developing these skills.

Editor Selection

How does one get to be an editor at a student newspaper? Most student publications have a relatively rigorous policy for selecting the top editor, usually called an editor in chief, executive editor, managing editor or, simply, editor. Generally candidates have to go through a formal process that may include writing a letter of application or an action plan, interviewing with a selection committee and making a presentation to the staff.

Typically, the top editor is selected by a newspaper adviser, a publication board or an ad-hoc committee made up of advisers, current editors, faculty members and sometimes professional journalists. Whoever makes the decision should look for these qualities in a top-ranking editor:

- Maturity
- Ability to deal with pressure
- Good organizational skills
- Strong leadership skills
- News judgment
- Creativity
- Excellent people skills
- Ability to multi-task, to deal with many issues at once

Once the top editor or editors are chosen, they are usually charged with hiring the rest of the staff, including section editors, art directors, photo editors, online editors and sometimes reporters and photographers (Figure 10.2). Some editors inherit a staff from the previous school term; others have to recruit a whole new team.

Staff Organization

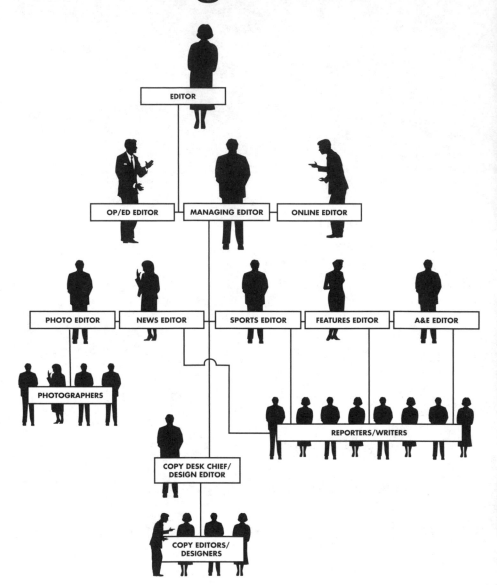

Figure 10.2. Most student newspapers have a hierarchical structure similar to those found in professional newsrooms. However, decision making at student newspapers may be more collaborative than at professional newspapers. Graphic by Bradley Wilson

Whatever the tradition is at your newspaper, the incoming editor should make the hiring process as professional as possible. Don't choose your three best friends to lead the news, sports and opinion sections, unless they are without a doubt the best qualified for the positions. When stories need to be assigned, copy needs to be edited, pages need to be proofed and tough decisions need to be made, you want to have people who can do the job.

To make the hiring process fair, create a professional looking application and have everyone who is interested in a leadership role fill one out. (An example of an editor application is at the end of this chapter.) Interview each applicant, asking about previous work experience, skills, strengths and weaknesses. You may even want to ask for references—professors, student newspaper advisers and employers who can speak to their character and ability to handle responsibility.

Developing a Leadership Style

As soon as you accept an editing position—whether you're an editor in chief overseeing an entire newspaper, a section editor com-

Tips from a Pro

■ Steve Buttry

As you work with a reporter on a story, you have two jobs: to help the reporter produce the best possible version of this story and to help the reporter produce better stories in the future.

Inexperienced editors who are good at editing copy sometimes think this job requires them to rewrite the story, using their superior touch with the copy. But rewriting by the editor doesn't help the reporter write a better story next time. You produce the best story now and better stories in the future by working effectively with the reporter throughout the storytelling process.

Below are some tips for helping reporters improve their stories.

Before the Reporter Turns in a Story

1. **Talk early and often.** From the idea stage through revision, talk with the reporter about the challenges the story presents and how she is addressing them.
2. **Discuss story ideas with the reporter.** Many story weaknesses rest with the fundamental idea. The direction you provide at this stage can save work later in the process. Ask why we're doing this story now. That forces the reporter to address two questions: Why are we doing this story at all and why now?
3. **Focus on the reader.** Ask reader-oriented questions early and often, to keep a strong focus on serving the reader. Why will the reader care? Who is likely to read this story? How might the reader act on this story? What information can we give the reader to help her act on it?
4. **Ask what the story is about.** At various stages of a reporter's work on a story, ask what the story is about. Sometimes the answer will change from the idea stage through the rewriting, and asking that question repeatedly will help the reporter keep the evolving story clearly focused. Sometimes the answer will remain the same and asking the question will help the reporter stay focused.
5. **Discuss records.** Ask what records the reporter will examine. Start with general questions that push the reporter to consider where she might find records to help with this story. If she doesn't identify some you think might help, follow with more specific questions that steer her toward specific records. Know the federal, state and local open-records laws and push reporters to gain access.
6. **Discuss data.** Discuss where the reporter might find data to help with the story. Discuss access issues such as open-records laws, cost and which officials might be most likely to provide the records promptly. Discuss whether the reporter has the skills to analyze the data or needs some help from a colleague or a professor.
7. **Debrief.** After an interview, ask the reporter how it went. What did she learn? What surprised her? What moved her? What did she hope to learn that the source would not tell? Who else might have that information? Encourage the reporter to start writing, even if much reporting remains.
8. **Ask about the lede.** The reporter probably is thinking about the lede without prompting from you, but talking may be helpful if he is struggling with it.
9. **Suggest sidebars and graphics.** Ask the reporter what facts you can tell better in graphics than in prose. Ask what points should be told in sidebars, rather than bogging down the main story. Can a photo make a point better than prose?
10. **Suggest an outline.** If a reporter appears unorganized, suggest that he write an outline. If he resists or has not written effective outlines in the past, talk through an outline. You might write down the outline yourself as the two of you identify main points.
11. **Suggest writing without notes.** Notes can distract a reporter. The story should be in her head. Suggest that she review the notes, then set them aside and write without pausing to find facts and quotes. When she's finished, she must return to her notebook to get the facts and quotes right.
12. **Encourage rewriting.** Perhaps the best way to see dramatic improvement in a reporter's work is to encourage a reporter who turns in first drafts to spend some time rewriting. Don't approach this as remedial work, but as professional development. Even good stories benefit from rewriting. Even great stories benefit from revision. Set a deadline for finishing the first draft, then another deadline for finishing the rewrite. Talk about specific things to look for in rewriting: strong verbs, sentence length, redundancy, etc.

After You Get the First Draft

1. **Encourage alternatives.** Encourage the reporter to try a different lede. Even if you both like the first one, encourage trying a different approach. Coaching should not concentrate only on making bad work good, but on making good work and even great work better.
2. **Ask the reporter to read aloud.** If a lede is long or a story is laden with long sentences or does not flow well, ask the reporter to read it aloud, to you or to herself. Often that will help her identify the fat sentences and weak passages. Also ask the reporter to read aloud the passages you love. That will underscore how well those passages work.
3. **Suggest areas to condense.** Avoid cutting stories yourself. Instead, suggest that a particular passage could be condensed, that a particular sentence seems too long.
4. **Don't rewrite the lede.** Tell the reporter what's wrong with the lede. Suggest possible alternative approaches. Demand a shorter, brighter or clearer lede. But make the reporter rewrite it.
5. **Don't insist on your approach.** If you do rewrite the lede, or suggest a different approach, don't insist that the story has to use your lede, or your approach. Explain why the original version didn't work and explain the thinking behind your revision. Then challenge the reporter to write something better than either.
6. **Explain editing changes.** Whether you changed because of style, grammar, clarity, brevity or some other reason, explain why you changed a story. Those changes will help the reporter turn in a better story next time. Learning is a primary function of the student newspaper and explanation hastens learning.

Steve Buttry is director of tailored programs at American Press Institute. He has spent more than 30 years in the newspaper business as a reporter, editor and writing coach for the Omaha World-Herald, *the* Des Moines Register *and other papers. While a student at Texas Christian University, Buttry spent four years on the staff of* The Daily Skiff, *including two semesters as editor. He is a founder, columnist and contributor to the "No Train, No Gain" Web site, from which this article was adapted.*

manding a small group of reporters or a photo editor in charge of a photography staff—it's time to start thinking about your leadership style.

Do you want to be an authoritarian leader, who confidently tells people what to do, or a more democratic chief, who asks for others' opinions before making a decision? Or do you see yourself as a leader who gives others autonomy to make their own decisions? Most people have a natural tendency toward one style or another, but good leaders use a mix of all three approaches, depending on the situation.

To be a good leader, you have to be able to read people and figure out what they need. If, for example, a reporter is feeling mortified about misspelling the name of the university president in a story, he probably doesn't need to be chewed out. You should, however, remind him of the importance of getting names right and of double-checking the spelling of all names.

Sometimes, however, you have to be stern. If few people are meeting deadlines, you may need to institute penalties. Some editors pull bylines or refuse to run stories if copy comes in late. You need to decide when to use the carrot and when to use the stick.

Keep in mind that praise can be a motivating force. If you're constantly pointing out errors and telling people they've done a lousy job, you're not going to get good work out of them. People work harder and better when they feel appreciated.

"One of the single most important things you can do as a leader is to recognize the accomplishments of other people," says Braseth, whose job includes advising *The Daily Mississippian*. "If you're not thanking folks, you're not leading. You have to do it every single day."

Recognition can come in the form of a pat on the back or paper certificates passed out in front of the whole staff. Misha Rosiak, managing editor of the weekly *Golden Gate [X]press* newspaper at San Francisco State University in 2005, handed out homemade cookies and chocolate bars to deserving staffers at semiweekly staff meetings. When someone's done excellent work or gone beyond the call of duty, slip a note in their box or send a congratulatory e-mail. Such words of encouragement keep people committed and motivated.

Editing Copy

Most newspaper stories are reviewed and edited by multiple people—a section editor, two or three copy editors and often the managing editor and/or editor in chief. At professional newspapers, section editors primarily edit for content (structure, logic, holes in the story) and copy editors usually focus on mechanics

Coaching Writers

The best editors see themselves more as coaches than as bosses, or even editors. They talk with reporters throughout the reporting and writing process, asking questions and listening.

Here are some questions you can pose to help a writer craft a story:

- What's the story about?
- What's your lede?
- What's your nut graph?
- What's new?
- Why are we writing this story now?
- Why should readers care?
- What's your headline?
- What's the most interesting thing you learned in your reporting?
- What's your best quote?
- Who are the most interesting characters in your story?
- What does the reader need to know?
- How would you explain this story to a friend?
- What would make a good ending?

(spelling, grammar, punctuation, math, adherence to the newspaper's style guidelines).

At student newspapers, the line between what section editors and copy editors do is often a bit blurry; everybody is doing their best to make the story better.

In their excellent book, *Coaching Writers*, Roy Peter Clark and Don Fry of the Poynter Institute for Media Studies suggest the best approach to editing is to *coach writers* rather than to *fix copy*. That means talking about stories throughout the reporting, organizing and writing process rather than simply whacking away at stories after they come in. This may sound time-consuming, but many editors find that brief but frequent conversations with writers can often save time in the long run.

"One mistake I know I made was fixing errors in articles rather than editing them," says Erika B. Neldner, who was editor in chief of *The Sentinel*, the weekly paper at Kennesaw State University, in 2004. "It always came down to crunch time, and I never had enough free time to sit down with each writer. If I had, I would have saved hours fixing the same errors every Tuesday morning."

Editorial Budgets

Editors generally plan each issue by creating an editorial budget, a list of every story assigned. Formatting varies, but the editorial budget generally includes this information for each story:

- A slug, a one-word title for the story
- Its length, usually in words or column inches
- The byline, the writer's name

- A one- or two-sentence description of the story
- Notations about photos (this may include whether a photo has been assigned or shot, the name of the photographer)
- Notations about graphics (whether a map, chart, graph or other graphic element has been assigned or completed)

It should look something like this:

DOWNTOWN—600 words, Chin—The College of Business has announced it will open a new downtown campus next year to better serve working students. **Photo** of new building shot by Green. **Graphic:** Locator map assigned.

Writers typically send a budget line to their section editor and the section editors send their section budgets to the managing editor or editor in chief. Some newspapers use a story planning form (Figure 10.4) to help plan stories, photos and graphics. The top editor then makes up an editorial budget for that entire issue of the paper. Editors usually discuss the budget—or at least the lead stories for each section—at a news meeting or budget meeting.

Editors at daily papers generally meet every morning to go over the editorial budget. These meetings should include the top editors; section editors; and the lead photo, graphics, online and design editors. At some papers, a smaller group of editors meets again later in the day to choose stories for the front page. At a weekly paper, editors typically meet once or twice during the week to plan each issue.

■ Checklist
Editing a Story

Editing a story can be a daunting task. There are so many things to look for. Editors should read stories at least three times:

- Once for content, including accuracy, organization, sense and meaning
- Once for mechanics—style, spelling and grammar
- Once for legal and ethical issues, such as libel, fairness and cultural sensitivity

After you're finished editing, it's a good idea to read the story over one last time to make sure you haven't introduced any errors.

In editing a story ask yourself these questions:

Content
1. Does the lede capture the essence of the story? Is it short and punchy, usually no more than 25 or 30 words? Does it entice the reader to read more?
2. Does the story flow smoothly and logically? Is it architecturally sound?
3. Are there any holes in the story—an important perspective that's not represented, an obvious question that isn't answered?
4. Are all the assertions in the story backed up by facts? Are all quotations and facts attributed to an appropriate source?
5. Has the writer provided the appropriate background information to put the story in context? Will readers who are just reading about this issue for the first time be able to understand what's going on?
6. Does the timeline of events make sense?
7. Are the basic facts correct? Make sure names, dates, times, phone numbers, titles, criminal charges, addresses, Web and e-mail addresses are accurate.

Mechanics
8. Are there errors of grammar, syntax, spelling or style?
9. Does the story follow Associated Press (and/or your newspaper's) style guidelines?
10. Does the math add up? Do the numbers all make sense?
11. Is there any unnecessary redundancy or repetition?

Law, Ethics and Taste
12. Is the story fair and balanced? Does it present all sides?
13. Are there any potentially libelous statements?
14. Is the story written in good taste?
15. Does the story include any profane language? If so, does it conform to your paper's standards? (For example, some newspapers only run swear words if they are in a quote from a source.) Is it journalistically justifiable?
16. Are there any references some people might find offensive?

Meetings

At their best, editors meetings are a quick and efficient way to communicate and collaborate. At their worst, they drag on for hours, boring everyone involved. Here are some guidelines to ensure your meetings are meaningful, productive and blissfully brief.

Make sure someone is in charge. The top editor of the paper should run most editors meetings. If that person is unavailable, the next person down the line should take charge.

Create an agenda. The leader of the meeting should have an agenda for each meeting. This might include going over the editorial budget for the paper, discussing front page possibilities, making decisions about packaging stories and doing a brief critique.

Invite key players. Newspaper planning meetings should include top editors; section editors; and the lead photo, graphics, online and design editors. If someone can't attend, another representative of that department should be there.

Start promptly. The top editor should set a reasonable hour for the meeting and make it clear the meeting will start on time. If meetings don't start promptly, people tend to arrive late for the next meeting.

Rein it in. The meeting leader should keep everyone on track, curbing digressions. If an important issue arises that isn't on the agenda, set another time to discuss that topic.

End promptly. Set an end time for each meeting and stick to it.

Dealing with Controversy

Every college paper will sometime stir up controversy. It may be an offensive cartoon, an article that makes the school look bad or a column that goes a little too far. Sometimes you see the hate mail coming. Other times the angry letters and phone calls seem to come out of nowhere. Whatever the situation, the editors have to deal with the flak.

"You have to be prepared to handle a lot of angry phone calls and a lot of hostile office visitors," says Mandy Phillips, who was editor in chief of *The Standard* at Southwest Missouri State University in 2003-2004. "I know when I first stepped into the editor's position and got my first few angry students and professors sort of 'in my face,' I probably backed off too much and too soon. I learned pretty quickly there's a fine line between being passive and being stubborn, and you've got to learn to walk it."

The key to handling controversy is to listen to all sides and keep your cool. If a source or reader has a complaint with the paper, or a staff member has a problem with a fellow staffer, make sure each person feels he is heard. Listen to the complaint and don't act rashly. Take time to formulate a response.

When you or the paper has made an error, admit it, run a correction or clarification, apologize to the injured party and move on. You have another issue to get out.

Evaluating Staff

Part of your job as an editor is to review your staff's performance. Every paper should have a process that includes written evaluations (see the evaluation forms for editors, reporters, photo editors and photographers at the end of this chapter) and private conferences.

Evaluating another person's work can be difficult, particularly when the person is a fellow student. Let's face it, most people don't like giving criticism and most people don't like getting it.

But a solid evaluation process can help both of you grow as journalists.

Here are some tips for conducting performance evaluations:

Set the time and place. Don't just grab the staffer on the fly. Make an appointment in advance and choose a place where you won't be disturbed.

Plan what you're going to say. Don't just talk off the cuff. When giving criticism, you need to be prepared.

Headline Styles

■ **Variety**
Each line, or deck, of a headline should have graphic appeal and should be functional on the page. All headlines should contain a subject and a verb. The biggest and boldest headline goes at the top of the page with less bold and smaller headlines appearing lower on the page. A consistent headline font is used throughout the publication, often with a contrasting font used for subheads.

SINGLE LINE
Campus alcohol use increases

DOUBLE LINE
Cell phones outlawed in classrooms; text messaging common way to cheat

HAMMER
TEEN CRIME
Judicial Commission hears 'absurd' stories

UNDERLINE
You win some, you lose some
Football team loses championship in last quarter

OVERLINE
For Rebecca Heslin, prom night was as bad...
Only in her wildest dreams

WICKET
I ntramurals give me a chance
to play in sports I normally couldn't"
Jocks of all kinds

TRIPOD
DRUM CORPS WINS
Local musicians take championship in DCI national competition

Figure 10.3. Headlines can be written in a variety of styles. Graphic by Bradley Wilson

Put the staff member at ease. Don't launch right into the review. Evaluations are stressful; recognize that and help the person relax.

Review the process. Explain that this is a discussion, not a lecture.

Start with a self-evaluation. Get the staff member's assessment of his performance. (You may ask the staff member to fill out a self-evaluation form before the meeting.)

Sandwich criticism between compliments. Start and end each category of performance by telling the person what she's done well. In the middle, focus on what she needs to work on.

Focus on the future. Don't dwell too much on what a person has done poorly in the past. Discuss what he needs to do to move to the next level.

Get specific. Prepare examples of what the staffer is doing well or needs to work on. Show her grammatical errors she makes again and again or ledes that are particularly good.

Look for trends. Take note of consistent problems and strengths—that the photographer has a great eye for feature photos, that the writer needs to dig deeper or look for more compelling quotes.

Write it down. Your review process should include a written evaluation. If your newspaper doesn't already have a form, use the ones at the end of this chapter or write a narrative evaluation.

Draft an action plan. Together, come up with specific steps the staff member can take to improve.

Ask for feedback. Discuss how you can be a more helpful and effective supervisor.

End on a high note. Thank the staff member for coming in and for contributing to the paper.

Writing Headlines

Some people are born headline writers; they practically come out of the womb spouting clever, catchy phrases that capture the essence of a story. Unfortunately, those people usually go into advertising.

That leaves us mere mortals to write newspaper headlines.

At professional newspapers, headline writing is generally the job of copy editors. At student newspapers, reporters and editors at various levels may share the task.

Here are some tips to get you started:

Read the story first. Yes, the whole thing. Often you'll get an idea for the headline or deck deep into the story.

Play with words. Choose a few key words and then play around. Look for synonyms, puns, twists of phrase, rhymes, alliterations that work well.

Avoid groaner puns. There's a fine line between what's clever and what's corny. If you think you've got something but you're not sure, try it out on some other people in the newsroom. You'll know soon enough when you've got a hit.

Use present tense. That keeps the news fresh.

Use active voice. Have the subject of the headline doing something rather than having something done to it.

Write a skeleton sentence. Then try to shorten that sentence to five to seven words, then make it shorter yet.

Leave out unnecessary words. Don't use articles like *the, a, an*. Use a comma instead of *and*.

Don't cannibalize the story. Avoid headlines that scoop the reporter on a great opening or a surprise ending.

Don't put information in the headline that isn't in the story. This isn't the place or time to add more information.

Avoid unfamiliar acronyms and abbreviations. In fact, use abbreviations sparingly and only when you're sure most readers will know what they mean.

Challenge your headline. Is it too obvious? Could it have a second, unintended meaning?

Avoid bad line splits. Don't divide: two-word nouns, adjectives/nouns, verbs/adverbs, prepositions/nouns, etc. And don't leave prepositions hanging.

Run a spell check. Typos are doubly embarrassing in large type.

Sample Copy Flow Schedule for a Weekly Newspaper

Day 1. Writer pitches story to assigning editor in a proposed budget line or story planning sheet that includes a brief description of the story, approximate length, photo and graphic possibilities and contact information for photographers. After a discussion and some fine-tuning the assigning editor OKs the story.

OR Editor assigns a story to the writer. Writer sends budget line to editor.

Writer sends graphics assignment form to the graphics editor and/or photo assignment form to the photo editor.

Day 2. Graphics editor assigns graphics to graphic artist. Photo editor assigns photo to photographer. Writer reports story, checking in with photographer and graphic artist on their related assignments.

Day 3. Editor coaches reporter through the story, asking questions, troubleshooting problems and helping the reporter organize the story.

Day 5. Reporter turns in first draft of story to assigning editor.

Day 6. Assigning editor edits story (editor in chief and/or managing editor may review story here, too).

Day 7. Assigning editor and reporter discuss suggested revisions. Reporter revises story.

Day 8. Reporter hands in second draft to editor. Graphic artist turns in graphic to graphics editor. Photographer turns in photos to photo editor; together they select the best photos. Photographer writes captions.

At budget meeting, editors discuss placement of stories and assignments for next week. Assigning editor edits second draft of story and turns it in to copyediting file. Copyeditor edits story and writes headline, calls reporter or assigning editor with questions. (Managing editor may review story here)

Day 9. Page designer puts story, photo and graphics on the page. After all pages are finished, paper is sent to the printer.

Day 10. Newspaper comes out and is distributed around campus. Staff meets in the afternoon to critique the paper.

Consider the tone of the story. Don't put a light, clever headline on a serious story. Likewise, don't get overly serious on a fun story.

Be specific. Vague headlines, even catchy ones, don't make readers want to read a story. Decks—lower headlines that run below the main headline—can help here. If you've got a snappy but imprecise headline, use a deck to explain it.

Consider photos and graphics. A headline, photo, graphic and story are one package. Make sure the headline doesn't contradict or undermine the photo or graphic.

Check other elements on the page. Make sure you're not repeating key words or creating an unintended meaning by placing your head next to a photo from another story.

Punch up your verbs. Strive for fresh, strong, specific verbs.

Be conversational. Avoid "headlinese," words like "solon" and "confab" that only headline writers use.

Be accurate. A mistake in a headline can be as serious—or even more so—than an error in a story.

See Figure 10.4 for samples of headline styles and Headline Writing Cheat Sheet for useful synonyms.

To Do:

1. Arrange for a group of your editors to sit in on an editors meeting at a newspaper in your area.

2. Before taking on a new editing job, call a professional editor in your position and ask if you can spend a day shadowing her. If that's not possible, set up a brief interview to ask about her job and get advice.

3. If you don't already have one, organize a training session for editors before the new term begins. Invite professional journalists, student newspaper advisers, journalism professors and others to lead sessions on managing people, leadership skills, project planning, time management and other skills editors need to succeed.

4. Organize occasional training sessions for editors throughout the school year to address particular problems that arise. If, for example, reporters are consistently missing deadlines, have editors meet to discuss strategies to combat the problem. If conflict management becomes a problem, organize a role-playing session to practice these skills.

5. If you supervise writers, set aside time for coaching, using tips listed in this chapter.

To Read:

Bowles, Dorothy A. and Diane L. Borden. *Creative Editing*, 4th ed. Belmont, Calif.: Wadsworth/Thomson Learning, 2004.

Fellow, Anthony R. and Thomas N. Clanin. *Copy Editors Handbook for Newspapers*, 2nd ed. Englewood, Colo.: Morton Publishing Company, 2003.

Fry, Don and Roy Peter Clark. *Coaching Writers: Editors and Reporters Working Together Across Media Platforms*, 2nd ed. New York: Bedford/St. Martin's, 2003.

Hill, Linda A. *Becoming a Manager: How New Managers Master the Challenges of Leadership.* 2nd ed. Cambridge, Mass.: Harvard Business School Press, 2003.

Rooney, Edmund J. and Oliver Witte. *Copy Editing for Professionals.* Champaign, Ill.: Stipes Publishing, 2000.

Ryan, Leland "Buck" and Michael J. O'Donnell. *Editor's Toolbox: The Reference Guide for Beginners and Professionals.* Ames, Iowa: Blackwell Publishing, 2000.

To Click:

American Copy Editors Society
http://www.copydesk.org/

American Society of Newspaper Editors
http://www.asne.org/

Associated Press Managing Editors
http://www.apme.com/

Confusing Words: A database of more than 3,000 words that are troublesome to readers and writers.
http://www.confusingwords.com/

Newsroom Leadership
http://www.newsroomleadership.com/

Institute for Midcareer Copy Editors: Resource Page for Copy Editors
http://www.ibiblio.org/copyed/resources.
  html#fact

The Slot: A Spot for Copy Editors
http://www.theslot.com/

"Coaching Writers: The Human Side of Editing" videotape (This 30-minute videotape teaches the fundamentals of coaching writers. It's available for $5 at the Poynter Institute Web site: http://www.poynter.org/shop/product_view.asp?id=710)

Tips from a Pro
■ Becky Sher

The top job at a student newspaper isn't easy. But it's a lot of fun, and an amazing opportunity to grow as a journalist, and as a leader. A few things to keep in mind as you get used to your new role:

1. Be fearless. Who cares if other people think a project will never work? If you think it will, give it a try. The same goes for newsroom policies. Just because the last editor didn't do it that way doesn't mean it won't work for you. Student journalism is your chance to try things that seem a little crazy or unconventional.

2. Act like a "real" journalist. If you want to be taken seriously by readers and sources, then take your job seriously. Act ethically and responsibly in everything you do. Whether you're reporting on the university president's alleged financial improprieties or the outdoors club's latest fund-raiser, treat the story like it's important to you.

3. Know your limits. You are a real journalist, but you're also a student. And you need to be a good student; that takes time and energy. Be realistic about what you can and can't commit to.

4. Learn from your mistakes. It sounds pretty basic, but it's more important than you think. There are very few times in your post-graduation life when you will have the chance to make mistakes without dramatic consequences. That's not to say mistakes are never a big deal at a college newspaper—they are. But for the most part, the kind of mistakes you'll make as a college editor won't cost you your job or your lifelong reputation. So take the heat while it lasts and then concentrate on the next issue. And don't do it again.

5. Critique! It's important to look at your work critically, and it's always nice to have an editor from another section of the paper look at your section with a critical eye. If you're the big boss, let your staff know that constructive criticism is welcome.

6. Ask for guidance. There are plenty of people out there who know a lot more than you do. Find them, and ask for their feedback. Look for professional journalists who are willing to critique your paper, give a seminar on a specific topic or offer help by phone when a reporter, editor or designer is struggling.

7. Do what you say you're going to do. You can't expect anyone else to be committed to the job unless you're setting a good example. If you say you'll do a final read on a story by 3 p.m., do it. If you say a meeting starts at 6 p.m., that's when it starts.

8. Be fair, but flexible. It's a management myth that you should treat everyone on your staff exactly the same. If a good reporter has mononucleosis, she needs to be cut some slack. Special circumstances don't mean lower expectations; they just demand a different approach.

9. Make your expectations clear. True, many of your staffers aren't getting much in return other than the satisfaction of a job well done, but that doesn't mean you can't expect good work. Don't be wishy-washy. Your staff should know that if a deadline is 7 p.m., that doesn't mean 7:15 or 7:45. Don't seethe under the surface when you read a bad lede, but never say anything to anyone. Your staff is talented, but they can't read your mind!

10. Make it fun. Yes, this is a job, and yes, you should take it seriously, but this is also college. Have some fun. But also make sure your staff knows that there are times to be serious, like when the 11 p.m. press deadline is approaching. Encourage fun outside the office as well—sign up for intramural sports, have parties, go to dinner. You'll make a lot of great memories that will get you through long nights in the office.

11. Treat your job like a job, not just an extracurricular activity. Even if you're not getting a paycheck, or your newspaper only comes out once a month, this is still your job. Set office hours when staffers know they can find you in the office. Answer e-mails, voice mails and letters in a professional fashion. If you're meeting with a source, dress up a little (at least take off your flip-flops).

12. Cultivate a good relationship with the business staff. The setup is different at every newspaper, but regardless of the way yours works, it almost always behooves top editors to be friendly with the business and production staffs. You need them to do your job—sometimes even more than they need you.

Becky Sher is senior editor of special sections at Knight Ridder/Tribune in Washington, D.C., where she edits news and features stories for young readers. Previously, as managing editor of the department, she supervised KRT Campus, KRT's wire service for college newspapers. Sher worked for The GW Hatchet, *the independent student newspaper at George Washington University, from 1995 to 1999, where she was a staff writer, assistant news editor and news editor before being elected editor in chief her senior year.*

Sample Job Descriptions

Editor in Chief

1. Sets overall editorial direction for the publication
2. Oversees hiring of all editorial staff
3. Conducts all editorial and staff meetings
4. Represents the paper to the public, including the school administration and campus community
5. Oversees layout, design and production of newspaper
6. Consults with adviser and student publication board (if the paper has them)
7. Works with adviser, business manager or student publication board to formulate a budget for the paper
8. Maintains communication with business and/or advertising manager
9. Sets, explains and enforces deadlines and policies for the editorial staff
10. Sets and maintains office hours to be available to the staff and community
11. Oversees training of new staff
12. Ensures the timely publication of the newspaper
13. Leads editorial board, which decides subject and stance of editorials
14. May write staff editorials
15. Reviews all controversial material for potential ethical and legal concerns
16. Acts as liaison to printer

Managing Editor

1. Assists the editor in chief and acts as second in command
2. Reviews stories after they've been edited by section editors and makes additional comments and changes
3. Makes all final decisions when editor in chief is not available
4. Attends budget meetings
5. Works with editor in chief, art director, section editors and designers to manage production of the paper

News Editor

1. Oversees assignment of all news stories
2. Oversees production of news pages
3. Peruses press releases, public service announcements and other newspapers for story ideas
4. Approves hiring of all news reporters
5. Supervises, coaches and evaluates news reporters
6. Reviews and edits all news stories
7. Reviews all news headlines and captions
8. Enforces deadlines among news reporters
9. Attends regular budget meetings
10. Coordinates all graphics and photos for news pages
11. Conducts regular news staff meetings and brainstorming sessions

Lifestyle Editor

1. Oversees assignment of all lifestyle stories
2. Oversees production of lifestyle section
3. Peruses press releases and other newspapers for lifestyle story ideas
4. Approves hiring of all lifestyle staff
5. Supervises, coaches and evaluates lifestyle staff
6. Reviews and edits all lifestyle section stories
7. Reviews all lifestyle section headlines and captions

8. Enforces deadlines among lifestyle reporters
9. Attends regular budget meetings
10. Coordinates all graphics and photos for the lifestyle section
11. Conducts regular lifestyle staff meetings and brainstorming sessions

Arts and Entertainment Editor

1. Oversees assignment of all A&E stories
2. Oversees production of A&E section
3. Peruses press releases and other newspapers for A&E story ideas
4. Approves hiring of all A&E staff
5. Supervises, coaches and evaluates A&E staff
6. Reviews and edits all A&E section stories
7. Reviews all A&E section headlines and captions
8. Enforces deadlines among A&E writers
9. Attends regular budget meetings
10. Coordinates all graphics and photos for the A&E section
11. Conducts regular A&E staff meetings and brainstorming sessions
12. Keeps track of arts events and maintains contact with arts and entertainment officials and producers in the community

Opinion Editor

1. Oversees assignment and collection of material for opinion pages, including editorial cartoons, letters to the editor, editorials and columns
2. Oversees, with the editor in chief and editorial board, writing of editorials
3. May write unsigned editorials or bylined opinion columns
4. Handles contributions from freelancers and community members
5. Oversees production of opinion section
6. Writes or reviews headlines and captions for opinion section

Sports Editor

1. Oversees assignment of all sports stories
2. Oversees production of sports section
3. Approves hiring of all sports staff
4. Supervises, coaches and evaluates sports staff
5. Reviews and edits all sports stories
6. Reviews all sports section headlines and captions
7. Enforces deadlines among sports reporters
8. Attends regular budget meetings
9. Coordinates all graphics and photos for the sports section
10. Conducts regular sports staff meetings and brainstorming sessions
11. Keeps track of sporting events and maintains communication with athletics officials

Photo Editor

1. Works with other editors to coordinate photography for the paper
2. Supervises, coaches and evaluates all staff photographers and freelancers
3. Distributes assignments to photographers and tracks the progress of all photo assignments
4. Helps photographers edit their work
5. Advises designers and other editors on selection, cropping and placement of photos

(continued on next page)

Sample Job Descriptions *(continued)*

6. Conducts regular photo staff meetings
7. Makes sure all photos are properly identified
8. Attends budget meetings
9. Maintains or oversees the maintenance of photo files
10. Keeps track of all photographic equipment owned by the newspaper and makes sure equipment is in good condition
11. Tracks stock and orders photo supplies, as needed
12. Advises editor in chief or others responsible on photography equipment purchases

Art Director

1. Sets overall design of the newspaper, including the use and placement of fonts, photos and graphic elements
2. Supervises and evaluates designers, graphics editor, graphic artists
3. Reviews and updates design style guide for the newspaper
4. Oversees layout of the newspaper, making sure the pages conform to the design style guide and are finished on time
5. Attends budget meetings
6. Assigns information graphics and graphic elements, such as charts, logos and maps; creates graphics if other staff aren't available
7. May coordinate with printer

Copy Chief

1. Oversees all copyediting and fact checking
2. Supervises, trains and evaluates all copy editors
3. Meets with copy editors on a regular basis to discuss common errors and copy flow problems
4. Reviews headlines and captions
5. Reviews and updates newspaper's stylebook
6. Meets regularly with editor in chief and other editors to discuss copy flow problems and changes to the copy system
7. Produces style and grammar memos to the staff, highlighting common problems and changes

Online Editor/Webmaster

1. Oversees production and maintenance of newspaper's Web site
2. Makes sure all stories and images are posted in a timely fashion
3. May supervise and evaluate team of online editors and/or producers
4. Devises ways to enhance Web content with links, interactive features, slide shows and other special elements
5. Ensures that important breaking news stories are updated between editions
6. Attends budget meetings
7. Responds to e-mail related to the newspaper's Web site
8. Assures adherence to all copyright law and corrects mistakes on the site

Headline Writing Cheat Sheet

Looking for a short word for earthquake? Need a catchy synonym for organization? Try these:

Accident: collision, crash, wreck
Accuse: charge, cite
Acquire: get
Advocate: urge, push, spur
Agreement: accord, compact, deal, pledge, pact
Alteration: revise, fix, change
Appointment: post, job
Apprehend: arrest, capture, catch, nab, seize, snag
Arrange: plan, set, shape
Arrest: seize, hold, net
Assemble: meet, gather, rally
Attempt: try
Beginning: opening, start
Business: company, firm, plant, shop, store
Celebrate: fete, mark, perform, stage
Celebration: bash, event, fete, party, do
Commander: chief, guide, leader, ruler
Company: firm, house, concern
Compete: vie
Competition: race, contest
Contract: deal, pact
Damage: harm, hurt, impair, injure, wreck
Decision: decree, order, rule, writ
Decline, decrease: dip, fall, plunge, slip
Defeat: fall, loss

Destroy: raze
Earthquake: jolt, quake, shock, temblor, tremor
Encourage: aid, help, spark, boost, push
Examine: scan, study
Expose: bare, reveal
Fire: blaze
Former: ex
Increase: add, hike, rise, up
Investigate: examine, probe, study
Leader: chief, expert, guide, head, ruler
Limit: curb, restrain, soften, temper
Meeting: confab, session
Murder: kill, slay
Organization: board, body, band, club, firm, group, unit
Organize: form, join, link, merge
Overcome: beat, win
Plan: deal, plot, scheme
Postpone: delay, defer, put off, shelve
Position: job, post
Prevent: ban, bar, curb, stop
Promise: agree, pledge, vow
Resign: quit, leave, give up
Revise: alter, change, modify, shift, switch, vary
Solicit: seek
Schedule: arrange, plan, set
Steal: loot, rob, take
Storm: gale, squall
Zealous: ardent, avid, fervent

⭐ **Northern Star Story Planner**

Story slug or working title:

Reporter: Please fill out a photo request!

Packaging Options
(check all that apply)

Visual Elements

photos / live

photos / archive

Illustration

Infographic

Map

Chart

Diagram

Table

Other:

Furniture:

column logo

series logo

tag line at end

page topper

other:

Text pullouts

Bio box

checklist

for more info ...

glossary

key players

Q&A

Quotes

timeline

what's next

other:

Promo elements:

Coming next

On the Web

Other:

Section: | Campus |

Due date:

Projected run day/date:

Writer / phone number:

Photographer / phone number:

What's the news and how will it affect readers?
(say it in one or two simple sentences)

Questions readers will have:

Key sources:

Projected story length: | Less than 8" |

Other notes:

Figure 10.4. *Northern Star,* the daily newspaper at Northern Illinois University, uses this form to plan stories, including graphics, photos, information boxes and promotional elements. Reprinted with permission.

Editor Application

Name _____

Phone number _____

Other phone number _____

E-mail address _____

1. What staff position or positions are you interested in? (rank your top choices in order from 1 to 3)

___ Editor in chief   ___ Special projects editor
___ Managing editor   ___ Online editor
___ News editor   ___ Copy chief
___ Lifestyle editor   ___ Copy editor
___ A&E editor   ___ Photo editor
___ Sports editor   ___ Art director
___ Opinion editor   ___ Graphics editor

2. List all relevant coursework:

_____
_____
_____

3. List other relevant experience, including internships, jobs, leadership positions, etc.:

_____
_____
_____

4. Why do you want this position(s)?

_____
_____
_____

5. If named to the position of your choice, what changes and improvements would you try to make?

_____
_____
_____

6. What ideas do you have for special projects or packages your section and/or the paper could tackle?

_____
_____
_____

7. What strengths will you bring to the position? What skills do you still need to develop to succeed?

_____
_____
_____

8. What do you think are the paper's greatest strengths? How could the paper improve?

_____
_____

Editor Performance Evaluation

Editor: _____

Evaluator (Name and Position): _____

Please rate the editor's contributions in each category according to the following system:

4	Exceeds expectations
3	Meets expectations
2	Needs some improvement
1	Needs significant improvement

	1	2	3	4
Coaching reporters through stories	1	2	3	4
Editing copy	1	2	3	4
Responsiveness to reporter's needs and requests	1	2	3	4
Ability to give constructive criticism	1	2	3	4
Ability to accept feedback	1	2	3	4
Organizational skills	1	2	3	4
Communication	1	2	3	4
Other comments				

Reporter Performance Evaluation

Reporter: _____

Evaluator (Name and Position): _____

Please rate the reporter's contributions in each category according to the following system:

4	Exceeds expectations
3	Meets expectations
2	Needs some improvement
1	Needs significant improvement

	1	2	3	4
Meeting deadlines	1	2	3	4
Quality of research and reporting	1	2	3	4
Quality of copy (spelling, grammar, punctuation, AP style)	1	2	3	4
Quality of writing (ledes, nut graphs, story organization, sentence structure)	1	2	3	4
Ability to accept feedback	1	2	3	4
Beat coverage/story ideas	1	2	3	4
Communication with editors	1	2	3	4
Other comments				

Photo Editor Performance Evaluation

Photographer: _____

Evaluator (Name and Position): _____

Please rate the photo editor's contributions in each category according to the following system:

4	Exceeds expectations
3	Meets expectations
2	Needs some improvement
1	Needs significant improvement

	1	2	3	4
Coaching photographers	1	2	3	4
Editing images	1	2	3	4
Organizational skills	1	2	3	4
Ability to give constructive criticism	1	2	3	4
Assignment of photos	1	2	3	4
Teamwork/willingness to work with others	1	2	3	4
Communication	1	2	3	4

Other comments

Photographer Performance Evaluation

Photographer: _____

Evaluator (Name and Position): _____

Please rate the photographer's contributions in each category according to the following system:

4	Exceeds expectations
3	Meets expectations
2	Needs some improvement
1	Needs significant improvement

	1	2	3	4
Meeting deadlines	1	2	3	4
Editing images	1	2	3	4
Quality of images	1	2	3	4
Creativity in handling assignments	1	2	3	4
Technical skills (lighting, use of flash, focus, etc.)	1	2	3	4
Teamwork/willingness to work with others	1	2	3	4
Communication	1	2	3	4
Other comments				

Figure 11.1. Just months after setting up an investigative team, *The Daily Tar Heel* at the University of North Carolina, Chapel Hill won a national award from Investigative Reporters and Editors, Inc. for this six-part series on the university's attempt to raise the cap on out-of-state enrollment. *The Daily Tar Heel,* University of North Carolina

Chapter 11

Investigative Reporting

In May 2003, John Frank, the newly appointed investigations editor at *The Daily Tar Heel* at the University of North Carolina, Chapel Hill, posted a mission statement near the entrance to the newsroom:

As the forefathers of *The Daily Tar Heel* Investigative Team, we hereby set these goals that we will uphold in our daily reporting:

• Be the paramount guardians in maintaining the watchdog mission of *The Daily Tar Heel*

- Ask the questions others are afraid to ask and dig deeper than others are willing to go for the truth
- Be the catalyst that sparks dialogue about underrepresented issues in the campus community
- Maintain the journalistic mission to "Comfort the afflicted and afflict the comfortable"
- Through professionalism and diligence, improve the paper's respectability in the campus community
- Impact the way policies and laws in the campus community are created.

The Daily Tar Heel, a five-day-a-week newspaper serving a campus of 26,000 students, had never had an investigative team before. But after taking a computer-assisted reporting class and attending an Investigative Reporters and Editors, Inc. conference, Frank, along with Editor in Chief Elyse Ashburn, decided the paper should take its watchdog role more seriously.

In that first year, Frank and his five-person investigative team completed numerous investigative reports. Among them:

- A story on how UNC Radiology Department employees had misused more than $300,000 in university funds
- An analysis of the university chancellor's weekly calendars that offered a glimpse into the inner workings of the university
- A four-month investigation into the university's summer reading book selection committee, a secretive group that had chosen several controversial books
- An investigation into a lawsuit that could have cost the university $11 million in parking ticket revenues
- A six-part series on the university's efforts to increase the university's enrollment cap for out-of-state students

The payoff was tangible. The following spring, the paper won the top award for student journalists from IRE for the "Raising the Cap" series. "We had never even entered a story before," says Frank, who later became a political reporter for *The Post and Courier* in Charleston, S.C. "We won on our first try."

Setting up an investigative team didn't just enrich the newspaper experience for the reporters involved, Frank says. It inspired the whole newsroom. "We had that investigative mindset going down to the freshmen reporters. They would see what we were working on and they would want to do it themselves."

The Daily Tar Heel's successes in setting up an investigative team are inspiring, but you don't have to be a big daily to do investigative reporting. The *Hampton Script*, a bi-

weekly paper serving the 6,000-student campus of Hampton University in Hampton, Va., won accolades for its investigative report on health violations at the campus cafeteria. Brian Krans, a reporter for *The Winonan*, a weekly at Winona State University in Minnesota, won awards for a 10-week investigation of underage drinking and the bars in town that most frequently served minors.

"You needn't have a big staff to do investigative reporting," says Frank. "Two or three reporters committed to doing professional journalism at a student level can get a lot done."

What is Investigative Reporting?

Investigative reporting sounds so sexy, so Woodward and Bernstein, so Pulitzer Prize. But what exactly is it? IRE, the leading organization of investigative journalists, defines it as "the reporting, through one's own initiative and work product, of matters of importance to readers, viewers or listeners. In many cases, the subjects of the reporting wish the matters under scrutiny to remain undisclosed."

That's it?

"People have this misguided notion that investigative journalism is this voodoo thing only select people can do," says Matt Waite, a reporter for the *St. Petersburg Times* who has been doing investigative journalism since he was a reporter for the *Daily Nebraskan* at the University of Nebraska. "It's pulling documents, reviewing routine matters and keeping an eye out for trends for when something different happens. It's watchdog journalism."

Brant Houston, executive director of IRE and a professor of journalism at the University of Missouri, advises students who want to do investigative journalism to start by asking a simple question: "What's not working?"

Why is the university parking garage already full at 9 a.m.? Why has tuition gone up? Why does a physically fit athlete have a handicapped parking placard for his car? Why is the roof on the new building leaking?

When Laws Don't Work

Brian Krans got the idea for his first big investigative project shortly after his 21st birthday when he found himself running into younger friends in the local bars. Clearly, thought Krans, then a junior at Winona State University in Winona, Minn., the laws that set the drinking age at 21 were not working.

"It started as kind of a joke, really," says Krans. When his advanced reporting professor assigned students to survey students for a Top 10 list, Krans blurted out, "How about the top 10 bars that minors go to?"

The professor liked the idea, and over the next two months Krans surveyed more than 300 students about which bars were the eas-

iest to get into. He accompanied underage high school and college students as they entered bars with fake IDs and even used a counterfeit identification card to get himself into a club.

Here's how his story in *The Winonan* began:

Andre "Dre" Klonecki, a senior at Winona Senior High School, wanted to go to the bars with friends from Winona State.

He did—using a fake ID.

The only shared trait between Klonecki and the ID, the top corner cut off and expired in 1999, was the red tint in Klonecki's strawberry blond hair.

Klonecki—a tall 18-year-old man—used the ID of a man three inches shorter, six years older and 25 pounds lighter.

Given a quick glance, the ID might have resembled Klonecki, and that is all it took.

On Jan. 18, manager Tony Haglund was checking IDs at the front door of Bulls-Eye Beer Hall, a popular college bar.

Haglund inadequately checked Klonecki's fake ID at the front door and let him in with little hesitation.

At Bulls-Eye, Klonecki was served by three different bartenders and despite having 15 drinks, no one asked for ID again.

When the story came out in the newspaper, much of the community was incensed. Both students and the town's bar owners challenged his reporting. One pub threatened to sue. Someone made up posters with Krans' photo saying businesses had the right to refuse service to anyone and distributed them to bars around town. The newspaper even received a death threat against Krans.

But some appreciated Krans' truth telling. After reading the story, a Winona City Council member recommended underage drinking violations be considered when a bar's liquor license came up for renewal. The Minnesota Newspaper Association awarded Krans first prize for investigative reporting.

And Krans learned something about himself: he loved investigative reporting. Now a reporter for *The Dispatch/Rock Island Argus/ The Leader* newspaper group in Moline, Ill., and Davenport, Iowa, he says, "I became addicted to this stuff."

Public Records

To hear reporters like Krans tell it, investigative reporting is lots of fun. And it can be. But there's also a lot of drudgery involved. For every hot tip, there are ten bum steers.

"It's painstaking work," says Krans. "It takes a lot of time. You've got to dig and then when you think you have your story you

Investigative and Enterprise Story Ideas

Crime

- Get crime statistics from your university police department for the last five years. Take note of trends—which crimes are up, which crimes are down.
- Ask for arrest records from your campus police or the law enforcement agency that covers your campus. Look for familiar names, trends, evidence of raids. Were a slew of students arrested for marijuana possession in the dorm last month? Was the dean of students arrested for driving under the influence?
- Run key school officials—the chancellor, president, provost, deans, controversial professors—through a criminal records check.
- Do the same for high-profile students, such as members of the football team or student governing board or leaders of student groups.
- Get information from the agency that handles parking on campus. Ask for lists of people who get handicapped placards, people who have their parking tickets waived, people issued faculty (or other premium) parking passes. Make sure these people are legitimate. (In 1999, 19 football players at the University of California, Los Angeles were cited for illegal use of disabled parking placards).

Budget

- Get your college or university budgets for the past five years. Note which departments are getting more or less funding than before. Take note of the biggest changes.
- Compare budgets for different departments. Divide by the number of students in each department to find out how much the university is spending on different groups of students.

Athletics

- Find out how much your school is spending on team recruiting.
- Check the graduation rates for each NCAA team on campus. Compare those numbers to the graduation rates for the campus as a whole.
- Look at funding for athletic scholarships. You might compare it to financial aid for academic achievements.

- Find out what kind of perks your athletes get. Schools have been known to lavish gifts on their top players, particularly if they win an important game.

Health and Safety

- Check the health inspection reports on the cafeterias and other food service establishments on campus.
- Find out which popular bars near campus have been cited for serving underage drinkers.
- If you've got a medical school on campus, check the licensing records of all M.D. faculty members with the state medical board.
- Use sex offender registries to find out about offenders who live on or near your campus.
- Check fire inspection reports on dorms, fraternity and sorority houses and other buildings.

Academics

- Look up the grade records on controversial or popular classes. You won't be able to get grades for individual students but you should be able to get records without names. If Human Sexuality 101 is reputed to be an easy A, report on the grade distribution. Compare different sections of the same course or different professors.
- Find out which departments are undergoing accreditation reviews. Study the accreditation reports to find the department's strengths and weaknesses.
- Request salary data for all faculty members. Find the highest paid professors and compare how professors in different departments are paid.
- Peruse the latest accreditation report for your school. Some colleges and universities routinely keep copies of these reports, which can run hundreds of pages, in the library. If you can't find it there, try the university registrar's office.

---

have to wait a little while and dig some more. There's usually more there."

Often that digging involves public records, documents that can shed light on an issue. "You've got to get into a document state of mind," advises IRE's Houston. "Every time you talk to someone and they say something is a certain way, you should ask: 'Is there a memo on this? Is there a report on this? Is there an audit on this?' Everything someone says can either be supported or contradicted by documents."

Among the documents students can look for:

- Health department records on cafeterias and restaurants on campus
- Lawsuits filed against the university
- University or department budgets

- University salary data (Figure 11.2)
- Accreditation reports
- On-campus crime reports
- Criminal records on faculty members, administrators, athletes, staff

Houston concedes that universities can be hard places to investigate. "It's difficult to get information out of universities. They have a certain arrogance about the information they have. They don't believe they have to share it."

But they do, particularly if the school is public. State colleges and university documents are all subject to open records laws. Want to know how much your biology professor makes? It's a public record. Curious about how much the student health center spends on condoms? It's a public record.

Wondering how many students have flunked out of school? You guessed it; it's a public record (although the names of the students are confidential). Public records laws vary state by state. But they share certain exemptions. Personnel files, student records and health records are usually exempt.

Investigating Private Schools

Private colleges and universities are not subject to the same open records laws that make public schools such gold mines for investigative reporters. But you can still get plenty of documents. Colleges and universities that participate in federal financial aid programs, for example, must be accredited by a nationally recognized accreditation agency and those reports are public records.

Whenever a private school contracts with

a public agency (for garbage pickup or police services, for example), that contract is public. And like other tax-exempt organizations, most private universities are required to file Return of Organization Exempt From Income Tax Annual Information Forms, better known as IRS Form 990s. These forms can provide valuable windows into a private university—and into the private foundations set up by public schools.

Knowing the Law

Waite, who won an IRE award while a reporter for the *Daily Nebraskan*, says one key to good investigative journalism is knowing the law. "Know it in and out, up and down, left and right," he says. "Know it better than your administrators."

In fact, he recommends literally carrying a copy of your state's open records law in your back pocket. (Some state press associations have pocket-sized guides to open records and open meeting laws. If yours doesn't, find the law and put it into a handy format). "That way, when a school administrator says, 'I'm not going to give you that document,' you can say, 'The law says this.'"

Cultivating Human Sources

While many investigative stories begin with documents, like all stories, they need human sources to really come alive. Once you've discovered that your school is spending thousands of dollars to recruit a few high school jocks to the football team or that the chief of the radiology department at the university hospital just had his medical license revoked,

you need to flesh out the story with interviews.

And, as you might imagine, getting people to talk may not be easy.

Waite recommends a combination of politeness and persistence. He remembers spending hours outside a key source's office waiting for the man to come out. When the source finally emerged, he refused to be interviewed. Waite thanked him politely and kept calling. "A week later I got the interview."

To Do:

1. If you don't already have one, create an investigative team with some of your newspaper's most experienced reporters. Pick one or two manageable projects to start with. Invite a professional investigative reporter to act as a mentor for the team.
2. Send a delegation to an investigative reporting conference or training workshop. (Investigative Reporters and Editors, Inc. and the National Institute for Computer-Assisted Reporting each hold an annual national convention and many regional workshops throughout the year.) Have participants share what they learned in a presentation to the staff.
3. Organize a brainstorming session for editors or for the whole staff focused on investigative reporting. Have people throw out ideas around the theme "What's Not Working?"
4. Organize an investigative reporting workshop for your staff or regional or state college press association. The IRE Web site

has information on how to do this. You might be able to collaborate with professional newspapers or other student papers in your area.

5. Invite an investigative reporter from a local news organization to give a lecture or workshop for your staff.
6. Find an interesting database (faculty salaries, campus crime statistics, parking ticket fine information) and assign a team to crunch the numbers in Excel or another spreadsheet program. Have them look for possible story ideas.
7. Get a copy of your school's most recent budget and one from five years ago and assign a team of reporters to delve into them in search of story ideas.

To Read:

Houston, Brant, Len Bruzzese and Steve Weinberg. *The Investigative Reporter's Handbook, 4th ed.* New York: Bedford/St. Martin's, 2002.

Houston, Brant. *Computer-Assisted Reporting: A Practical Guide, 3rd ed.* New York: Bedford/St. Martin's, 2003.

Sankey, Michael L. *Public Records Online: The National Guide to Private & Government Online Sources of Public Records, 5th ed.* Tempe, Ariz.: Facts on Demand Press, 2004.

Weinberg, Steve. *The Reporter's Handbook: An Investigator's Guide to Documents and Techniques, 3rd ed.* New York: St. Martin's Press, 1996.

2005 Salary Guide

A Supplement to The Diamondback | Tuesday April 26, 2005

TABLE OF CONTENTS

Figure 11.2. Some public documents are interesting in and of themselves. Several student newspapers, including *The Diamondback* at the University of Maryland, routinely publish faculty salaries, which are available from public documents at public universities. *The Diamondback,* University of Maryland

To Click:

Investigative Reporters and Editors, Inc.
www.ire.org

National Institute for Computer-Assisted Reporting
http://www.nicar.org/

Freedom of Information Center
http://foi.missouri.edu/

The Search Systems Free Public Records Directory: An online directory of free public record databases on the Internet
http://www.searchsystems.net/

Center for Investigative Reporting
http://www.muckraker.org

How to Use the Federal Freedom of Information Act: Reporters' Committee for Freedom of the Press
http://www.rcfp.org/foiact/index.html

Tapping Officials' Secrets: Reporters' Committee for Freedom of the Press
http://www.rcfp.org/cgi-local/tapping/
    index.cgi

The Scoop: Derek Willis' weblog on investigative and computer-assisted reporting
http://thescoop.org./

Making the Grade: Access to College Accreditation Reports
http://splc.org/legalresearch.asp?id=17

Student Media Guide to the Clery Act
http://splc.org/legalresearch.asp?id=19

Tips from a Pro
■ **John Frank**

Covering higher education is the best of all reporting worlds. It's a lot more than the chancellors and trustees and faculty council. There are elements from nearly every other beat—local government to business to cops to politics.

One of the best parts about covering higher education is the wealth of information out there.

These are just a few of my favorite sources of information:

1. **The weekly calendars.** Review the calendars for the chancellor (and/or president) and perhaps the top two lieutenants. It just lets you stay on top of what's going on at the institution and it's important to look at who is getting that precious face time. If nothing else, it gives you an idea of when is best to reach them.

2. **Audits.** Get these at the college, university system and state levels. I find the best ones are at the university level. Auditors have an annual schedule of what departments will be examined. Get the schedule, but also regularly (maybe every two months) ask for a list of the "special request" audits under way. These are typically the juicy ones because they've been launched by a tip or some sort of indication of wrongdoing. Then call regularly and see if they've been completed.

3. **Salary database.** This is probably a no-brainer, but the stories it can produce are limitless. It also adds valuable context to plenty of other stories by just plugging in average salaries for, say, a top administrator or assistant professor.

4. **Correspondence.** The best are the e-mails, but just request general correspondence.

5. **IRS Form 990s.** Form 990 is the annual information return, which must be filed with the Internal Revenue Service by most tax-exempt charities and social welfare organizations. The best place to get them is from Guidestar (www.guidestar.com) but the non-profit must keep a copy for public inspection as well. It is one of the best sources for information about private universities—salary disclosures are a main reason for that. Don't forget the athletic booster clubs, investment offices and scholarships that are run by foundations.

6. **Contracts.** There is a contract for nearly everything, from chancellors to athletic directors to coaches, not to mention those with corporations, such as licensing contracts.

7. **Fundraising brochures.** These give you a glimpse of the people who are playing a larger role at the university than most know.

8. **Google news alerts.** You can do this through Lexis-Nexis and Factiva, too, but getting an email anytime your school is mentioned helps tremendously when other schools are trying to steal away your university's personnel.

John Frank was the investigations editor at The Daily Tar Heel, *an independent student newspaper covering the University of North Carolina, Chapel Hill, from May 2003 to May 2004. He has received numerous honors for his investigative work, including top awards from Investigative Reporters and Editors, Inc., Society of Professional Journalists and the Hearst Foundation. After graduating in May 2004, he did a summer internship at* The News & Observer *in Raleigh, N.C., and a 22-week political reporting fellowship in Washington, D.C. He is now a political reporter for* The Post and Courier *in Charleston, S.C.*

This is adapted from a presentation Frank did at IRE's annual conference in June 2004 in Atlanta.

A Dozen Tips to Avoid Being Burned by a Hot Story

■ **Student Press Law Center**

As more student media move from being merely a showcase for football players and prom queens to being serious news organizations, not afraid to address controversial or sensitive subjects, they face many of the hazards that have long confronted their commercial counterparts: threats of libel lawsuits, invasion of privacy claims, charges of bias, etc. While such problems are daunting, they need not be crippling. With the exercise of proper caution, the risks of covering a hot, or sensitive, story can be significantly reduced. Toward that end, the Student Press Law Center offers our suggestions for how you can avoid getting burned when the story you are covering is a hot one.

1. **Activate your common sense.** While the nitty-gritty details of libel or privacy law can be confusing, the main ideas are fairly straightforward, generally conforming to common sense. For example, libel law in a nutshell: (1) don't publish things that aren't true or that you don't have the evidence to reasonably support and (2) don't be a sloppy reporter. Privacy law: don't publish or gather information that is nobody else's business. Common sense also dictates that if you don't understand something or if a story simply doesn't make sense ask enough questions of enough people until it does. If you are confused, rest assured that your readers will be as well.

2. **Remember your role as a journalist.** Your job is to accurately relate the facts of a story to your readers. Go into a story with an open mind and not just looking for information that supports any preconceived version of the story that you might have. Your job is to find and report the facts as they exist. Do not be content with anything less. Good reporting is hard work. Be prepared to invest the time and energy necessary to get the story right. No excuses. If you're not willing or can't do so, leave the story for someone else.

3. **Take good notes.** The "Golden Oldie" of libel lawyer advice. Record facts and interviews scrupulously, including who said what and when. If you know you are a weak note taker, invest in a tape recorder.

4. **Documents, documents, documents.** Get it in writing. If your source tells you during an interview that she acquired her information from an internal memo, ask for a copy of the memo. And then read it to make sure that what your source told you jibes with what's in the memo. Also, whenever possible, cite a public record as your source for information. In most cases, doing so will protect you from liability even if it later turns out the information contained in the public record was wrong.

5. **Don't overstate the facts.** You are a reporter not a salesman. Get rid of the "bigger is better" mentality. Your football coach who can't account for $1,000 of the team's budget does not need to be labeled "corrupt" or the "ring-leader of the largest financial scandal in school history."

    "Two sources" is not "many sources" or "a number or sources"—it is "two sources." And it is perfectly okay for a problem to just be a "problem" and not a "crisis." You get the idea. Finally, you should generally avoid the temptation to interpret the facts or reach a conclusion or an opinion for your readers. In covering a sensitive story, it is safer to let the facts speak for themselves.

6. **Don't overstate the credibility of a source.** Either to yourself or to your readers. When interviewing a source, ask yourself if you think he's telling the truth. Does he have a reputation as a liar? Does he have any reason to harm the subject? If you are relying on statistical data or some other published report, establish that source's reliability. If, for example, the manner in which the statistics were compiled has been reasonably questioned, say so in your story. Remember that one exceptionally credible source is worth far more than a dozen semi-credible sources. Finally, anonymous sources should be used sparingly. And at least you should know the identity of your confidential source.

7. **Be fair.** Always give the subject of your story an opportunity to present his or her side. Not only does this give a story an essential element of fairness, it also provides you with an opportunity to catch—or at least confirm—parts of a story that may be subject to debate or question.

8. **Eliminate the non-essential.** Sensitive stories are not the place to show off your literary talents. Leave the flowery prose and melodrama for the features page. Write carefully and purposefully. Edit out sources or subjects that do not contribute to the "core" of a story. They are potential plaintiffs. Delete unnecessary (even though interesting) allegations. Tell what you know and how you know it. No more. No less.

9. **Seek the input of others.** Prior to publication, ask others to look at your story and offer their criticisms or suggestions. After working endless hours on a story, "fresh eyes" are essential for catching gaps, inconsistencies, confusing phraseology, mistaken attributions and all of the other small traps that are forever hidden to one who has already read the copy 20 times. This is also the time to contact your adviser, an attorney, the Student Press Law Center or someone else well-versed in media law if you have specific questions about the legality of a story. An ounce of prevention sure beats sitting in court.

10. **Prior to publication, step back and look at the "Big Picture."** Forget the little details upon which you have focused so long and hard. Read the story through one last time. Taken as a whole, are there any obvious questions you failed to ask or glaring sources you didn't contact (for example, a person in a room who witnessed a key—and disputed—meeting)? Look at your story from different points of view. Do you believe each of your subjects and sources would feel they were treated fairly (even if they didn't like the story itself)? What about headlines and subheads—are they fair and accurate? Are the graphics, photos and accompanying captions correct and not misleading? The bottom line: make sure the story makes sense to you and fairly presents the facts as you know them.

11. **After publication, respond to complaints courteously and fairly.** Studies have shown that a person who perceives that he or she has been treated rudely or arrogantly by a media organization is far more likely to sue than one who believes that they have been shown the proper respect. Select one person—preferably a "people person"—to whom all complaints should be referred. While that person should not admit fault or provide information about specific newsgathering practices, he or she should listen carefully to the caller's complaints, promise to investigate the matter—and then do so. Where a correction or retraction is appropriate, publish it in a timely fashion.

12. **Finally, if you need help—legal or otherwise—don't be afraid to ask for it.** As a student, you're not supposed to know it all. And ask for that help sooner rather than later. It's much easier to put out a brush fire than a forest fire.

Copyright 1996. Reprinted with permission from the Student Press Law Center.

Question & Answer

How can a student newspaper develop a watchdog or investigative spirit?

It really helps to take a group of editors, get them out of the newsroom and sit them down to have a fundamental discussion. What are we going to cover? What do we want to emphasize? What kind of newspaper do we want to be?

The thing that builds that watchdog attitude is success. If you can teach reporters at your paper to get into a document frame of mind, to look at internal audits, to ask for documents the university isn't used to having people ask for, to assess what kind of a job they are doing, then those stories end up in the paper. Those stories get noticed by people, other papers, other editors. And you know what? That kind of success gets addictive.

What are some documents student reporters should look for?

Lawsuits are a perfect example. Go to the courthouse to look for professors suing the administration, harassment suits, breach of contract actions. It's boring and there will be weeks when you don't find a thing. But it's worth making sure. When I started going down to the courthouse the stories started dropping out of the sky.

Get the budget. It's the very lifeblood of the entire campus. Money makes the world go 'round. Every department has a budget and they spend money.

Look for audits. All kinds of stuff on a university campus is audited. Research grants are ruthlessly audited, extension services are audited. If you look at them you may find some people are wasting money.

■ Matt Waite

Even before he had unpacked the boxes in his dorm room his freshman year at the University of Nebraska, Matt Waite showed up at the Daily Nebraskan looking for a job. An editor assigned him to write a story about the city police's new electronic parking ticket writer. It was a routine story, but Waite was thrilled to be working as a reporter. He continued to write for the paper for the next four and a half years, and in 1996 he received an award from Investigative Reporters and Editors, Inc. After graduating in 1997, Waite landed a night cops reporting gig at the Arkansas Democrat-Gazette. In 2000, he became a general assignment reporter for the St. Petersburg Times.

What tips do you have for getting government and university officials to release documents?

Saying please and thank you and being polite works wonders. I have avoided having to write dozens and dozens of open records request letters and gotten out of countless fights over records by saying "please" and "thank you." Get to know people on your beat. Look at what's on the walls, what they have pictures of. When I was a police reporter, I got so much out of the cops by finding out what their favorite football teams were and remembering them. I'd walk in and say, "Hey, the Longhorns won this weekend." That had an impact. You start to present yourself as a decent person.

What advice do you have for reporters dealing with reluctant sources?

Be polite. If you ask somebody for a comment and they say, "No," say, "I'm sorry. Thanks a lot." It's much easier for someone to turn you away if you're rude and act stupid. If you're polite to a fault, it's only a matter of time until they start feeling bad about it and talk to you.

How can student papers start doing computer-assisted projects?

You have to build a lot of shacks before you can build the Taj Mahal. Start small with campus crime numbers or by comparing budget figures over the last five years. Use that to learn about the budgeting process or crime and how to do percent change comparisons or summing and sorting and ranking in Excel. Treat these stories as skill-building exercises. Each time you'll learn something new.

One fairly easy story to do is to compare your campus to other schools. Get a list of peer institutions and compare tuition, graduation rates, campus crime statistics, graduation requirements. All these things are interesting to your readership.

PHOTO ESSAY

A City in Crisis

Two Daily Reveille staffers documented the broken city of New Orleans on Sunday

Photos by Michael Beagle • THE DAILY REVEILLE

New Orleans residents sit outside a boarded-up Copeland's Restaurant on the corner of Napoleon and St. Charles avenues on Sunday afternoon.

Light covers and trash litter the standing water on Canal Street in New Orleans. The water had receded to only a few inches deep in lower parts, but water marks showed that it had once been more than two feet deep in some areas.

Although reports of looting were rampant in the days following Hurricane Katrina, one Uptown shop owner sent a more direct message in an attempt to deter break-ins.

"The people of our city are holding on by a thread. Time has run out. Can we survive another night? And who can we depend on? Only God knows."

Ray Nagin, mayor of New Orleans

A construction crew works to plug the more than 500 foot-wide hole in the 17th Street Canal in New Orleans. City officials said Monday the hole is about 84 percent closed.

Soldiers from the Army's 82nd Airborne Divison march down Canal Street at sundown on Sunday. A large military presence is being used to supplement local law enforcement, restore order and enforce a curfew.

Figure 12.1.
Sometimes photos can tell a story better than words. In September 2005, photographer Michael Beagle of *The Daily Reveille* went to New Orleans to document the aftermath of Hurricane Katrina. *The Daily Reveille*, Louisiana State University

Chapter 12

Photojournalism

I t was the second round of the 2004 NCAA men's basketball tournament and the University of North Carolina Tar Heels were locked in a tight battle with the University of Texas Longhorns. *The Daily Tar Heel* photographer Brian Cassella had gotten plenty of good action shots during the game. But when the Tar Heels lost 78-75, Cassella knew he'd need a reaction photo to truly capture the mood of the season-ending game.

After snapping a few shots of the disappointed players leaving the court, Cassella went to the locker room. "The atmosphere was overwhelmingly morose," he said. "It was difficult to raise my camera. (It was like) shooting a funeral."

Cassella noticed one player sitting on a bench with a jersey over his head and he shot a few frames. Then another player went to comfort the visibly upset team manager sitting a few feet away. "The moment lined up perfectly right in front of me, and I was able to squeeze off just one frame (before other people got in the way). One minute later the coaches kicked us out, but I had a photo that was part of our front-page package the next day."

Photojournalism is about seizing moments, about showing readers what writers try to—and sometimes can't—describe. Cassella's photo (Figure 12.2), with its slumped shoulders and bowed heads, captures the Tar Heels' utter sense of defeat as no text story could.

Photojournalists need sensitivity and intuition to find these moments, as well as the technical skills to arrest them and make stirring images. They also need access. Unlike reporters, they can't get the story over the phone. Photographers must be enterprising and assertive enough to get to the action when it's happening.

In this chapter we'll discuss what it takes to make great newspaper photos.

What is Photojournalism?

Photojournalism is telling stories through photos. Photos don't just break up gray text; they add value to a newspaper by providing additional information and insights. They can be poignant or entertaining, silly or serious. They take readers to places they can't go and show them things they can't normally see.

And they bring readers to your newspaper. Numerous studies have shown readers are more likely to read a story if it's accompanied by a photo. In a landmark 1991 study, researchers from the Poynter Institute for Media Studies used Eye-Trac technology (a device that tracks eye movements) to monitor how readers read newspapers. They found:

- Photos are usually the first thing readers see on a page, even before headlines.
- Readers process photographs 75 percent of the time (as compared to 56 percent of the time for headlines and 25 percent of the time for text).
- The larger the photo, the more likely readers will scan it. Pictures that run three columns across or wider are read 92 percent of the time (Figure 12.3).

Photos lure people to pick up the paper and read it, so it's in everyone's interest to

Figure 12.2. This shot taken in the locker room after the University of North Carolina Tar Heels lost a key NCAA basketball game captures the team's utter sense of defeat. Brian Cassella, *The Daily Tar Heel,* University of North Carolina, Chapel Hill. Reprinted with permission.

make sure your paper is chock full of good photos.

One trick to making good photos is to take a lot of shots. In the past, when professional photojournalists mostly used film, they'd often shoot three or four 36-exposure rolls on a routine assignment. Now, with digital, it's not unusual for a photographer to shoot hundreds of photos to get one or two great images for a story.

One difference between shooting as a photojournalist and shooting for fun is that now you're trying to document reality. That means you don't set up photos. Unless you're shooting a portrait or creating a photo illustration, you want to capture life as it unfolds, not as you want it to look.

Though digital photography offers myriad opportunities for manipulating images, **resist the temptation**! Photojournalists take varying positions on digital manipulation but most agree photographers shooting news should limit themselves to basic photo techniques traditionally used in the darkroom—cropping, taking out dust spots, adjusting contrast, dodging and burning (lightening and darkening areas of the photograph). Be aware that altering photos beyond these simple changes—especially in ways that fundamentally alter the meaning of the image—may be unethical and can even cause legal problems.

Shooting Perspectives

For virtually any assignment, you want to get a variety of shots, including a long shot, a medium shot and a close-up. Each type of photo offers a different perspective on an event.

The Long Shot

A long shot is one that sets the scene, giving the reader an overall impression of the event and where it takes place. If there's a demonstration on campus, the long shot might show the quad where the protest is happening. If you're covering a fraternity house fire, you might take a picture from across the street showing the firefighters hosing the building. If you're covering a football game, you'll want an overall shot of the entire stadium.

Long shots demand height. When taking the long shot, try to find a way to lift yourself above the crowd. That may mean standing on a chair, scrambling on top of a car (better make it your own) or taking a picture from a balcony across the street. Photojournalists have been known to climb trees, rent ladders, even hire helicopters all in the quest for a good long shot.

The Medium Shot

The medium shot is one that tells the story in a single image. Like a news lede, it should capture all the major elements in one tight package.

A medium shot at a fire might show tearful survivors in the foreground with firefighters battling the blaze in the background. At a basketball game, it might show a player making a basket with the crowd watching in awe.

TECHNICIAN

WEDNESDAY
JULY
14
2004

technicianonline.com   Raleigh, North Carolina

Edwards returns home

Teresa Heinz-Kerry, John Kerry, John Edwards and Elizabeth Edwards arrive at the Court of North Carolina for their rally on Saturday. Campus police estimated the rally attendance to be 15,000 people.   JOSH MICHEL/TECHNICIAN

John Edwards brought John Kerry to N.C. State Saturday and Democrats vowed to make North Carolina a blue state.

Ben McNeely
Staff Writer

The prodigal Wolfpack son returned – and this time, he brought a friend.

John Edwards brought John Kerry back home to North Carolina Saturday and both vowed to instill hometown values back into America.

One of the largest political crowds ever assembled in the state braved 90-degree Southern heat and filled the Court of North Carolina on campus to see

John Kerry and John Edwards smile and wave to the crowd upon their arrival at their rally held at the Court of North Carolina.   ROB BRADLEY/TECHNICIAN

the newly formed Democratic presidential ticket. According to Campus Police, 15,000 attended the rally, while the Kerry/Edwards campaign estimated around

25,000.

It was the first time Kerry had campaigned in North Carolina,

EDWARDS continued on page 4

inside technician

A political homecoming
The Kerry/Edwards rally was one of the largest political gatherings in North Carolina history.
Check out our team coverage.
See pages 4-5.

The heat is rising
Fahrenheit 9/11 is scorching theaters, box office records and political opinions across the nation.
See page 3.

Students bring rally to campus

College Democrats invite Kerry/Edwards campaign to N.C. State to "energize" the Democratic Party.

Jessica Horne
News Editor

As the crowd began to chant and wave provided signs for "a stronger America," at least one individual looked on with a smile.

Melissa Price, a senior in political science and vice-president of

the College Democrats, helped bring the Kerry Edwards Rally to N.C. State on Saturday. After John Kerry announced John Edwards as his running mate for the presidential election last Tuesday, the College Democrats invited both men to NCSU for a welcome home rally.

"This is an amazing event," Price said. "It's even more amazing that [Edwards] is running. It will really help North Carolina and will energize the Democratic

COLL DEMS continued on page 4

Fox departs as replacement search continues

Chancellor Marye Anne Fox, on her last official day at the post, gives Mr. Wuf a goodbye hug at her farewell reception held in Caldwell Lounge Tuesday.   ROB BRADLEY/TECHNICIAN

Matt Middleton
Staff Writer

In a formal ceremony with posh hor'derves, lily-white tablecloths and a red-bowtied wait staff, N.C. State officially said goodbye to outgoing chancellor Marye Anne Fox in a ceremony Tuesday in Caldwell Lounge.

Fox ended her term as the 12th chancellor at NCSU; she will take over the same position at the University of California San Diego Aug. 16. Former College of Textiles headman Bob Barnhardt is now officially in charge of the university on an interim basis.

A crowd of about 150 gathered in the CHASS building for the formalities; attending parties included UNC President Molly Corbett Broad, athletics director Lee Fowler, university trustees -- and even Mr. Wuf.

"I look around the crowd, and at each face I have a great memory of that person," Fox told the campus throng from behind a

podium. "When I came to NCSU, we had a chip on our shoulder. Now, we know it's not just good enough to be the best university in Wake County, northeastern North Carolina or even the state of North Carolina. We're now performing at the top level."

Fox gave her farewell remarks after 11 university-related groups gave laudatory speeches. Some presented her with gifts, which included anything from a crystal bowl from Provost James Oblinger to an engraved wooden chair for her husband, chemistry professor Jim Whitesell, a vocal supporter of Wolfpack athletics.

But perhaps the most notable piece of recognition was the first – The Old North State Award, given by a representative from the governor's office. The presenter, North Carolina Department of Revenue Secretary E. Norris Tolson, noted Fox is the first civilian state citizen to be honored with the award.

"I wouldn't be leaving if I didn't

leave behind a capable leadership team," Fox said.

Now he's here
Standing some 25 feet away from the podium applauding during the myriad of presentations was Barnhardt. The blue-eyed former dean of the College of Textiles with a constantly present sense of humor admitted yesterday even he was at first skeptical in accepting his new position of interim chancellor.

Barnhardt said that the constant phone calls and messages from friends urging him to consider the post made he and his wife agree on accepting. So when Broad ultimately contacted him while he was in Hong Kong, he agreed to sit down and talk about the position.

"And now I'm here," he said.

Fox has spent the last several weeks meeting with Barnhardt on a regular basis, giving him the basic ins-and-outs of the

FOX continued on page 2

Figure 12.3. Studies show nearly all newspaper readers will look at a photo that runs across the entire width of a page. *Technician*, North Carolina State University

---

At a demonstration it might focus on a heated argument between a protester and a police officer.

Ideally, the medium shot should capture action. That means photographers have to be on their toes, ever watchful for movement. A photojournalist must learn to anticipate action, waiting for the swimmer to dive off the diving board or the campus police officer to slap the handcuffs on the demonstrator. Medium shots are best caught with a wide-angle lens, such as a 24mm or a 28mm, but a 50mm will suffice.

The Close-up

The close-up shot captures drama and emotion. It puts the reader right in the event, showing the grimace on the athlete's face (Figure 12.4) or the blissful glow on the singer's.

But a close-up needn't focus on a person's face. It might be a hand taking a brush to a mural or a plume of smoke coming from a beaker in a scientific lab.

A telephoto lens enables a photographer to be less conspicuous when shooting a close shot.

Close-ups are often used as part of a photo story or as a secondary shot grouped with a medium or long shot.

High and Low Angles

One of the challenges of photojournalism is to offer readers a unique perspective on a subject. That often means shooting from an unusual angle—down from a tall building or up from the ground. Good photojournalists shoot from a variety of viewpoints for each assignment. They move their bodies, climbing up on furniture for a high shot, scrunching down on the floor for a low shot, standing in back of a speaker to capture reaction from the crowd.

When shooting an assignment, try to get the subject from as many angles as you can.

Breaking News

It may be a raucous rally on the quad or a motorcycle accident near the entrance to the campus, professors picketing against budget cuts or a dorm being evacuated during a flood. News happens, even on a seemingly sleepy college campus. The role of the photojournalist is to document that news when it's happening (Figures 12.5, 12.6, 12.7, 12.8 and 12.9).

Student photographers often don't have the resources of professional newspaper photographers—police scanners crackling in their cars, high-powered lenses and other fancy equipment—but they can cover breaking news.

In fact, student photojournalists have certain advantages over pros because they're

Figure 12.4. A close-up shot can capture facial expressions, giving the reader insights into the subject. Sean Gallagher, *Columbia Missourian*, University of Missouri. Reprinted with permission.

the key ingredient to a powerful photo—happen without warning. A good photographer is constantly watching for them.

Speeches and Meetings

Whether it's the president of the school giving the annual state of the university speech or a political activist speaking at an anti-war rally, speeches are a big part of campus coverage. They're also a challenge for college photographers. How do you get an interesting shot of a person standing on a stage? How do you capture reaction when the speaker is up there and the crowd is back here? How do you make this photo look different from the speech in the same hall last week or last month?

Scott Strazzante, a staff photographer for the *Chicago Tribune*, advises photojournalists to try to gain access to the speaker before and after the talk. "Arriving at a speech early and staying late is the best way to avoid having to depend on the traditional podium shot," says Strazzante, who was a photographer for *College Days* when he was a student at Ripon College in Ripon, Wis.

When shooting the actual speech, he says, "try to mix up your approach. Shoot extremely tight on the speaker's face or shoot loose, giving the photo context. Shoot from the crowd using the audience as a framing device. If possible, photograph the speech from outside a doorway or window."

If speech photos can be dull, meeting photos can be even duller. Who wants to see a bunch of people sitting around a conference table talking?

When it comes to covering meetings, photographers may want to skip the actual meeting altogether. A more effective approach is to cover the issue being discussed.

Say, for example, the faculty senate votes to restrict smoking on your campus. Don't shoot the senators discussing the issue; shoot the smokers on the quad. Get shots of smokers lighting up outside buildings, standing in the rain, gathering in doorways. If the student government board is discussing whether to fund the new Filipino student group on campus, shoot participants doing something—making decorations for the Filipino Cultural Night, eating lumpia and roast pig at a celebratory dinner.

Shooting Sports

Like the athletes they cover, sports photographers must be nimble, energetic and fast. They have to be able to capture fast-moving action one second and the emotional reaction to a decisive play the next (Figures 12.10, 12.11 and 12.12).

Knowing the sport you cover is essential. That way you can foresee where the ball is going to end up and what's likely to happen

part of the community they cover. A professional photographer may be responsible for covering a city, a county, a whole state. A student newspaper photographer can focus on a single campus.

The key is to be prepared at all times. That means carrying a camera (or two or three) wherever you go and being on the lookout at all hours. A good photojournalist is always on duty.

Shooting News as It Happens

Do you hear people chanting political slogans outside your dorm window? Grab your camera and shoot the protest. Do you see police handcuffing someone across the street? Pull out your long lens and take a few shots. That just may be the suspect in the recent string of robberies on campus.

When shooting breaking news, try to take a single picture that encompasses all the elements of the story. Look for an angle that shows the injured student as well as the damaged motorcycle in one photo.

Record a visual moment that reflects the most intense part of the event—the angry faces of the demonstrators or the tearful faces at an accident scene. These moments—often

Figure 12.5. A photographer needs to anticipate action and be quick on the draw. At this rally, photographer Jordin Thomas Althaus was able to catch the peak point of the confrontation between protesters and police. Jordin Thomas Althaus, *Golden Gate [X]press*, San Francisco State University. Reprinted with permission.

Figure 12.6. Photographer Derek Montgomery knew the Halloween revelry on Madison, Wisconsin's State Street often turned violent so he stuck around to capture the news as it broke. "I knew the best images would come from these two people who decided to stay and confront the police," he says. "Using a wide angle lens I was able to get most of the street scene before being blasted myself with a pepper spray cannon. It was an irritating experience, but I'm happy with the results." Derek Montgomery, *The Badger Herald*, University of Wisconsin, Madison. Reprinted with permission.

next. "For sports photography you have to anticipate," says Joe Jaszewski, a staff photographer for the *Idaho Statesman* in Boise. "Once you've observed, it's too late."

It's also useful to know the players, says Jaszewski, who was a photographer, photo editor and reporter during his three and a half years working for *The California Aggie* at the University of California, Davis. "It helps to have one photographer who shoots all the football games or all the basketball games and knows this player likes to shoot off his left foot or this football player likes to catch passes over the middle," he says.

You need the appropriate lens for shooting sports. To cover football you should have a 300mm or longer; for basketball a much shorter lens will do. Shooting a burst of pictures with a motor drive helps nail the peak-action play.

Shooting inside a poorly lit gymnasium can be a hassle. Sometimes you can go in before the game and set up strobes high above the court and trigger them from your camera. By lighting the gym you will improve the quality of your images.

Just like sports writers, sports photographers need to go beyond covering the game and hang out at practices, in the locker room, at post-game celebrations. The more the players know you, the more they'll be willing to let you into their world.

Feature Photos

Some of the best newspaper photographs don't come from an assignment sheet or even run with a story. They're stand-alone, or feature, photos. Feature pictures document the life of the community you're covering and provide a visual break for readers.

To find feature photos, look around you. Look at the couple kissing under that stone arch, the soccer players who gather for a late afternoon pick-up game, the tired student who has fallen asleep over her book in the library carrel. Once again, the photographer is looking to capture a moment.

But that moment needn't be completely spontaneous or unexpected. A good photographer can plan for feature photos. "Instead of just wandering around looking for people doing things, read your paper, the activities bulletin board or posted notes for things going on at your school," Strazzante advises.

Find an area of the campus that you can go back to over and over so that you can anticipate what is going to happen and when you'll have the best light. Late afternoons on the quad may give you long shadows and intimate moments, for example. If you hang around the drama department, you'll know when students are going to try out for the play, when set designers will be painting the sets, when actors will be rehearsing in costume.

Shannon Guthrie, a staff photographer for the *State Journal-Register* in Springfield, Ill., advises feature-hunters to keep a close eye on the weather. "If the wind is blowing really badly or it's raining or snowing, get out there," says Guthrie, who won numerous awards while working for the *College Heights Herald* at Western Kentucky University. Umbrellas, snowdrifts, ice crystals on trees all make for interesting photos.

Candids

Often the best way to photograph a story is to focus on a single person at the center of the tale or issue. Candid shots of subjects work-

Figure 12.7. Photographer Cera Renault was able to capture an argument between a Bush opponent and Bush supporter at a get-out-the-vote rally the day before the 2004 presidential election. Cera Renault, *Golden Gate [X]press,* San Francisco State University. Reprinted with permission.

people. During an hour-long chat, the man mentioned he got his inspiration from a higher source. He told how he kneels down alone each night before going to bed. Wagner asked if he could photograph that and the man agreed. So Wagner came back in the evening and photographed the man kneeling at his bedside.

"If I hadn't spent an hour talking with him, he probably wouldn't have told me that and he certainly wouldn't have let me take a picture of him praying," Wagner says. "As young journalists we tend to think that the picture is the only thing that matters. These days, I find that I'm talking to people more than I'm shooting."

Wagner says talking with subjects also helped him overcome his fear of intruding.

"When I was a college photographer, I was more leery of imposing on people than of coming back to the newsroom empty handed. I had to overcome the mindset that sticking a camera in someone's face is a nuisance. Eventually, I became more confident and realized it isn't such a bother. I realized I wasn't just taking from the situation, I was giving. I was showing people that they were important in my eyes, important enough to show other people."

Portraits

Once you have some good candids, try some posed shots. Look for props—an astronomer's telescope, an athlete's basketball—that will help tell the story. Or look for an interesting background or setting. If you're shooting a swimmer, for example, it makes sense to shoot in a pool; if you're shooting a geography professor, a geography lab with maps all around will help tell the story.

Lighting is a key part of shooting portraits. When shooting indoors, turn off overhead lamps and look for natural light. Position your source next to a window. Side lighting is more dramatic and telling. Putting the camera on a tripod will allow you to use a slow shutter speed. The subject easily can hold still for a half-second exposure.

Even when shooting a posed portrait, try to capture a "real" moment—an expression, a hand gesture, a movement that says something about the person. If you're shooting more than one person, watch for a look or a natural gesture of affection between them. You want to catch a revealing moment.

Photo Illustrations

Digital photography has given photographers a multitude of tools for manipulating images. Now even an amateur can use multiple photos to create new images, putting the university president's face on the body of a bodybuilder or allowing people who have never met to shake hands.

ing, studying, and interacting with other people can offer readers windows into their world.

To start, talk with the subjects. Ask about their roles in the story and how their work or hobby has brought them into the headlines. "Often as young photojournalists we bury ourselves so deep in our cameras we forget to ask questions," says Brian Wagner, a staff photographer for *The Daily Herald* in Provo,

Utah. "The more you talk to a subject, the more important and relevant the photos are. You communicate what you're trying to do and they communicate who they are."

Wagner, who worked for *The Beacon* at the University of Tennessee, Knoxville and the *College Heights Herald* at Western Kentucky University, mentions a story he shot about a senior volunteer who visits elderly

Figure 12.8. Photographer Tom Whisenand was with Stephanie Seiler (center), the mother of a University of Wisconsin, Madison student who was missing for four days, when she learned her daughter had been found alive and well. He was able to show her relief at the news. Tom Whisenand, *The Minnesota Daily,* University of Minnesota, Twin Cities. Reprinted with permission.

Figure 12.9. Photographer Autumn Cruz sought permission from the family before covering the funeral of 18-year-old Kelly Holt. Friends and family later thanked her for her sensitive depiction of the funeral. Autumn Cruz, *The Spartan Daily,* San Jose State University. Reprinted with permission.

If you do decide to go with a photo illustration, make sure it's clear to the reader that this is an illustration and not a representation of something real. "If a reader can look at the image and have any questions about whether it's real, you shouldn't use it," says Jim Merithew, a picture editor for the *San Francisco Chronicle* who worked on *The News*

Record when he was a student at the University of Cincinnati.

When creating a photo illustration, be careful not to violate copyright protections. Don't scan or steal someone else's images from the Web. You may only use images you have shot or ones that you have express permission to use. Taking other people's

work to enhance your photo illustration is illegal, regardless of how much you change the original.

In his book, *Photojournalism: The Professionals' Approach,* photojournalism professor Kenneth Kobré offers these practical and ethical guidelines for using photo illustrations:

- Eliminate the docudrama. Never set up a photograph to mimic reality, even if it is labeled a photo illustration.
- Create only abstractions with photo illustration. Studio techniques, for example, can help to make situations abstract—the use of a seamless or abstract backdrop, photo montage, or exaggerated lighting. Contrast in size and content, juxtaposition of headline and photo—all can give the reader visual clues that what appears on the page is obviously not the real thing.
- Always clearly label photo illustrations as such, regardless of how obvious you may think they are.
- Never play photo illustrations on news pages. Restrict them to feature pages or to section fronts. Display them so that they are obviously distinct from news or feature pictures.
- If you haven't the time to do a photo illustration right, don't do it. Find another solution.

Photo Stories

Photo stories are stories told in pictures. They may be pegged to an event, like move-in day at the dorms or homecoming weekend, or be tied to a theme. After a University of California, Davis student died of an alcohol overdose the night he turned 21, Jaszewski, the former *California Aggie* photographer, set out to document how other students spent their 21st birthdays. "I'd spend the evening with them and document what happened," he says. "There was some pretty reckless behavior."

Often, photojournalists look for a story line with a beginning, middle and end, such as preparations for a big race or performance or the creation of a class project. Follow a nursing student learning to give an injection or an art student creating a sculpture from beginning to end. Such stories offer a natural narrative arc.

Photo stories may have an accompanying text story or simply a collection of captions that explain the photos.

When planning a photo story, look for a variety of types of photo that illustrate the challenges your subjects encounter and how they overcome them. Show the fear on the nursing student's face as she encounters her first patient, the grimace as she holds the syringe to the arm, the relief after she's completed the injection.

Figure 12.10. In sports photography, the challenge is to arrest the action and capture emotion. Sean Gallagher, *Columbia Missourian,* University of Missouri. Reprinted with permission.

Figure 12.11. Sports photographers must capture reaction as well as action. Brian Cassella, *The Daily Tar Heel,* University of North Carolina, Chapel Hill. Reprinted with permission.

A photo story should offer a variety of shots that may include:

- An establishing shot, or overall photo, that shows where the action is taking place
- A medium shot that focuses on one activity or aspect of the story

- A close-up of a person's face
- A detail shot that shows one element of the story, such as a person's hands
- A portrait of a key person
- An action shot that captures people doing something
- A shot that captures emotion

Photo Assignments

How does a photographer find out where to go, what to shoot, what the story is about? Most newspapers have a set photo assignment process.

At some papers, reporters or editors fill out old-fashioned paper photo assignment forms that photo editors distribute to photographers. But more and more, newspapers rely on Web-based or e-mail forms that can be filled out and sent electronically.

At a minimum, photo assignment forms should include:

- Slug (one word name) of the story
- A description of what the story is about
- Time, date and location of event
- Contact name and phone number
- Name and contact information for the reporter
- Section the story is planned for
- A space for additional information

Once the photo editor assigns a photographer to the story, the photographer and reporter should talk about the story. Sometimes photographers and reporters go out to cover stories together. This kind of teamwork is effective for certain types of assignments—breaking news events, for example, or in-depth stories where the reporter and photographer should focus on the same subjects.

For other stories, however, it may work better for the photographer and reporter to meet with the subject separately. Reporters and photojournalists are looking for different things, after all. Reporters generally want their subjects to sit and talk, while photographers want them to move and do what they normally do. Separate photo and interviewing sessions allow both journalists to get what they need without either interfering with the other's work.

Where Can You Shoot?

Whether you're photographing a professor lecturing in a classroom or students drinking in a campus pub, it's important that you understand where you are allowed to shoot and where you're likely to face restrictions (Figure 12.13).

Photographers can shoot photographs in most public places. You can take pictures on any public street, on a public beach, in a public airport, bus station or train station.

You can also shoot in many areas at a public college or university—in the quad, in the student union, in the hallway of an academic building—without permission. However, you may be restricted from shooting in certain places or at certain times. If a class is in session, for example, you must get the professor's consent before taking pictures. If you want to shoot a concert in the student union,

Figure 12.12. Photographer Derek Montgomery had shot enough University of Wisconsin basketball games to know Bo Ryan, the expressive head coach, was a man to watch. In this situation, Wisconsin's Devin Harris was getting into foul trouble and Ryan was reacting to a call against him late in the game. Derek Montgomery, *The Badger Herald,* University of Wisconsin. Reprinted with permission.

you'll have to get permission from organizers of the event. And photographers usually need to get an OK from residents and/or housing officials before they can take photos in dorm rooms, on-campus apartments and other residential areas.

Private colleges and universities—and most other private businesses—are allowed to limit access. Photographers generally need permission to shoot anywhere on a private campus.

Photos on the Web

With its virtually unlimited space, the Web is an ideal venue to showcase the work of your newspaper's photographers. Do you have lots of great photos from a campus event or game? Create a photo gallery. Do you have a story that's best told with a set of sequential images? Post an online slideshow.

A number of student newspapers have regular places on their Web sites to show off photographers' work. *The Oklahoma Daily* at the University of Oklahoma has a photography tab on its navigation bar that leads to "the week in pictures." The *Arizona Daily Wildcat* at the University of Arizona has a Photo Spreads section with slideshows on big games, the annual student-run fund-raising carnival and a visit to town by President George W. Bush.

As discussed in Chapter 17, the Web also offers multimedia capabilities. An audio clip with ambient sound and dialogue can add a whole new dimension to a photo story.

Golden Gate [X]press, the student newspaper at San Francisco State University, has used multimedia storytelling to great effect on its Web site. Photographers and online producers frequently work together to create multimedia stories, not just for in-depth projects but for breaking news, such as protest rallies and other campus events.

Photo Editing

Like word editors, photo editors play many roles, from managing the photo staff and ensuring all assignments are shot to making decisions about which photographs will run and how they will be cropped.

The photo editor often acts as a liaison between the top editors and the photographers and must have excellent communication skills and judgment.

In choosing images, photo editors look for several qualities:

News value: Does the photograph have journalistic value? Does it illustrate the who, what, where, when, why or how of a story?

Information: Does the photo provide information beyond what's in the story it accompanies? For example, does a portrait give readers a fuller sense of what a person looks like? Does a fire photo show readers the scope of the damage?

Emotion: Does the photo capture emotion—laughter, pain, love, anger?

Action: Does the photo capture movement, action, something happening?

Intimacy: Does the photo offer a glimpse into the subject's private world?

Writing Cutlines

Good cutlines, or photo captions, do more than simply explain a photo; they lure readers into the story. Cutlines accomplish four important things:

1. Explain the action
2. Name the principal people in the photo
3. Explain how the photo relates to the story

Tips from a Pro
■ **Kenneth Kobré**

"The first step in becoming a professional photojournalist is to shoot twice as much as you now shoot," says Kenneth Kobré, professor at San Francisco State University, whose book *Photojournalism: The Professionals' Approach*, now in its fifth edition, has been used by more than 200,000 students and is a standard text at more than 125 universities around the country. "One difference between an amateur and a professional is the professional shoots and throws away a lot more images than the novice."

Kobré offers these 10 suggestions for transforming ordinary snapshots into memorable, award-winning front-page images:

1. **Get closer.** This was the advice of Robert Capa, legendary war photographer and founder of Magnum photo agency, who said, "If your pictures aren't good enough, you're not close enough." Often the key to giving a photo pizzazz is to move in and capture the details of your subject, leaving out extraneous things in the background. Don't be afraid to invade a person's personal space. If you are shooting the college president, put your camera within a few inches of his face for an up-close-and-personal portrait that might reveal his "true" nature.

2. **Have patience.** When you're photographing students or professors, let them get used to you before you start shooting pictures. When they forget the camera is there, you can take more natural candid shots.

3. **Frame the photo.** With a photograph, like a painting, the edges of the image are just as important as the central action. Suppose you are taking pictures of a merit scholar on the college green. Before snapping the shutter, ask yourself if you need to include the blank sky above the student's head or the boring building on either side of the scholar. If the sky and building don't help to tell the story of your brainiac, move your camera closer to eliminate the extraneous elements, leaving only the parts of the scene that are really important to your image.

4. **Avoid the "jumbled effect."** This occurs when surrounding shapes and colors compete for attention with the subject of the photo. If you are taking pictures of a juggler on the quad, for example, you may see other people in the view finder eating, studying, taking naps. These extraneous students add nothing to the picture of the juggler. Try setting a wide aperture and

selecting a telephoto lens. Then get as close as you can to the juggler; that will help throw the other players out of focus.

5. **Cut the on-camera flash.** When you use the strobe light on the camera, the resulting pictures often look unnaturally lit. If you're using film, try an 800 ISO film for shooting the indoor college graduation ceremony. With a digital camera, select 800 ISO or even 1200 ISO for indoor low-light shooting without an on-camera strobe.

6. **Avoid the noontime sun.** Middle-of-the-day light, from about 10 a.m. to 2 p.m., comes straight down from the sky, leaving your subject's eyes in shadow and giving them the look of a raccoon. Scenic landscape pictures lose detail under this harsh light. Instead, try capturing your subjects in the rich tones and long shadows at sunrise and sunset. If you must shoot an outdoor portrait of the winning football coach during the day, move your coach into a shaded area out of direct sunlight.

7. **Shoot at night.** Nighttime offers interesting shadows and light for taking unique shots. At night, without flash, shoot by the rays of a street lamp or the light from an unshaded window. In low light, you can use a tripod to allow longer exposure and avoid camera movement. Explore what is happening inside the buildings on your campus, from late-night dorm parties to all-night study sessions.

8. **Take candids.** For more interesting shots, don't insist on having students and faculty pose in front of your camera. Instead, capture them in the middle of an activity so the photo says something about their personalities or interests. Rather than set the chemistry professor in front of her blackboard, follow her around for a few hours and see what she does. Snap pictures when she flails her arms in an attempt to explain a difficult concept to a student or colleague.

9. **For portraits, include a telling prop.** When you do choose to take an arranged portrait, find an object that will tell the reader something about the person. If you're shooting a professor who specializes in nuclear physics, pose the person in front of the school's cyclotron.

10. **Make your subject comfortable.** If you want the new library director to pose with a volume of Shakespeare, have her find a comfortable, natural position. Here's when a little leaning on the stacks or slouching against a chair is permitted. Avoid having her stand or sit straight up; these tense postures make the subject look uncomfortable and don't say anything revealing about the person.

---

4. Note the important or telling details in the photo

For more information on writing cutlines, see Checklist: Cutline Writing.

To Do:
1. Invite a photographer or photo editor from a professional newspaper to critique your paper.
2. Arrange for your photo staff to spend a day at the local paper, sitting in on budget, Page 1 and photo selection meetings.

3. Re-evaluate your photo assignment system. Does it work well? How could it be improved? If it's not working well, assign a team of photographers, photo editors, word editors and reporters to come up with a new system.
4. Plan a workshop for photographers, reporters and editors to discuss communication problems. Use Elinor J. Brecher's Ten Commandments for Photographers and Reporters Working Together as a way to open the discussion. Try role-playing or other techniques to open the lines of communication.

5. Pair up photographers and reporters and assign them to work together on a story. Make sure the story has strong possibilities for text and photos.
6. Set up a coaching program for your photo staff. Invite photographers from local newspapers to act as mentors who will meet regularly with your staff photographers to discuss their work.

To Read:
Giles, Matthew, ed. *Facing the World: Great Moments in Photojournalism.* New York: H.N. Abrams, 2001.

The Ten Commandments for Photographers and Reporters Working Together

■ Elinor J. Brecher

For the Reporter:

1. **Thou shalt not wait until the last minute to assign photographs.** Reporters should be thinking about photos as soon as a story is assigned and begin talking with the photo department then about picture possibilities.

2. **Thou shalt not tell the story subject what the photographer will shoot.** There is nothing worse than showing up at an assignment and having the subject say, "The reporter said you would photograph me doing. . . "

3. **Thou shalt give as much information as possible on the assignment card, including street address, contact name and number, and a summary of what the story is about.** Due to assignment load, photographers cannot always check with reporters or editors before going to assignments. Often, the card is all that they have to go on. The more information they have, the better job they can do.

4. **Thou shalt respect a photographer's professionalism.** Reporters should let photographers shoot assignments as they see fit. Suggestions are welcomed, but the final call on whether something will work should be the photographer's.

5. **Thou shalt not schedule interview photographs if there is something more active to shoot.** Interview photographs are generally predictable and visually uninteresting.

6. **Thou shalt not introduce the photographer as "my photographer."** You're part of a team and the photographer has a name.

7. **Thou shalt get to know photographers and photography.** Stop by and visit the photo department.

8. **Thou shalt give photographers feedback.** If you like or dislike a photograph, let the photographer know. Constructive criticism and communication can only help everyone do their jobs better and foster better understanding between reporters and photographers.

9. **Thou shalt stay out of the picture.** When on assignment with a photographer, be conscious of what he or she is shooting and make every effort to stay out of the line of fire.

10. **Thou shalt bear with photographers while they deal with equipment problems; help out if you can.** Lights, cameras, and other gear are necessary to get the job done. Lend a hand if a photographer asks. You may learn something.

For the Photographer:

1. **Thou shalt not depend only on the photo request information.** The request is only a starting place. Photographers should talk with reporters and get as much information as possible about the story before going to the assignment.

2. **Thou shalt not barge into interviews, cameras and flashes blazing.** Be sensitive to the reporter's needs and understand that interviews can be easily thrown off-kilter with an ill-timed interruption.

3. **Thou shalt share information with the reporter.** Photographers should pass on to the reporter information, quotes and any tidbits that he or she may pick up when the reporter is not around.

4. **Thou shalt act like a journalist.** Be aware of the world around you. Understand your community and what is going on and making news in it.

5. **Thou shalt use common sense and know the law.** Photographers tend to be gung-ho risk-takers, which is all well and good. However, common sense and restraint should prevail as shooters are not much good if they are in police custody or the emergency room.

6. **Thou shalt not set up photos.** Staged photographs are as misleading and unacceptable as fabricated quotes.

7. **Thou shalt have thy technical act together.** Fooling around with lights and equipment endlessly can ruin an interview.

8. **Thou shalt respect reporters' professionalism.** Photographers should listen to reporters' photo suggestions and consider them carefully since many reporters have good visual sense and care about how the final package looks.

9. **Thou shalt bring story ideas to reporters.** Photographers as journalists should be in touch with the community and have as many story ideas as reporters. Talk them over with reporters to develop stories and projects that you can team up on.

10. **Thou shalt get to know reporters.** Get out of the darkroom and into the newsroom.

Elinor J. Brecher has been a reporter for The Miami Herald *since 1989. She was a Nieman Fellow at Harvard University in 1988. She is the author of the book,* Schindler's Legacy: True Stories of the List Survivors. *As a student at the University of Arizona, Tucson in the mid- to late 1970s, Brecher was a reporter and city editor for the* Arizona Daily Wildcat. *She graduated from the university in 1977 with a degree in journalism.*

Where and When a Photojournalist Can Shoot

	Anytime	If No One Objects	With Restrictions	Only With Permission
Public Area				
Street	X			
Sidewalk	X			
Airport			X	
Beach	X			
Park	X			
Zoo	X			
Train Station	X			
Bus Station	X			
In Public School				
Preschool			X	
Grade School			X	
High School			X	
University Campus	X			
Class in Session				X
In Public Area				
Police Headquarters			X	
Government Buildings			X	
Courtroom				X
Prisons				X
Military Bases				X
Legislative Chambers				X
In Medical Facilities				
Hospital				X
Rehab Center				X
Emergency Van			X	
Mental Health Center				X
Doctor's Office				X
Clinic				X
Private But Open To The Public				
Movie Theater Lobby		X		
Business Office		X		
Hotel Lobby		X		
Restaurant		X		
Casino				X
Museum			X	
Shopping Mall				X
Store in Mall				X
Private Areas Visible To The Public				
Window of Home	X			
Porch	X			
Lawn	X			
In Private				
Home		X		
Porch		X		
Lawn		X		
Apartment		X		
Hotel Room		X		
Car		X		

Figure 12.13. Where and when a photojournalist can shoot. Reproduced with permission from *Photojournalism: The Professionals' Approach, 5th ed.,* by Kenneth Kobré, 2004.

■ Checklist
Photo Editing

In editing photos, ask yourself these questions:

1. Will photos enhance or advance this story?
2. Which photos best complement the story?
3. Has the photographer chosen the most graphic, most compelling images from the shoot?
4. Do the photos support or conflict with information in the story? Do they add information?
5. Do the photos have news value?
6. Are they graphically appealing? Emotionally appealing?
7. Will the photos draw the reader's eye?
8. Should the photos be cropped? How?
9. Are the photos composed well?
10. Do the brightness or contrast need adjusting?
11. Would anyone find the photos offensive? If so, do they need special explanation? Should other people be brought in to discuss the photos?
12. Does one photo say enough or are multiple images needed to tell the story? If multiple images are used, how can they tell different parts of the story?
13. What is the best size for the photos?
14. How do these photos and this story relate to others on the page?
15. Does this photo warrant placement as the dominant art on the page?
16. Is the caption complete?

■ Checklist
Writing Cutlines

1. Does the caption answer the relevant who, what, where, when and why questions?
2. Is it written in present tense?
3. Is it written in active voice?
4. Does the cutline thoroughly identify all prominent people?
5. Does it identify subjects from left to right?
6. Are the names spelled correctly?
7. Does it include titles, ages, hometowns, academic majors or other identifying information appropriate to the story?
8. If it includes quotations, are they accurate and properly attributed?
9. Are all mysterious objects or circumstances clearly explained?
10. Does it tell when the scene happened?
11. Does it tell where it was taken?
12. Does the cutline go beyond the obvious, expanding on what is visible in the photo? If the basketball player is holding a basketball and wearing a uniform you don't need to say that he is basketball player in the caption—let the picture tell the story. Add what is not evident in the photo, such as how many points he scored during the season.

To Click:

American Society of Media Photographers
http://www.asmp.org/

American Society of Picture Professionals
http://www.aspp.com/

Americanphotojournalist
http://www.americanphotojournalist.com/

Associated Press Photo Managers
http://www.apphotomanagers.org/

College Photographer of the Year
http://www.cpoy.org/

The Digital Journalist
http://digitaljournalist.org/

Ethics Matters: Column from *News Photographer* magazine
http://commfaculty.fullerton.edu/lester/ writings/nppa.html

National Press Photographers Association
http://www.nppa.org/

NPPA Code of Ethics
http://www.nppa.org/professional_ development/business_practices/ ethics.html

Poynter Online's Photojournalism Resources
http://www.poynter.org/subject.asp?id=29

Poynter Online's Photojournalism Tip Sheets
http://poynteronline.org/content/content_ view.asp?id=31901

Pulitzer Prize Photos: Examples from the Newseum
http://www.newseum.org/pulitzer/index.htm

Sports Shooter
http://www.sportsshooter.com/

Visual Edge
http://www.visualedge.org/

Horton, Brian. *Associated Press Guide to Photojournalism*. New York: McGraw Hill, 2000.

Kobré, Kenneth. *Photojournalism: The Professionals' Approach, 5th ed.* Woburn, Mass.: Focal Press, 2004.

London, Barbara, John Upton, Kenneth Kobré, and Betsy Brill. *Photography, 7th ed.* Upper Saddle River, N.J.: Prentice Hall, 2002.

National Press Photographers Association. *The Best of Photojournalism*. Durham, N.C.: National Press Photographers Association, Annual.

Parrish, Fred S. *Photojournalism, An Introduction*. Belmont, Calif.: Wadsworth/Thomson Leaning, 2001.

Figure 13.1. Shortly after San Francisco State University photojournalism student Omar Vega took photographs of other students allegedly burglarizing a car, university officials had him evicted from the dorm. He was also charged by the district attorney's office with burglarizing and tampering with a vehicle, even though he claimed he was acting as a photojournalist, not a participant. The charges were ultimately dropped as part of a plea agreement, but the case launched a national debate about the rights of student photojournalists to document activity by students. *Golden Gate [X]press,* San Francisco State University

GOLDEN GATE [X] [X]PRESS

Muni Fare Hike On Horizon
SEE **NEWS**_PAGE 2

NEXA on the Chopping Block
SEE **NEWS**_PAGE 3

Ring in the Lunar New Year
SEE **A&E**_PAGE 12

[February 17, 2005]   [www.xpress.sfsu.edu]   [Issue 3 Vol. LXXVIIII]

WAS THIS STUDENT SILENCED?

SPECIAL REPORT PAGE 2

KELLY ADAMS/STAFF PHOTOGRAPHER

Photojournalist Says Arrest Violated His First Amendment Rights

Chapter 13

Legal Issues

In Tennessee, stacks of a state university student newspaper were stolen the day the paper printed a story about a star basketball player's arrest for drug possession. In California, a photojournalism student was evicted from his dorm and threatened with expulsion after photographing a group of students burglarizing a car. In New York, a community college student governing board locked the newspaper staffers out of their office for a week during a funding dispute.

On paper, student journalists have virtually

the same legal rights and responsibilities as professional journalists. But in reality, they face a host of added challenges.

Some administrators try to exercise prior restraint against student newspapers to keep controversial material from appearing. Official sources sometimes try to bar student journalists' access to public meetings and public records. Even fellow students—student governing boards, fraternity members and others—occasionally attempt to squelch expression by cutting funding, firing editors and stealing newspapers when they don't like what's being written.

The best way to prevent or combat these problems is to know your rights—and to know where to turn when these rights have been abridged. In this chapter we'll explore some of the major legal issues facing student journalists.

Censorship at Public Schools

Every year, the Student Press Law Center (SPLC) in Arlington, Va., the leading legal resource for student journalists, fields dozens of complaints from students who believe their free-press rights have been censored.

SPLC Executive Director Mark Goodman says censorship can take many forms, including:

- Demanding prior approval of content by an adviser, publication board, administrator or others
- Confiscating newspapers
- Restricting distribution of papers
- Cutting funding on the basis of content
- Disciplining editors or advisers for the content of the paper.

The First Amendment protects journalists from government censorship and more than 60 state and federal court decisions have concluded that freedom of the press applies to student publications at public colleges and universities.

As the Student Press Law Center writes in its Legal Brief on Student Press Freedom at Public Colleges:

School officials cannot:

(1) Censor or confiscate a publication, withdraw or reduce its funding, withhold student activities fees, prohibit lawful advertising, fire an editor or adviser, "stack" a student media board, discipline staff members or take any other action that is motivated by an attempt to control, manipulate or punish past or future content. . . .

(2) Demand the right to review publications before distribution. . . .

Student government officials are subject to the same First Amendment restraints as school administrators. For ex-

ample, they cannot punish a paper's staff or adviser or withdraw a publication's funds for content-based reasons.

However, school officials can:

Regulate non-content based aspects of a publication. For example, school officials can review the financial records of its student media and prohibit staff hiring policies when they discriminate on the basis of race.

In Canada, the Charter of Rights and Freedoms works much like the American First Amendment in protecting the rights of journalists, both professionals and students. Despite these protections, however, attempts at censorship continue in both countries.

Censorship at Private Schools

Student journalists at private colleges and universities in the United States do not enjoy the same free speech protections as those at public schools. The First Amendment only limits censorship by government officials or others, such as student governing board officials, who act on their behalf.

However, some private schools voluntarily give student journalists rights to free expression through written school policies, which may be published in a student handbook, code of conduct or other document. Your newspaper should know if your school has a free expression policy. Courts have suggested that schools that adopt such policies are contractually bound to abide by them.

Some states, most notably California, have statutes that protect free expression at private schools. The California law reads, in part, "It is the intent of the Legislature that a student shall have the same right to exercise his or her right to free speech on campus as he or she enjoys when off campus."

For more information about the rights of private school journalists, see the Student Press Law Center's *Press Freedom at Private Schools*, available at the center's Web site, listed at the end of this chapter.

Censorship Prevention

Student journalists can try to prevent censorship by building relationships with the campus community before problems arise. Effective strategies include:

- Meeting regularly with top school officials and leaders of student groups
- Publishing periodic columns, articles or editor's notes explaining the editorial decision-making process. This step is particularly important with the publication of controversial material.
- Hosting a panel discussion, open house or other public event where you can educate the campus about press freedom in

general and specifically about your editorial policies
- Reaching out to student groups that feel least served by the publication and soliciting their concerns, thoughts and story ideas.

You can often keep censorship at bay just by opening communication lines.

Fighting Censorship

If you do encounter any sort of censorship, contact the Student Press Law Center immediately. The center provides free information, advice and legal assistance to students and the educators who work with them.

In Canada, the Canadian University Press, a cooperative of more than 60 student publications, offers legal advice and assistance to member newspapers; about three-quarters of the student newspapers in the country belong to the cooperative. "In terms of censorship, student papers here have a lot of the same problems as those in the States," says Sean Patrick Sullivan, CUP president for the 2005-06 academic year.

If a Canadian University Press member paper reports a censorship problem, CUP officials typically make phone calls or write letters in support, Sullivan says. "A lot of times in those situations, lobbying works," Sullivan says. "If it doesn't, we get a lawyer involved."

The professional media in both the United States and Canada can also be important allies in the battle against censorship. Journalists are usually quick to jump on a censorship story and the public scrutiny media coverage can bring may intimidate censors. Professional news organizations may provide other kinds of assistance, such as legal advice and letters of support.

Newspaper Theft

Maybe some fraternity brothers don't like your coverage of a rowdy party. Or perhaps your college president is embarrassed by the safe sex editorial that came out the day of an open house for prospective students. So they quietly remove stacks of newspaper from around campus, tossing them in a trash Dumpster or out-of-the-way recycling bin.

Every year thousands of student newspapers disappear under suspicious circumstances. But if a paper is free, is this theft? Campus police departments often don't see it that way, but the Student Press Law Center says stealing newspapers, even free ones, is a crime.

"Just because a newspaper doesn't have a sales price doesn't mean it doesn't have value," says Goodman. "That value can be measured in different ways—in the cost of printing, in the advertising revenue the copies of the publication represent."

Newspaper Theft Checklist

The Student Press Law Center offers these tips on preventing and handling theft of newspapers.

Before a Theft:

- Include a price tag. In lieu of a price, include language such as the following on your flag: "Single copies free." In your masthead and rate card include additional information indicating that single copies are free to members of the school community. Also indicate that multiple copies may be available for purchase at an established price by contacting the newspaper's business office. The following language is an example: "Because of high production costs, members of the State University community are permitted one copy per issue. Where available, additional copies may be purchased with prior approval for 50 cents each by contacting the Student Times business office. Newspaper theft is a crime. Those who violate the single copy rule may be subject to civil and criminal prosecution and/or subject to university discipline." Of course, determining the actual price is up to you. It's not necessary that you always collect the money. You remain free to give copies away when you feel it is appropriate.
- Establish ties. Meet now with campus and law enforcement officials. Explain your concerns regarding newspaper theft and the danger it poses to your publication. Try to obtain their assurance that they will take newspaper theft incidents seriously. Be available to answer any questions they might have and to provide additional information.
- Be alert. In some cases, thieves have actually warned a newspaper staff that they intend to confiscate the publication when it is distributed. Tell staff that they need to report such warnings to editors immediately. Carefully record the source, nature and time of the warning. If you learn of a theft in progress or have reason to believe that such action is imminent, notify law enforcement authorities. Then, position your staff at likely theft locations to take photographs of those involved. Safety dictates that staff not interfere with the thieves but simply record the criminal activity as it occurs.

After a Theft:

- Get a number. Attempt to determine how many copies of the paper were stolen.
- Get a dollar figure. "Free" distribution newspapers are not free. In dealing with law enforcement officials and prosecutors, it can be very important to provide a reasonable estimate of the monetary harm your publication has suffered as a result of the theft. To come up with a price tag, the following costs should be determined: (1) printing costs, (2) delivery costs, (3) production costs (e.g., wire/photo service charges, graphic art fees, telephone and postage expenses, office supplies, photo supplies, etc.), (4) special printing/production fees associated with a "rush" job should you decide to reprint the paper, (5) salary for publication staff, (6) revenue that may need to be refunded to advertisers, etc. Do your best to be accurate and reasonable in your estimates, but also don't hold back. For example, if an advertiser paid $2,000 to run an ad and only 50 percent of the newspapers were actually circulated, advertiser goodwill, if not the law, suggests that you may owe the advertiser a refund of $1,000. That is a legitimate, quantifiable loss and should be included in your tally. Prepare an itemized list to submit to law enforcement officials, news media and school officials.

- Notify campus and/or local law enforcement agencies. File a formal police report and request a copy. Also notify the local prosecutor's office as they will eventually be the agency responsible for determining whether a prosecutable crime has occurred. Be careful to note who you talk to and what is said. Inform officials that newspaper thieves around the country have been successfully prosecuted. If you determine the thieves are government officials (public college administrators, campus police, etc.), additional legal claims may also be available. For information about past prosecutions that you can share with "reluctant" law enforcement officials, contact the Student Press Law Center.
- Launch an investigation. Unless your efforts would impede police efforts, attempt to identify and interview witnesses to the theft. Send a campus e-mail or use other campus communication resources to ask for information that may lead to the thieves' apprehension. In a few cases, professional journalism groups or interested alumni have offered modest rewards for valid "tips." Carefully document all witness statements.
- Notify school officials. Contact the college president and/or other high-ranking university officials in writing and request that they issue a strong public statement condemning the thefts that encourages law enforcement officials in their investigation, promises to appropriately discipline the thieves if caught and generally reaffirms the school's commitment to free speech on campus. Their refusal or agreement to do so is news.
- Set up a "Dumpster Patrol." Search all university trash collection sites or other likely "dumping" locations. If copies are found, call for a photographer and the police to record the scene before removing them.
- Alert local and state news media. Prepare a short press release for distribution. As with a news story, report only what you know and how you know it. Be careful about publishing unconfirmed reports about the identity or motivation of the thieves. Include information about how many copies were printed, the number of copies stolen, the cost to the publication, the response (or lack of response) of law enforcement and school officials. You may also want to include contact information for the Student Press Law Center to assist reporters who may want to obtain a national perspective of the serious problem of newspaper theft.
- Inform your readers. Publish your own story—and perhaps an editorial—about the theft in the next issue of your publication.
- Let us know. If you haven't done so already, please report the theft to the Student Press Law Center. The SPLC is the nation's leading authority on newspaper theft and the only group to consistently track such incidents. It is very important that we know about yours. Law enforcement and campus officials have sometimes refused to act, viewing a theft as an isolated "prank." Help us remind them that there is nothing isolated or prankish about newspaper theft, that yours is part of a serious and threatening trend. Additionally, the SPLC can provide you with additional information and legal help in successfully prosecuting the theft of your publication.

Punishing Newspaper Thieves:

- Criminal prosecution. Possible charges include: larceny, petty theft, criminal mischief or destruction of property. Though not necessary to prosecute a theft, Maryland and Colorado have a specific state law making the taking of a free distribution
(continued on next page)

newspaper a crime. Ultimately the decision to pursue criminal charges is up to the local prosecutor.

- Campus disciplinary action. Even if there is insufficient evidence or grounds for criminal prosecution, newspaper thieves can be punished by campus officials for their misbehavior. While pursuing such punishment is also up to those issuing the discipline, student media can keep pressure on campus officials to take appropriate action and then follow up on the outcome.
- Civil lawsuit for damages. This type of claim is solely in your hands and can be a way to recover financial losses suffered

by the newspaper. Depending on the amount of loss (frequently a maximum of $2,500), student media may be able to pursue this claim on their own in small claims court for minimum cost and without the expense of an attorney. You will need to have carefully documented evidence of your losses. If small claims court is not an option, you will probably need to hire an attorney. The SPLC can discuss this option with you in more detail.

Reprinted with permission of the Student Press Law Center

In several states, including Florida, Kentucky and Texas, individuals have been successfully prosecuted for stealing "free" student newspapers. In 2005, Binghamton University adopted a policy banning newspaper theft after two student publications were reported stolen.

Stealing newspapers can be seen as an act of censorship. By taking newspapers out of circulation, thieves are preventing the dissemination of information, opinion or images.

If you've been the victim of newspaper theft, don't just let it go. Follow the Student Press Law Center's Newspaper Theft Checklist.

Libel

One of the greatest fears of every journalist—professional or student—is being sued for libel.

Libel is anything written or printed that defames a person; defamation that is spoken is considered slander. Stories, editorials, headlines, photos, captions, graphics, cartoons, display advertisements, classified ads, letters to the editor, even comments posted on your Web site can potentially contain libelous statements. Even if the statement didn't originate with your staff, if your newspaper or Web site publishes it, you can be held liable.

To successfully sue for libel, a person must prove the following:

Defamation. The statement must damage the person's reputation. Any statement that says something negative about a person, group or business, causing them shame, disgrace or ridicule or injuring the person's livelihood, is potentially libelous.

Identification. The statement must clearly identify a person, either by name or by some other designation that will make at least some readers understand the statement is about the victim. In addition, if the story involves someone with a common name (like John Jones), it is important to give other identifying information, such as an address

or middle initial, to make it clear that the story is about a specific John Jones and no others in the community.

Publication. The statement must be published or broadcast, meaning it was read or heard by people other than the author and the subject of the story.

Falsity. The statement must be false.

Injury. The person must prove that the defamatory statement has led to "actual injury," meaning injury to his or her reputation, humiliation, mental anguish or financial loss.

Fault. The plaintiff must prove some degree of fault; the degree depends on whether the person is a private or public figure. Private individuals only have to prove negligence on the part of a reporter (such as failing to check public records). The U.S. Supreme Court has said public figures, including public officials, must prove "actual

malice" in publishing the defamation. That means the reporter:

a) Knew facts that would disprove the story but published it anyway
b) Did not check information that might have disproved a story
c) Used obviously unreliable sources
d) Made up a story

The best defense against libel is truth. If a defamatory statement is true and you can prove it, it's not libelous. The other defenses for libel are:

Consent. If a person consents to the media using a defamatory statement about him, he can't later sue if the statement injures his reputation.

Privilege. A newspaper is not liable when it publishes fair and accurate accounts of official public proceedings and reports, even if

---

Tips from a Pro

■ James M. Wagstaffe

James M. Wagstaffe, a San Francisco attorney who specializes in media law, offers these Ten Commandments for Staying out of a Lawyer's Office:

1. Be a skeptic.
2. Get it right.
3. Get permission.
4. Write sensitive subjects sensitively.
5. Do not promise confidentiality lightly.
6. Watch for an unexpected plaintiff. (If you write a story about a teen drug addict, for example, you may inadvertently defame the teen's parent.)
7. Be wary of sources you yourself don't trust.
8. Obtain public record or documentary support.
9. Make sure your headlines and teasers are factually accurate.
10. Treat demands for correction seriously.

James M. Wagstaffe is partner and co-founder of Kerr & Wagstaffe, LLP, a San Francisco law firm that specializes in First Amendment and media law. He successfully defended The New Yorker *magazine in the libel trial Masson v. New Yorker. He teaches constitutional law and civil procedure at Hastings College of the Law and media law at San Francisco State University.*

the information turns out to be false. To qualify for this privilege:

- The information must come from an official record or proceeding, such as a court hearing, official public meeting or public document.
- The media report must be "fair and accurate," meaning it is balanced and presented in context.
- The source of the statement should be clearly noted in the media report.

Opinion. Statements of pure opinion cannot be libelous. But that doesn't mean phrases like "in my opinion," labeling a piece as a "review" or "commentary," or publishing something on an opinion page will automatically protect you from a libel charge. According to the Student Press Law Center's Legal Brief on Libel Law, "The test is whether the expression is capable of being proven true or false. Pure opinions, by their very nature, cannot be proven true or false."

Satire and Cartoons. A statement made in a publication that is clearly a parody or spoof cannot be libelous. This defense also covers cartoons.

If someone threatens to sue you and/or your newspaper for libel, treat the threat seriously. Investigate the person's claims and if you've found you've made an error, run a retraction or correction as soon as possible. While a retraction or correction will not absolutely protect you from a libel suit, people are far less likely to sue if you correct the mistake. Many states have retraction laws that limit the damages a plaintiff can win if a publication corrects the mistake within a specified time. If a potentially libelous error is published on your newspaper's Web site, be sure to correct it there, too.

Privacy

Everyone has a legal right to privacy, to be left alone. Unlike the freedom of the press, which is guaranteed in the First Amendment, the right to privacy has developed over time in a series of court cases.

There are four kinds of invasion of privacy:

1. **Public disclosure of private or embarrassing facts.** This may include information that is:
   a) Sufficiently private: known only to a small circle of family or friends
   b) Sufficiently intimate: personal habits, details or history that the person doesn't ordinarily reveal
   c) Highly offensive: the information would humiliate or seriously offend the average person if it were revealed about him/her

"Red Flags": Reporter Beware

■ Student Press Law Center

The following is a list of particularly sensitive categories and topics that, if published inaccurately, will almost always satisfy the "Harm to Reputation" requirement for libel. These topics should be given special attention:

1. **Statements that accuse or suggest that a person has been involved in serious sexual misconduct or is sexually promiscuous.** A special problem: identifying an unmarried woman as pregnant.
2. **Statements that associated a person with a "loathsome" or socially stigmatizing disease.** For example: leprosy, some mental illnesses and any sexually transmitted disease such as herpes or AIDS.
3. **Statements that accuse another of committing a crime, of being arrested, jailed or otherwise involved in criminal activity.** For example, depending on the context or inferences made, it might be defamatory to falsely report that a person was "questioned by police." And be careful: even if you do not flatly accuse a person of, for example, committing the crime of perjury (lying while under oath), you might still invoke a red flag by reporting that a person had answered "yes" to a question on the witness stand yesterday but had responded "no" to the same question over a year ago.
4. **Negative statements that affect a person's ability to engage in his livelihood, business, trade, profession or office.** For example, a story that accused a teacher of being erratic, disorganized, absent from the classroom for extended periods and otherwise unable to teach was held to be libelous. As libel attorney and author Neil Rosini has pointed out, this is an especially broad category and lawsuits can come from unexpected sources. For example, a story that reported that a section of a new hospital was "plagued with air conditioning problems relating to the design of the system" was found to have injured the professional reputation of the building's architect even though the architect was never named. And a high school football coach successfully argued that his professional reputation was damaged when a newspaper falsely reported that he cursed and belittled his players from the sidelines, yelling such statements as "Come on, get your head out of your &!(!!(. Play the game." The coach claimed he said, "Get your head up."
5. **Statements that attack a person's honesty or integrity.** For example: calling a person a "liar" or a "thief" or stating that a person has a "selective memory."
6. **Negative statements about grades or academic ability.** A special problem: stories about "special education" or remedial learning programs.
7. **Statements that allege racial, ethnic or religious bigotry.**
8. **Statements that accuse a person of associating with criminals, "shady characters," or publicly disfavored groups.**
9. **Statements that question a person's creditworthiness, financial stability, or economic status.**
10. **Any negative statement about a lawyer.** As one writer has noted, "lawyers, in a class by themselves, are the most prolific libel plaintiffs in America. ..." Because lawyers do sue and do know their way to the courthouse, all references to them should be flagged and verified.

Reprinted with permission from Law of the Student Press, *published by the Student Press Law Center.*

2. **False Light.** The portrayal of a person—in words or pictures—in an inaccurate and unflattering way. False light is similar to libel but the plaintiff need not prove injury or damage to reputation, only that the statement was highly offensive.

3. **Intrusion into a person's solitude.** This can occur when a reporter gathers information about a person in a place where that person has a reasonable right to expect privacy, such as a home. Generally, reporters are allowed to enter privately

owned public places such as a private school campus or a restaurant. However, private business owners can ask a journalist to leave if they feel someone's privacy is being violated. The three most common types of intrusion are:

Trespass—going onto private property without the owner's consent

Secret Surveillance—using hidden cameras or bugging equipment to surreptitiously record information

Misrepresentation—using a disguise to gain access

4. **Misappropriation of Name or Likeness.** You may not use a person's name, photograph, likeness, voice or endorsement in an advertisement.

The best defense against all four forms of invasion of privacy is consent. When getting consent, explain to the subject what you're going to use and how you plan to use it. If possible, get it in writing, making sure you seek permission from a person with a legal right to give it.

Obscenity

Obscenity is generally more of an issue of taste than law. Most potentially offensive content, such as profane language or ideas, is not obscene; obscenity refers exclusively to sexually explicit material.

The standard test for obscenity involves three elements described by the Supreme Court in the 1973 case of Miller v. California:

- Whether a reasonable person, applying contemporary community standards, would find the work, taken as a whole, appeals to a prurient interest
- Whether the work depicts or describes in a patently offensive way sexual conduct specifically defined as obscene by the applicable state law, and
- Whether the work, taken as a whole, lacks serious literary, artistic, political or scientific value.

Student newspapers have successfully printed nude photographs, sexually explicit descriptions and profane cartoons, without being charged with obscenity. "If the material is not more graphic than what appears in *Playboy* or *Penthouse*, it will not be considered legally obscene," says the Student Press Law Center's Goodman.

Sexually explicit material is far more likely to generate an attempt at censorship than an obscenity charge, Goodman says, but in most cases the courts, including the U.S. Supreme Court, have ruled in favor of free expression.

Access to Information

As explained in Chapter 11, student journalists have the same access as professionals (indeed, the same access as anyone) to public meetings and public records. However, some sources don't know this or intentionally try to keep information from students, thinking they won't know their rights.

Students frequently report being denied access to campus police records despite a federal law designed to make information about campus crime public, according to the Student Press Law Center. Under the federal Clery Act, any college or university that receives federal funding (that includes most private schools) must provide three different types of records:

- An annual statistical report of campus crime
- A daily campus crime log
- "Timely reports" regarding crimes that present an ongoing threat to the campus community.

Schools that fail to release this information can be investigated by the Department of Education and fined for noncompliance.

It's essential that student journalists know what records and meetings are public. To understand the open records and open meetings laws that affect you, contact your state or provincial newspaper publishers association or the Student Press Law Center.

You can also go to the Reporters Committee for Freedom of the Press's Web site, which includes "Tapping Officials' Secrets," an online version of its 1,300-page report on every state's open records and open meetings laws. The Web site address is listed at the end of this chapter.

Copyright Law

For college journalists, understanding copyright law is important both as it applies to the work they create and how they use other people's work. Copyright protects the creator of an original work (music, articles, photos, graphics, etc.) from unauthorized use of the work.

Copyright is a kind of property right. In its Legal Brief on Copyright Law, the Student Press Law Center explains:

A person owns a copyright in much the same way he owns a car. Just as it is against the law to use or borrow someone else's car without the owner's permission, it is generally against the law to use someone's copyrighted work without first obtaining her consent. Additionally, just as no one but the automobile owner can legally sell, give away or change the ap-

pearance of a car, no one but the copyright owner, with a few exceptions, may legally transfer or alter a copyrighted work.

To be able to copyright something, it must be original and it must be "fixed in any tangible medium of expression," such as a newspaper or magazine, a book, a video, a CD-ROM disk, etc. You cannot copyright a slogan, word, phrase or title. As a result, you can use a familiar advertising slogan like "Got Milk?" for a headline.

Copyright ownership is a rather fuzzy issue for student newspapers. In the professional world, the creator of a work owns the copyright, but an employer may own the copyright of works created by employees while working in the scope of their employment. Professional publications generally own the copyrights for staff-produced material and often contract for those rights when they hire a freelance writer, photographer, cartoonist, etc.

When writing or editing a story, ask yourself the following questions:

1. Could any statements damage someone's reputation? If so, do you have public records or other credible information to back up the claim?
2. Do you trust the reporter's sources? If you have doubts, confirm suspect information with other sources.
3. Have you inadvertently identified any person who the writer meant to be unidentifiable?
4. Has the reporter or photographer invaded anyone's privacy?
5. Do you have permission to use photos or graphics taken from the Internet or other publications?
6. When writing about crime, are all potentially defamatory statements based on police records, court testimony or other credible sources? Be careful of unofficial statements made by police, attorneys or court officials outside of a court proceeding; these are not privileged.
7. When printing sexually explicit material, can you justify the content journalistically?

At student papers, it's often not clear who owns the copyright to published material. What happens if a photographer wants to sell photos or a writer wants to sell a story first published in the student newspaper?

If the photographer or writer is on staff, receives a salary and gets direction from a supervisor, it's presumed the copyright belongs to the publication, Goodman explains. If the person contributes to the newspaper on an occasional basis, makes their own assignments and is paid by the piece (or not at all), the individual generally owns the copyright.

"The problem is most situations fall somewhere in the middle," says Goodman. "The best thing is to have a written agreement that staff members and contributors can sign." See the sample license agreement at the end of this chapter.

To Do:

1. If your newspaper doesn't already have a relationship with a media law attorney, find someone who will be on call for legal emergencies. Your state press association, state newspaper publishers' association or local newspaper may provide legal services or be able to help you find an attorney. The Student Press Law Center, listed in the "To Click" section, will also answer media law questions.

2. Invite your media lawyer, a local media law expert or a law professor on campus to give a workshop to your staff on what student journalists need to know about the law.

3. Sponsor a First Amendment event for your campus community. It's a good way to educate readers and sources (including your school's administrators), as well as your own staff about press freedom. For ideas on First Amendment programs, see the Freedom Forum Web site listed in the "To Click" section.

4. Try to build relationships with officials and groups that might feel poorly served by your newspaper. Invite leaders to meet with your editors or ask if you can visit their offices. Ask about their concerns and what they'd like to see in the paper.

To Read:

Fishman, Stephen. *The Copyright Handbook: How to Protect and Use Written Works*, 7th ed. Berkeley, Calif.: Nolo Press, 2003.

Fishman, Stephen. *The Public Domain: How to Find and Use Copyright-Free Writings, Music, Art and More.* Berkeley, Calif.: Nolo Press, 2004.

Press Freedom in Practice: A Manual for Student Media Advisers on Responding to Censorship. Available for free download at http://splc.org/legalresearch.asp?id=72

Student Press Law Center. *Law of the Student Press*, 2nd ed. Arlington, Va.: Student Press Law Center, 1994.

To Click:

Canadian University Press
http://www.cup.ca/

Copyright Crash Course
http://www.utsystem.edu/ogc/intellectual property/cprtindx.htm

College Freedom
http://www.collegefreedom.org/

Freedom Forum
http://www.freedomforum.org/

How to File a FOIA Request
http://www.firstamendmentcenter.org//press/ information/topic.aspx?topic=how_to_ FOIA&SearchString=student

National Coalition Against Censorship
http://www.ncac.org/

National Freedom of Information Coalition
http://www.rcfp.org

Student Press Law Center
http://splc.org

Tapping Officials' Secrets
http://www.rcfp.org/cgi-local/tapping/ index.cgi

U.S. Copyright Office
http://www.copyright.gov/

Staff Copyright Policy

All content produced by (NAME OF PUBLICATION) staff members is copyrighted by (NAME OF PUBLICATION).

As a condition of being a member of the (NAME OF PUBLICATION) staff or applying to join the staff, you must agree that (NAME OF PUBLICATION) has exclusive and unlimited copyright ownership of any content you submit for publication or other uses by (NAME OF PUBLICATION), including material that is not published or not otherwise used.

Content includes words, photographs, graphics, illustrations, cartoons, designs, "spec" ads and any other creative work that may be subject to copyright.

(NAME OF PUBLICATION) staff members include all students in the Business Division and the News Division: reporters, columnists, photographers, artists, account executives, representatives, specialists, editors, managers and any other positions that may be created.

This policy means if you submit anything for publication by (NAME OF PUBLICATION), you may not give someone else permission to publish that material. Further, (NAME OF PUBLICATION) may sell reprints or copyright permissions. (All revenue received by (NAME OF PUBLICATION) is used exclusively to fund (NAME OF PUBLICATION) operations and programs.)

For photographers: If you submit a photograph for publication, you must also agree that (NAME OF PUBLICATION) owns the negative, even if you used your own film. (NAME OF PUBLICATION) will reimburse you for the cost of your film, if you submit a valid request.

NAME OF PUBLICATION grants you the following permissions: Unlimited use of your own work (a) for your own personal portfolio, (b) for exhibitions, (c) as entries for awards contests and scholarship programs, and (d) for internship applications and job searches.

AGREEMENT

As a condition of my participation in a (NAME OF PUBLICATION) educational program or as a (NAME OF PUBLICATION) staff member, I hereby agree that (NAME OF PUBLICATION) has exclusive and unlimited copyright ownership of anything subject to copyright that I create or prepare and submit to (NAME OF PUBLICATION) for any use in any medium, including items not published or otherwise used. Further, I hereby agree to the terms of the (NAME OF PUBLICATION) Staff Copyright Policy.

Signature _____ Date _____

Printed name _____

Adapted with permission from a license agreement used by Collegian, Inc., publisher of *The Daily Collegian* at Pennsylvania State University

Figure 14.1. Would you run this photo? *State Press Magazine* at Arizona State University published this image on the cover of its weekly magazine to illustrate a story on extreme body piercing. University officials responded with a threat to cut the newspaper's funding if the paper continued to run such controversial material. But the newspaper's editors refused to apologize. Instead, they established formal guidelines for making news decisions, working with administrators and explaining their actions to others. The newspaper won a Payne Award for Ethics in Journalism for its responsible handling of the controversy. Photo by Andrew Benson, *State Press Magazine*, Arizona State University

Chapter 14

Ethical Issues

Student journalists face all the ethical challenges of professional journalists—and more. Just like the pros, you have to deal with the moral dilemmas associated with reluctant sources, conflicts of interest and potentially offensive words and images.

You also have the complications of being a student at the very college or university you're covering. What are the ramifications of writing negative things about administrators who can discipline you or professors who can dock your grade or the health professionals who treat your sore throat in the campus health center?

In this chapter we'll look at some of the ethical problems unique to student journalists and offer some suggestions and guidelines for walking this landmine-strewn path.

Developing a Code of Ethics

Sooner or later your newspaper will face an ethical dilemma. Perhaps the police reporter will want to use an anonymous source in a story about drugs in the dorms. Or a photographer will start freelancing for the local newspaper. Or the arts and entertainment editor will take home a stack of review CDs sent to the newspaper.

Are you prepared?

The key to addressing such dilemmas is to have a comprehensive code of ethics, a set of guidelines that helps newspaper staffers make ethical decisions.

Many student newspapers incorporate their code of ethics into the employee manual distributed to each new staff member. Some, including *The Correspondent* at Indiana University, Kokomo, the *Daily Trojan* at the University of Southern California and the *Campus Times* at the University of La Verne, post their code prominently on the newspaper's Web site. This allows the entire community—including advertisers, sources and readers—to understand how the newspaper operates.

Some college papers adopt the code of the Society for Professional Journalists (included in this chapter). The SPJ code is comprehensive, but it does not specifically address issues unique to student newspapers, such as selling work to competing professional newspapers. For this reason, many papers develop their own codes or adapt the Associated Collegiate Press' "Model Code of Ethics for Collegiate Journalists." (For information about getting a copy, see the resources list at the end of this chapter.)

A student newspaper code of ethics typically addresses the following areas:

- Conflicts of interest, including membership in campus organizations, work for competing media and freebies (free tickets, travel opportunities, gifts and review products)
- Plagiarism and fabrication
- Confidentiality of sources
- Photo ethics, including photo illustrations and digital alteration (for more information see Chapter 12)
- Obscenity and profanity
- Advertising (for more information see Chapter 18)

Conflicts of Interest

Professional papers often have strict guidelines to avoid conflicts of interest. Newsroom employees are typically restricted from writing for competing media, accepting gifts or meals from sources, and engaging in political and social activities that could be seen as compromising their coverage.

But at a college newspaper, conflicts can be harder to avoid. For one thing, most student journalists are part of the college community. They typically live, eat, take classes and get health services from the college or university. Many of the people they write about may be acquaintances, classmates, dorm mates, friends of friends. That makes it pretty hard to cover the campus objectively.

In addition, college is a time to explore a variety of interests and many students want to take part in student government, clubs and other political and social activities. Career-minded young journalists often want to intern or freelance for local media organizations while they are in school.

Student papers take different stances on these potential conflicts. For example, a newspaper serving a large college campus may ban student journalists from taking any leadership role in student organizations. But on a smaller campus—where newspapers may have difficulty recruiting "untainted" staffers—some newspapers allow staff members to serve in student groups as long as they don't write about issues that relate to those groups.

Competition clauses also vary among student newspapers. Some student papers don't allow staffers to write for competing professional media. Others encourage students to get professional experience but draw the line at "double-dipping"—writing the same story for the campus and community newspapers.

There's no single right answer to these questions; each paper is entitled to its own approach. But your newspaper's leadership should anticipate these conflicts and have policies in place before such situations arise.

Plagiarism and Fabrication

Plagiarism and fabrication have become major issues in journalism in recent years, both in the professional world and at the student level. The revelations about plagiarized and fabricated work by Jayson Blair (who was a reporter and editor at *The Diamondback* at the University of Maryland, College Park, before going to work for *The New York Times*), and Stephen Glass (who served as executive editor of *The Daily Pennsylvanian* at the University of Pennsylvania the year before he started writing for *The New Republic*), have brought increased attention to these journalistic crimes.

In 2003, *The Cavalier Daily* at the University of Virginia fired two student reporters for plagiarizing ideas, sentences and entire paragraphs from various media outlets. In 2004, a contributing writer and a columnist for the University of Georgia-Athens' *Red and Black* were disciplined for stealing passages from other writers. In 2005, the opinion editor for the *BG News* at Bowling Green State University was fired for plagiarizing a column.

Your newspaper should have a written policy on how to handle plagiarism, fabrication and other journalistic sins. These are serious offenses; at some student newspapers even a first offense may be cause for termination.

While it may seem obvious that copying other people's work and making things up is verboten, it pays to discuss such issues as each new staff comes on board. It's not sufficient to simply say, "Don't do it." Advisers or editors should explain exactly what plagiarism and fabrication are and how to avoid those temptations. In addition, they should outline the consequences if a staff member is found to copy or make up material for a story. Some student newspapers have staff members sign an oath saying they understand the newspaper's policy and pledging they will not plagiarize or fabricate.

One strategy for plagiarism prevention is to have reporters submit with each story a source list that includes phone numbers and e-mail addresses for all people interviewed, Web site addresses for online sources, and citations for all books and articles used for research.

Editors who suspect a staff member has plagiarized or fabricated should investigate the situation immediately and report it to the top editor and adviser, if there is one.

A number of Web sites listed at the end of this chapter offer guidance in preventing and detecting plagiarism.

Obscenity and Profanity

Many student newspapers relish the freedom of being able to set four-letter words in type. Others see using obscene language as unprofessional. Whatever your stance, you need to have a policy.

The Whetstone, the student-run newspaper at Wesley College in Dover, Del., for example, includes this obscenity clause in its code of ethics:

There is never a good reason to print vulgar language just to get a reaction. The staff should be sure that the words are a justifiable part of the story.

The Banner at Des Moines Area Community College is even more specific in its position on obscenity:

The Banner makes every attempt to exclude profanity from its articles, columns,

Tips from a Pro

■ **Harry Kloman**

When you decide to become a journalist, you have to give up certain things. One of them is your freedom of speech.

Well, maybe that's a little bit extreme. But *only* a little bit. In a profession where people count on you to present information fairly and accurately, and where you publish your name for all to see, thus making yourself a public figure, journalists have a certain obligation to conduct their private lives along some guidelines that can restrict their freedom.

Here are some general rules your paper should consider to reduce the risk of creating real or apparent conflicts of interest:

1. When reporters join the staff of your paper in any capacity, even just to write one or two stories, they must disclose to the newspaper any campus, city or hometown organization to which they belong so editors can avoid conflicts of interest. In fact, you may want to include an entry for such information on application forms. Editors should also explain the importance of this to new reporters and urge them to make full disclosure.

2. Reporters should not interview relatives, friends or roommates for a story, nor should they interview a professor if they currently have that instructor. As a corollary to this, editors should avoid assigning a story on, say, the history department to a student who majors or minors in history. Such an assignment might cause a reporter to hesitate to ask challenging questions, or the reporter might intentionally *not* ask certain questions to avoid making the department look bad.

3. Reporters should avoid socializing with people—students, university professionals or citizens of the community—on the beat they cover. There's certainly nothing wrong with attending a large, casual social event or having lunch with a source. (Reporters must make sure, of course, that *they* pay for their own meals.) But attending a party at the source's home is discouraged because it threatens to build a personal relationship that will make it more difficult for reporters to treat all sources fairly when doing a story.

4. News reporters should limit their political activities to the voting booth. They should not take part in political campaigns, speak out publicly on political issues, and/or take part in any activity or event that in some way might be considered "political"—for example, marching for or against abortion rights, gay rights, women's rights and so forth. If someone on staff decides to run for an elective political office on campus, he should resign before declaring candidacy. If he loses the election, he may choose to return to work for the newspaper.

5. Culture and arts reporters should not take part in the kind of activity on which they report. For example, a student who performs as a local musician should not review local bands. A student who performs in local theater should not review local plays. Permitting this puts the newspaper at risk of being charged with bias.

6. Sports reporting often involves a high level of fandom on the part of the reporter. Nonetheless, readers count on sports reporting to tell the whole, on-the-record truth. So sports reporters should try especially hard to maintain a professional distance from the coaches and athletes whom they cover.

7. Editors can't know everything or be everywhere. So when reporters accept a story, they must think seriously about whether they face any conflict of interest. If reporters fear that even the slightest of conflicts might exist, they should tell the editor immediately.

8. In addition to not joining organizations that might put them in a conflict situation, reporters should disclose any jobs they hold to see if those positions might create a conflict. Sports writers, of course, should not work or intern for any sports-related department of the university, nor should news writers work or intern for the university's office of public relations or police department.

9. Reporters and editors should never show a story to a source before publication. Doing so could lead to a discussion or argument about what the newspaper can or cannot print. Reporters can, however, read quotes and facts to a source if they feel a need to confirm them, although some newspaper attorneys advise against doing this. A reporter should never promise a source a copy of a story before publication.

10. The newspaper should try never to use its own people as sources for a story. If a staff member is involved with a group that is in the news, that person can suggest other sources of information. Do not let the staffer who is involved in the story read it before publication. Don't put your reporters in a position of conflicting loyalties.

11. Newspapers should try to avoid writing stories about themselves unless the news is unavoidably big and important. When a newspaper does write a story about itself—the appointment of new leadership, for example, or when it wins awards—it should work diligently to make the story as fair and balanced as possible.

In conclusion: When you work for a newspaper, you should think about every non-newspaper thing you do and consider how it might put you in a conflict situation. Always err on the side of caution, and always feel free to discuss your situation with an editor or adviser. The willingness to introduce these discussions and the sensitivity to conflict of interest issues distinguish top journalists from the rest of the field.

Harry Kloman is the news adviser for The Pitt News, *the daily student newspaper at the University of Pittsburgh, and the journalism program coordinator for the university's English Department. This piece is adapted from* Ethics, Standards and Practices in Newspaper Journalism, *an ethics manual he wrote for* The Pitt News.

---

and editorials. In order for an obscenity to be printed, it must give added insight into the character of the speaker. The full word is not printed. The first letters are printed, and the rest of the word is replaced by dashes (-). Words such as hell, damn, and bitch are not considered obscene. The sec-tion editor, managing editor, and editor in chief must be consulted before an obscenity is printed.

Newspapers should also have a policy—and a process—for dealing with sexually explicit material. The *State Press Magazine* at Arizona State University learned this the hard way in 2004 when it published a story about extreme body piercing. "The problem was how to illustrate the story without watering it down and without totally grossing people out," says Megan Irwin, who was editor of the magazine at the time.

Society of Professional Journalists' Code of Ethics

The SPJ Code of Ethics is voluntarily embraced by thousands of writers, editors and other news professionals. The present version of the code was adopted by the 1996 SPJ National Convention, after months of study and debate among the Society's members.

Preamble

Members of the Society of Professional Journalists believe that public enlightenment is the forerunner of justice and the foundation of democracy. The duty of the journalist is to further those ends by seeking truth and providing a fair and comprehensive account of events and issues. Conscientious journalists from all media and specialties strive to serve the public with thoroughness and honesty. Professional integrity is the cornerstone of a journalist's credibility. Members of the Society share a dedication to ethical behavior and adopt this code to declare the Society's principles and standards of practice.

Seek Truth and Report It

Journalists should be honest, fair and courageous in gathering, reporting and interpreting information.

Journalists should:

- Test the accuracy of information from all sources and exercise care to avoid inadvertent error. Deliberate distortion is never permissible.
- Diligently seek out subjects of news stories to give them the opportunity to respond to allegations of wrongdoing.
- Identify sources whenever feasible. The public is entitled to as much information as possible on sources' reliability.
- Always question sources' motives before promising anonymity. Clarify conditions attached to any promise made in exchange for information. Keep promises.
- Make certain that headlines, news teases and promotional material, photos, video, audio, graphics, sound bites and quotations do not misrepresent. They should not oversimplify or highlight incidents out of context.
- Never distort the content of news photos or video. Image enhancement for technical clarity is always permissible. Label montages and photo illustrations.
- Avoid misleading re-enactments or staged news events. If re-enactment is necessary to tell a story, label it.
- Avoid undercover or other surreptitious methods of gathering information except when traditional open methods will not yield information vital to the public. Use of such methods should be explained as part of the story

- Never plagiarize.
- Tell the story of the diversity and magnitude of the human experience boldly, even when it is unpopular to do so.
- Examine their own cultural values and avoid imposing those values on others.
- Avoid stereotyping by race, gender, age, religion, ethnicity, geography, sexual orientation, disability, physical appearance or social status.
- Support the open exchange of views, even views they find repugnant.
- Give voice to the voiceless; official and unofficial sources of information can be equally valid.
- Distinguish between advocacy and news reporting. Analysis and commentary should be labeled and not misrepresent fact or context.
- Distinguish news from advertising and shun hybrids that blur the lines between the two.
- Recognize a special obligation to ensure that the public's business is conducted in the open and that government records are open to inspection.

Minimize Harm

Ethical journalists treat sources, subjects and colleagues as human beings deserving of respect.

Journalists should:

- Show compassion for those who may be affected adversely by news coverage. Use special sensitivity when dealing with children and inexperienced sources or subjects.
- Be sensitive when seeking or using interviews or photographs of those affected by tragedy or grief.
- Recognize that gathering and reporting information may cause harm or discomfort. Pursuit of the news is not a license for arrogance.
- Recognize that private people have a greater right to control information about themselves than do public officials and others who seek power, influence or attention. Only an overriding public need can justify intrusion into anyone's privacy.
- Show good taste. Avoid pandering to lurid curiosity.
- Be cautious about identifying juvenile suspects or victims of sex crimes.
- Be judicious about naming criminal suspects before the formal filing of charges.
- Balance a criminal suspect's fair trial rights with the public's right to be informed.

(continued)

Irwin and other editors reviewed a batch of photos, dismissing some as too graphic, before choosing a simple close-up of a breast with a pierced nipple (Figure 14.1) for the magazine's cover. "We understood that some people would be offended but we felt it was still in good taste and made sense within the context of the story," Irwin said.

After one of the university's largest donors complained, the president demanded an apology and threatened to withdraw the newspaper's funding if it contin-

ued to publish similarly explicit material. But the newspaper's editors refused to apologize. Instead, they established formal guidelines for making decisions, working with administrators and explaining their decisions to others. The newspaper won a Payne Award for Ethics in Journalism for its actions.

"I always knew I would stand up for the First Amendment," Irwin said. "It was just kind of funny standing up for First Amendment rights over a nipple."

Interviewing Victims of Tragedy

One of the scariest things for a fledgling reporter is having to pick up the phone and call—or, even worse, having to knock on the door of—a person experiencing a tragedy. It's also one of the best lessons you can get for a career as a reporter.

No one really wants to interview the mother of a college freshman who just overdosed on drugs or the girlfriend of a young man who was shot to death outside a nightclub. But as you screw up your courage to make those tough calls, remember this: You're doing a service, both to your readers and to the people touched by the tragedy.

The Dart Center for Journalism & Trauma, a network of journalists, journalism educators and health professionals dedicated to improving media coverage of trauma and violence, offers these tips for interviewing victims of tragedy and their families:

* Journalists can help victims and survivors tell their stories in ways that are constructive, and in ways that make for great journalism.
* Sometimes you can't avoid intruding upon someone in grief. If you can't postpone your contact, remember to be sensitive and respectful in your approach.
* "I'm sorry for your loss," is a good way to start the conversation.
* Don't assume a victim or family member won't want to talk; often they are eager to share their story and memories with a journalist.
* If someone doesn't want to talk to you, be respectful and polite. And don't forget to leave your business card; at some point, the person may decide to talk to a reporter, and they will likely call the one that made the best impression.
* Make sure the person understands the terms of the interview. Tell them: "This is an interview for a story I'm writing. Your quotes will appear in the newspaper along with your name." Remind them of the terms periodically.
* Pay attention to your own emotions during the interview and let your reactions inform your reporting (while remaining profes-

sional). If you find something emotionally stirring, chances are readers will, too.

Covering Suicide

Deciding whether and how to cover a suicide is one of the most common and most poignant ethical dilemmas a student editor may face. And unlike with many other ethical issues, looking to the professional press isn't necessarily instructive. Most professional newspapers don't cover suicide unless:

* It causes a public spectacle (a jump onto a freeway streaming with cars, for example, or after a standoff with police)
* It's committed in connection with a homicide, kidnapping or other serious crime
* It involves a public figure

Student newspapers, however, frequently do cover suicides of students or faculty, particularly if they happen on campus. Why? For one thing, the suicide of a member of the campus community often has a significant impact on a large segment of the school—an entire academic department or a whole dorm may feel traumatized by the event.

For another, suicide is a major social problem among college students (it's the third leading cause of death among 15- to 24-year-olds, after accidents and homicides, according to the U.S. Department of Health and Human Services), and many newspapers use a suicidal incident as a news peg for an educational piece about the problem.

A year after a freshman at Northwestern University killed himself in his dorm room, for example, *The Daily Northwestern* ran a seven-part series on mental health. The se-

ries, "State of Mind," looked at eating disorders, obsessive-compulsive disorders and mental health care, as well as depression and suicide.

"There were all these issues that didn't find a place in our regular news coverage," says Elaine Helm, who worked on the series in the fall of 2003 and became editor in chief of the newspaper the following year. "We wanted to find an appropriate way to reflect on those issues and find a context for this one incident that touched so many lives." The series won several awards, including one from the National Mental Health Association.

When deciding whether to cover a suicide in your own paper, ask yourself these questions:

* Was the suicide committed on campus?
* Was the suicide committed in a public place, such as a park or downtown street?
* Was the student or faculty member prominent on your campus?
* Does the suicide appear to be part of a trend?
* Will coverage of the suicide help the campus community in any way?

If the answer to one or more of these questions is yes, your newspaper may decide it's important to run a story.

Some newspapers also consider the family's wishes when deciding whether to write about a suicide. Journalists rarely contemplate the impact their stories will have on family members, but in the case of a suicide, editors may want to take into account how open the family is to talking about the circumstances of the death.

College Newspaper Ethics Policy: The *Northern Star*

Every newspaper should have an ethics policy. Some college newspapers adopt the Society of Professional Journalists' Code of Ethics (reprinted in this chapter) or the Associated Collegiate Press Model Code of Ethics (see the link at the end of this chapter). Others write their own.

The Northern Star at Northern Illinois University developed the policy below by adopting sections of the ACP ethics policy. The Northern Star code, which is designed to supplement the SPJ Code of Ethics, is an excellent example for student journalists everywhere.

This ethics policy was developed by the *Northern Star* at Northern Illinois University. It supplements the Society of Professional Journalists' Code of Ethics. Together, these two documents are the expected code of conduct for all *Northern Star* and NS*Radio employees. Note: "*Northern Star*" refers to the newspaper, the online edition and NS*Radio.

Travel

The *Northern Star* does not accept free travel, accommodations or meals during coverage of events. Journalists must remain free of any perception that sources are buying favorable coverage. For sports coverage, *Star* reporters, photographers and broadcasters may travel on team buses or planes, or stay in the same hotels as a team, but the *Star* will pay for employees' transportation, food and lodging costs.

Products

The *Northern Star* often reviews new consumer products—music CDs, DVD movies, video games, computer software, books, electronic gadgets, etc. Some are sent by companies' PR offices and some are purchased locally by the *Star*. It is important that staff members adhere to a firm ethical policy regarding these materials.

In choosing which products to review or otherwise feature in the paper, use normal standards of news judgment. Do not choose based on what was received for free. That amounts to a company "buying" publicity.

Any materials given to or bought by the *Northern Star* for review become the property of the *Northern Star* and not of any individual staff member. Materials are to be stored at the *Star* office. Editors, at their discretion, may dispose of old material in an equitable way. (Adapted from the Associated Collegiate Press Model Code of Ethics.)

Reviews and Event Coverage

Movies: The *Star* will pay for a ticket for the reviewer. Do not accept free admission.

Concerts: If the *Star* is covering the concert as a news event, arrange for media credentials beforehand with the concert promoters. We do not need to buy tickets for reporters or photographers. However. . . if a reporter or critic attends a concert in order to review it, then the *Star* will pay for that person's ticket. The reason: There could be public perception that organizers "bought" a positive review by giving the reporter free admission.

Sporting events: These generally are covered as news, and reporters and photographers may arrange for media credentials and free admission.

Abuse of media credentials: If a *Northern Star* employee is found to have accepted media credentials for a concert,

sporting event or other public event, but then attends the event for non-*Star* purposes, the employee is subject to disciplinary action, possibly including dismissal.

"Free tickets or passes may be accepted by staff members for personal use only if tickets are available on the same complimentary basis to non-journalists." (From the ACP Model Code of Ethics.)

Radio Promotional Events

NS*Radio and the *Northern Star* sometimes will promote concerts with ticket giveaways for listeners/readers. Under no circumstances should tickets or other prizes be given to or won by *Northern Star* employees, their relatives or friends.

Gifts

"Gifts should not be accepted. Any gift should be returned to the sender or sent to a charity. If the gift is of no significant value, such as a desk trinket, a small food item or a pen, the staff member may retain the gift. As a guideline, if the value is under $10, the gift may be kept. More than one gift in one year, even if under $10, from the same giver, may not be accepted." (From the ACP Model Code of Ethics.)

Use of *Northern Star* Equipment

Northern Star equipment—computers, software, printers, photo equipment—is the property of the state of Illinois. It may not be used for outside-NIU, for-profit activity by any individual or group. Such use violates university policy and could result in penalties to the *Northern Star*. Further, the *Star* sometimes reports on similar, questionable practices within other NIU organizations. It cannot ethically report on these situations if it is not itself beyond reproach.

Northern Star equipment may not be used to produce any publication—print, online or broadcast—which competes or potentially competes with the *Northern Star* for advertising revenue. Exceptions: Publications or services that enter into formal partnership with the *Northern Star*.

Northern Star equipment may be used on occasion to assist other NIU offices or outside, not-for-profit entities, but always on the employee's own time, with the prior knowledge and approval of the editor in chief, and never at times when the equipment is needed for *Northern Star* work.

Outside Employment and Activities

The *Star* strives to remain free of any potential conflict of interest—real or perceived. No *Northern Star* employee may serve any elected or appointed post within the NIU Student Association—paid or unpaid. The press serves as the "Fourth Estate"—an independent watchdog of government. That responsibility will not be compromised.

Star employees may not cover or do other *Star* business with any organization which they belong to or work for. It is the responsibility of the employee to alert his/her manager or editor of potential conflicts of interest.

Star employees may participate in political rallies, protests or demonstrations, but this practice is discouraged. Such participation disqualifies them from ever covering such an event. Again, the employee is responsible to alert his/her manager of this potential conflict of interest.

(continued)

College Newspaper Ethics Policy: The *Northern Star* (*continued*)

Relationships

Staff members should not cover or have *Star*-business dealings with "family members or persons with whom they have a financial, adversarial or close sexual or platonic relationship. Intrastaff dating is not recommended if one person assigns or evaluates the work of the other person or if one is in a position to promote the other to a higher staff position." (From the ACP Model Code of Ethics.)

Drinking While on the Job

"Even though a staffer may be able to drink legally, no or only light drinking in a social setting such as a dinner or reception is recommended to avoid any suspicion by a source or the public that the staffer's judgment, credibility or objectivity is impaired by alcohol. When covering an event where alcohol is served, staffers should not accept free drinks unless all drinks are free to everyone in attendance. Staffers should avoid the appearance that they are being "wined and dined" by any source or group." (From the ACP Model Code of Ethics.)

Influence of Advertisers

"Editors should guard against attempts made by advertisers. . . to influence the editorial content of the print or online publication. The editorial staff reserves the right to make all decisions about any editorial coverage an advertiser may get in the publication, including advertising supplements. Readers should not perceive that an advertiser is getting favorable editorial mention simply because the advertiser has bought space in the publication." (From the ACP Model Code of Ethics.) In addition, business-side employees should, when needed, explain this policy to clients and potential clients.

Corrections

An inaccuracy is never knowingly published. If any error is found, the *Northern Star* is obligated to correct the error as soon as possible—regardless of who made the error. At editors' discretion, corrections may be made to the Web site immediately. Any online story which results in a correction should clearly state that it has been corrected, and how. (Adapted from the ACP Model Code of Ethics.)

Plagiarism and Fabrication

What is plagiarism?

- Presenting someone else's work as your own, without proper acknowledgement and/or permission.
- Using some else's opinions, word arrangement, design or sequence of ideas without proper acknowledgement and/or permission.

What is fabrication?

- Making up quotes or information from a real source.
- Attributing real quotes or information from a source other than the person who actually said it.
- Making up quotes or information from an imaginary source.
- Making up information and not citing a source at all.

Any *Northern Star* employee found to have plagiarized or fabricated content for print, online or radio is subject to immediate termination.

Acknowledgement: The ACP Model Code of Ethics, 3rd edition, 1999, by Albert DeLuca and Tom Rolnicki, Associated Collegiate Press. Excerpts used with permission.

Another factor to consider is the risk of "suicide contagion" or copycat suicides. Researchers have found that suicides tend to increase when a particular incident gets a lot of media play. This copycat phenomenon is particularly evident when coverage is sensational and when media stories highlight the mode of suicide. For example, in the year after a student fell to his death at New York University, four other students there took their lives the same way.

The Dart Center for Journalism & Trauma offers these guidelines for covering suicide:

- Be careful when approaching friends and relatives for comment; they might not have heard the news.
- In your story, avoid speculating about the motivation for the suicide. Likewise, avoid quoting the speculation of others. Often, there is not a simple "reason" for a suicide. If you include one in your report, you may cause someone else to feel unwarranted responsibility for the suicide.
- Be careful not to romanticize the suicide with lurid or gratuitous detail.
- Consider running a sidebar with contact information for local suicide hotlines and other mental health resources.
- Journalists can include information that can help the public view suicide more accurately by including such contextual details as trends in suicide rates, myths about suicide, warning signs, actions that individuals can take to prevent suicide by others.

Doing an Ethics Audit

How do you know if you're doing a good job of covering your campus? How can you tell if you're being fair and equitable to all segments of the community?

Deni Elliott, the Poynter-Jamison Professor of Journalism Ethics and Press Policy and ombudsman at the University of South Florida, St. Petersburg, suggests newspapers do ethics audits. Such audits can help editors take a critical look at how they cover the campus.

Before embarking on an audit, collect demographic information about your campus, including racial, ethnic and gender composition of students and faculty; average age of students; numbers of part- and full-time students, etc. Much of this information will be readily available from the admissions, public information or institutional research offices—or even your university's Web site.

Then study several issues of the paper, asking these questions:

1. How many men and women appear as subjects in news photos or as sources in stories? What is the racial balance of people pictured in the paper? What are those people doing?
2. What words are being used to describe the people in the news?

Reflections on an Ethical Dilemma

■ **Joel Elliott**

In May 2003, Joel Elliott, editor of The Talon *at Toccoa Falls College in Toccoa, Ga., published a story in the student paper revealing that the evangelical college's president, Donald O. Young, did not hold the master's degree that was listed on his résumé. Many on the campus criticized Elliott for his actions, saying it wasn't Christian of him to reveal the unpleasant facts. A few weeks later Young resigned from his job.*

In the end, it took a five-minute call to Fuller Seminary to determine that my college president had not earned a master's degree as he claimed. It had taken me several months of examining financial statements, working contacts and poking through the college's hallowed archives to find it.

The president's skeleton had initially peeked from its closet when one professor hinted vaguely of a scandal he planned to disclose upon his own retirement. He wouldn't specify, so I had to dig for it.

I first caught wind of the story while shooting the breeze with a fellow reporter at *The Toccoa Record*, where I worked to pay my school bills. He said it was rumored the college ran into difficulty trying to renew accreditation because the president was underqualified.

The rumor was a little misleading, but I eventually dug out the kernel of truth.

I didn't have much time to contemplate whether to publish the story, as we had only one issue of *The Talon* left before students went home for the summer. The situation didn't look good. President Donald O. Young had threatened to shut down *The Talon* earlier in the semester, so I could only guess what he'd do in retaliation for this. My mother asked me not to do it, for fear Young would expel me with only one semester before graduation. I'd already been kicked out of one college, so it was a real concern. However, I felt I'd made my decision and commitment to reporting the news the previous year, when I'd taken the position as editor. Fear for personal loss couldn't be a consideration.

As for *The Talon*, I knew it would cease to exist as a truthful news-reporting organization the instant I spiked the story. I felt that gambling on the consequences of telling the whole truth was a better bet than going for the seemingly safer certainty of destroying our integrity.

Folks at the school seemed to think that the school's Christianity should throw a warm fuzzy into my editorial decision-making process. Quite the opposite, I feel. Jesus and the prophets never depended on the suppression of truth for the promotion of their agendas. I saw no reason why a newspaper or a school should, either.

The day the story ran, Donald Young compared its impact to an earthquake. He announced the catastrophe during chapel that morning and evoked a more emotional response than the time he announced the bombing of the Twin Towers.

Students and faculty members cried, wailed and prayed for God to deliver them from evil as they surged to the front to embrace and lay hands on Young, while I scribbled notes for a follow-up story. Soon, I was alone in my seat with nearly every Toccoa Falls College student and professor at the stage, facing back toward me.

One student gave Young a hug and borrowed his microphone to shout up at the few who dared remain in their seats.

"Satan's trying to destroy this school and this man of God," he said. "You're either for us or against us."

"This school" was also my school, and I was sickened by the hypocrisy. Even a dean, who, the previous day, had offered to help blackmail the man into resigning in exchange for me killing the story, stood behind Young with head dutifully bowed.

The dean would later denounce me to a *New York Times* reporter as having chosen the way of the newspaperman over the way of the Christian. However, his false dichotomy served only to further solidify my knowledge that I had made the right decision. If journalism is worth doing, it's worth doing right. I believe it's worth doing.

Joel Elliott graduated from Toccoa Falls College in December 2003 with a degree in journalism. He won numerous awards for the story on Donald O. Young, including the Payne Award for Ethics in Journalism from the University of Oregon School of Journalism and Communication, the Weltner Hero Award from the Georgia First Amendment Foundation and a citation from the Georgia General Assembly. He is a reporter for the Toccoa Record.

3. What gets the greatest attention in the paper? What gets the least?
4. Who's missing from your coverage?
5. How does your coverage of the campus square with the demographic statistics you collected?

Discuss in groups how you can better cover the community you serve. Then come up with an action plan to make sure you follow up on suggestions for improving coverage.

To Do:

1. Assign a team to review your code of ethics. Is it as complete as it could be? Are there important issues it doesn't address?

Once your code is revised, consider different ways of distributing it, including posting it on your Web site, making it part of your staff manual and publishing it in your newspaper.

2. Invite an ethics expert on campus (perhaps a journalism or communications professor) or a journalist from a professional paper to speak to your staff about media ethics.
3. Devote a training session to discussing ethics. You might assign staffers to small groups to discuss real or theoretical ethical dilemmas such as those presented at Journalism Ethics Cases Online (see the Web site listed below).

4. Assign a team of people to conduct an ethics audit of your paper. Present the results of the audit to your entire staff and break people into small groups to discuss how to improve your coverage.
5. Break your staff into small groups and assign each group to pretend to be a certain kind of student—a person who uses a wheelchair, an African-American, a lesbian, a student who lives at home with his parents, a Muslim student, a 40-year-old student who is returning to school after 20 years in the working world. Have each group brainstorm story ideas that might appeal to that type of person. Then have each group share its ideas with the whole

staff and put together a list of story ideas for the paper.

6. Rent a movie with a media ethics dilemma, such as "The Paper," "Absence of Malice," or "The Insider" and show it to your staff. Then discuss the movie as a group.

To Read:

Black, Jay, Bob Steele and Ralph Barney. *Doing Ethics in Journalism: A Handbook with Case Studies*. Greencastle, Ind.: The Sigma Delta Chi Foundation and The Society of Professional Journalists, 1993.

Cote, William and Roger Simpson. *Covering Violence—A Guide to Ethical Reporting About Victims and Trauma*. New York: Columbia University, 2000.

Patterson, Philip and Lee C. Wilkins. *Media Ethics: Issues and Cases, 4th ed.* New York: McGraw-Hill Humanities/Social Sciences/Languages, 2001.

Smith, Ron F. *Groping for Ethics in Journalism*. Ames, Iowa: Iowa State Press, 1999.

To Click:

Ethics Advice Line for Journalists
http://www.ethicsadvicelineforjournalists.org

Associated Collegiate Press Model Code of Ethics for Collegiate Journalists
http://studentpress.journ.umn.edu/pubs.
    html#ethicscode

Dart Center for Journalism & Trauma
http://www.dartcenter.org

Journalism Ethics Cases Online: Indiana University, Bloomington
http://www.journalism.indiana.edu/gallery/
    Ethics/

Poynter Institute Ethics Section
http://www.poynter.org/subject.asp?id=32

American Society of Newspaper Editors Codes of Ethics
http://www.asne.org/ideas/codes/codes.htm

Editorial and Commentary Issues: The American Press Institute (This collection of articles discusses how to put perspective on difficult issues.)
http://www.americanpressinstitute.org/
    content/287.cfm

Code of Ethics from the Society of Professional Journalists
http://www.spj.org/ethics.asp

Plagiarism Prevention Web Sites
Avoiding Plagiarism: Purdue University Online Writing Lab
http://owl.english.purdue.edu/handouts/
    research/r_plagiar.html

Avoiding Plagiarism: University of California, Davis, Student Judicial Affairs
http://sja.ucdavis.edu/avoid.htm

Excerpts from Ethics Codes on Plagiarism
Journalism.org
http://www.journalism.org/resources/tools/
    ethics/plagiarism/excerpts.asp?from=print

Guidelines for Racial Identification:
Poynter Online, Feb. 2000.
http://www.poynter.org/content/content_
    view.asp?id=4343

Figure 15.1. Students at the University of Wisconsin-Eau Claire started the *The Flip Side* in 2003 to compete with *The Spectator,* the long-established campus newspaper. *The Flip Side,* University of Wisconsin-Eau Claire

Starting a New Newspaper

As a student at the University of Wisconsin-Eau Claire, Jeremy Gragert wasn't satisfied with the semiweekly campus newspaper. Though *The Spectator* had won several state and national awards, Gragert felt the 80-year-old paper didn't cover many of the events and issues he cared most about. After hearing a talk by a professional journalist about the dangers of media consolidation, Gragert decided what the campus needed was a second newspaper, one that would bring an alternative perspective to the university community.

In the spring and early fall of 2003, Gragert and a few friends hosted a series of meetings for people interested in working on the new paper. Some wanted to create a humor publication patterned after *The Onion*. Others favored a political magazine with a decidedly liberal slant, more akin to *The Nation*. Over the course of the meetings, the students came up with a guiding vision and hammered out a constitution establishing the new paper as "an alternative news media outlet" serving the campus and the greater Eau Claire communities.

In October 2003, the team of fledgling journalists put out the first issue of *The Flip Side* (Figure 15.2). The premier issue was 16 sheets of 8.5-by-11-inch paper stapled together. "We printed it on campus printers," says Gragert, a history major who graduated in 2005. "A bunch of us spread out to different printers on campus. It took about three or four hours to print it. Then we got together stacks of the papers and formed an assembly line to put the pages in order and staple them."

The next day, Gragert and his colleagues set up a table in the middle of campus and started distributing the new paper to students. The inaugural edition was heavy on commentary but also offered news stories and features on campus, statewide and national issues—everything from tips on registering for classes to an analysis of a Coca-Cola boycott protesting the treatment of union members in Colombia.

Among the first to notice the appearance of the new paper were reporters from *The Spectator*, which ran an article about the upstart paper the following day titled "Alternative publication creates new campus medium."

And, so, the University of Wisconsin-Eau Claire, a campus of about 10,000 students, became host to a good, old-fashioned newspaper war.

Newspaper Competition

In the professional world, newspaper competition is quickly becoming a thing of the past. In 1956, 94 American cities had competing daily newspapers. But by 2004 only a dozen had two or more separately owned, competing papers.

Most North American cities have but a single daily newspaper reporting on local issues and events. The majority of college campuses are one-newspaper communities, too, but in recent years alternative publications have sprouted on campuses around the country, turning many into true marketplaces of ideas.

When it comes to newspaper competition, the University of Wisconsin, Madison,

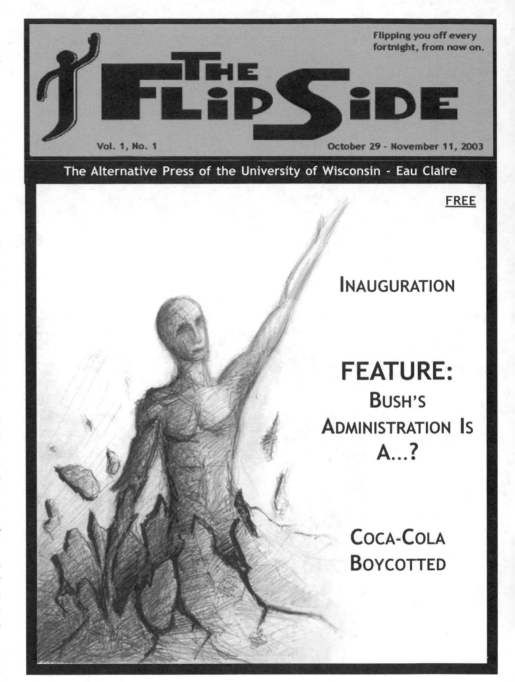

Figure 15.2. The premier edition of *The Flip Side* featured news and commentary. *The Flip Side*, University of Wisconsin-Eau Claire

may be the most spirited campus in the nation. On any weekday the 40,000 students there can pick up two dailies—*The Daily Cardinal*, founded in 1892, and the *Badger Herald*, founded in 1969 as a more conservative voice. (It's since swung to the center, according to one *Badger Herald* staffer.) The two newspapers celebrate this spirit of competition with an annual *Cardinal/Badger Herald* football game in the fall and a softball game in the spring. According to tradition, the losing newspaper must run a report of each game by one of its rival's reporters.

In 2003, a group of students launched *The Madison Observer*, a biweekly alternative paper, and in 2005, another group started *The Mendota Beacon*, a voice for campus conservatives.

A spirit of competition also thrives at Vanderbilt University in Nashville, Tenn. In 2001, a coalition of liberal and minority groups launched *The Vanderbilt Orbis* to compete with the *Vanderbilt Hustler*, the official student newspaper for more than 100 years. Soon after, another band of students announced plans to start *The Vanderbilt Torch*, a conservative/libertarian paper. "The belief was that the *Hustler* wasn't doing a very good job covering some aspects of the campus," says Chris Carroll, director of student media.

Four years later, all three newspapers (as well as two magazines, a literary review, a humor magazine and a yearbook) were still around; in fact, the *Hustler* increased from twice-a-week to three-times-a-week publication in 2004. *The Nation* named *The Vanderbilt Orbis* one of "Ten Papers We Like" in an article about alternative campus newspapers.

Carroll has doubts about whether Vanderbilt, a campus of only 6,000 undergraduates and about 10,000 students total, can support so many publications. In fact, the *Hustler* is the only one that brings in substantial advertising revenue. "To have so many publications, you're stretching to get the best writers, the best photographers. There's an overload of media, an overload of message."

However, he notes, the new publications have encouraged many more students to get involved in campus media than ever before. "Our chancellor makes a big deal about how many publications we have, how many outlets for expression, which he sees as a demonstration of the vitality of the campus."

Alternative Newspapers

Since most colleges and universities have a campus paper, the majority of the new publications that have sprung up in recent years are alternative papers—ones that provide an alternate perspective to the mainstream campus newspaper. John K. Wilson, coordinator of the Independent Press Association's Campus Journalism Project, divides alternative publications into six categories:

Conservative—publications that provide right-of-center perspectives.

Progressive—newspapers created to discuss progressive or liberal ideas

Humor—non-partisan newspapers that offer satire. "Harvard's *National Lampoon* was a forerunner," Wilson says. "Today *The Onion* inspires many imitators."

Religious—newspapers that offer a religious slant are rare but growing in number with a recent Supreme Court decision decreeing that religious newspapers are entitled to student fee funding.

Alternative weeklies—campus papers patterned after urban alternative weeklies.

Identity—newspapers based on identity politics, such as African-American, gay and lesbian and feminist newspapers.

"Alternative newspapers work best by filling an ignored niche," says Wilson, who in 1995 co-founded the University of Chicago *Free Press*, an alternative monthly, and in 2001 founded the *Indy*, an alternative weekly at Illinois State University. "The mainstream campus newspaper has all of the advantages of being established, and no alternative newspaper can really hope to beat it at overall campus news coverage. Therefore, alternative newspapers specialize in things that mainstream papers do poorly." Alternative papers tend to run longer pieces, including investigative, magazine-style and opinion articles.

Starting a New Paper

So what does it take to launch a new college newspaper? Ideas, people, production facilities and money.

First off, you need a vision. Think carefully about what kind of publication you want to create. Does your college or university need a mainstream, general-interest publication that covers the whole campus or a forum for alternative voices? Do you want to start a newspaper that caters to a particular group—such as Asian Americans, night students, summer students—or one that has a specific political bent?

Next, you need to recruit a staff that believes in your vision. Announce an organizational meeting. Print fliers and post them all over campus. Make recruiting visits to journalism, English, political science, creative writing, photography and graphic design classes, as well as clubs where you're likely to find people interested in writing, photography and design.

Once you have a core group, it's time to come up with a name. Student newspapers typically play on the school's mascot, landmarks or nicknames such as *The Pitt News* (The University of Pittsburgh), *The Spartan Daily* (San Jose State University), *The Foghorn* (University of San Francisco), *The Daily Tar Heel* (University of North Carolina). Conservative newspapers often use the words review (such as *The Carolina Review, The Duke Review, The Stanford Review, The Aggie Review* and the *Dartmouth Review*), patriot (*The California Patriot, The GW Patriot*) or spectator (as in *The Spartan Spectator, The Amherst Spectator*). Left-leaning alternative newspapers sometimes take more playful or militant names, such as *The Flip Side, The Boiling Point* (University of North Carolina at Chapel Hill) and *Toast*, a summer newspaper launched at Trent University in Peterborough, Ontario, in the summer of 2004.

Writing a Mission Statement

The next step is to write a mission statement for your newspaper. The mission statement should reflect the goals and aspirations of your staff. What does your publication stand for? Who do you want to serve? What values do you want to uphold?

In discussing your mission statement be sure to give everyone on the staff a say in what the paper should be; a newspaper is a team effort, not just one person's soapbox. Early on, decide how you want to make group decisions—by consensus or by majority rule—and stick with your process.

As you make decisions, start writing down rules and policies that can be used in a constitution and/or staff handbook. Some newspapers have one of each; others have a single document that serves both functions.

Sample Mission Statements

The Vanderbilt Orbis, Vanderbilt University

The Vanderbilt Orbis aspires to change the atmosphere on Vanderbilt's campus and provides a voice for the liberal, multicultural, and minority viewpoints. This publication strives to inform the public about issues that these groups face as well as to promote diversity and unity within our community. It is a forum for the discussion of social, political, and religious commentary relevant to Vanderbilt, the nation, and the world. Orbis was founded by a coalition of students seeking to raise consciousness about the diverse ideas, cultures, and backgrounds in our society. We hope to challenge the existing social atmosphere at Vanderbilt and promote a rebirth of acceptance.
Reprinted with permission.

The Flip Side, University of Wisconsin-Eau Claire

The Flip Side is a publication dedicated to providing a news media outlet and forum on the UW-Eau Claire campus by welcoming the writings, views, and involvement of all students and community members. By reporting on news, perspectives, and opinions on local, national, and international issues, we seek to develop participatory democracy and freedom of speech.
Reprinted with permission.

Drafting a Constitution

A constitution is a formal document that outlines the body of rules that govern a student newspaper; you may be required to draft a constitution to get funding or recognition as a club or activity from your student government.

A typical constitution articulates its policies in a format like this:

Article I Name of the Organization

Article II Membership. Explain who can join your staff, such as whether they must be students or whether they have to take a prerequisite course. You might want to include a non-discrimination clause explaining that the organization does not discriminate against anyone on the basis of gender, race/ethnicity, sexual orientation, political affiliation, religion or disability status.

Article III Officers. Outline the titles and responsibilities of your paper's officers/editors.

Article IV Editor Selection. Explain how you select your editor in chief (and, if applicable, other top editors).

Article V Removal of staffers. Explain the terms under which a staffer can be removed from a position.

Article VI Ratification and Amendments. Explain the terms for ratifying and amending the constitution.

Creating a Staff Manual

Generally less formal but more detailed than a constitution, a staff manual is a guidebook that will help staffers do their jobs. At a minimum it should include:

- Mission statement
- Job descriptions
- Code of ethics
- Stylebook
- Policies on deadlines, meetings, copy submission and other issues related to the functioning of the organization.

You may also want to include important campus phone numbers, maps, department listings and other documents to help new staff members.

Drafting a Business Plan

Early on in the process you need to figure out your expenses and how you're going to pay for them. The biggest cost at most professional papers is salaries, but new student papers typically pay staffers little or nothing. Many student papers compensate staffers by giving them independent study or course credit. If you're interested in doing this, contact a journalism, English or writing program faculty member about how to arrange credit for the work you're doing. Other fledgling papers compensate staffers with small stipends.

At student newspapers that don't pay their staffers, the largest expenses are generally printing costs. The cost of paper and printing can vary widely; it pays to shop around. It may also pay to beg. Some community newspapers may be willing to print your paper at little or no cost as a community service.

Many student newspapers rely on some or all of their funding from student activity fees, often doled out by student government. Since your paper is serving the student body, this can be a legitimate use of student fees. However, there's a danger to using these funds. If student governing board members don't like what you run, they may decide to stop funding your paper. (See Chapter 13 for a discussion of this kind of censorship.) In the best situations, student government bodies understand the basic principles of press freedom. But student newspapers critical of student government or administrators have been the victims of reprisals.

Grants are another possible source of income. A number of ideological groups, including the liberal Center for American Progress and the conservative Collegiate Network, provide grants to help establish new student newspapers. Friends and family members or local corporations may also help out. Once again, however, these sources of funding may have strings attached. If your Aunt Thelma agrees to contribute $2,000 toward your effort on the condition you make the dean's list, you may want to want to think twice about the offer.

Probably the easiest way to support a student newspaper is to do what professional papers do—sell ads. Once you've put together a prototype or a first issue you can approach campus organizations and local businesses about buying ads. (For more about developing a media kit and selling ads, see Chapter 18.)

Production

Not that long ago, producing a student newspaper was a complex process that required expensive equipment. But new advances in printing technology and Web publishing make starting a newspaper easier than ever. All you really need to get started is a single personal computer (though the more computers your staff has access to the better) loaded with some kind of design or publishing program. If you don't have Adobe InDesign or Quark Xpress, you may be able to get access to them at a school computer. Even an old copy of Adobe Pagemaker will do.

While money can be an obstacle, don't let it keep you from publishing. *The Flip Side* started on stapled sheets of copy paper with almost no money. The *DoG Street Journal* at the College of William and Mary delayed the burden of printing costs by publishing first on the Web (Figure 15.3) and adding a print edition later (Figures 15.4 and 15.5).

Creating a Newsroom

One of the most challenging parts of starting a new campus newspaper is finding—and being able to afford—a newsroom. Sometimes you can secure an unused classroom or office space on campus for little or no cost, but on-campus space is a finite commodity. If you can't find a free or affordable space, you may need to start by sharing an office with another campus organization or running the newspaper out of someone's dorm room or apartment.

The Otter Realm, the newspaper at California State University, Monterey Bay, operated for years out of a tiny office space on the far edge of the campus. The cubicle had room for just three computers, castoffs that were donated, along with the office space, by the university. The newspaper shared a fax machine with several other campus organizations housed in the building. Students did much of the production work in a campus computer lab. It was far from an ideal situation, but the newspaper got out, first every month and later every two weeks. *The Otter Realm* finally got a newsroom in 2005.

If you don't have a space large enough to accommodate your whole staff, hold staff meetings in an empty classroom, library discussion room or quiet public gathering spot.

Once you are able to find office space, make up a budget of what you'll need to outfit it. Look for grants to help you buy equipment and supplies. You may be able to get castoff computers, software and other equipment from the university. In addition, make a plea to local professional newspapers, which may be willing to give you old equipment. When the *San Francisco Chronicle* photo department switched from Nikon to Canon cameras, it donated tens of thousands of dollars worth of photo equipment to the San Francisco State Journalism Department and its laboratory newspaper, *Golden Gate [X]press*. The cameras and lenses might no longer have been state-of-the-art, but they were certainly more sophisticated than individual staffers or the student newspaper could afford to buy.

Every newsroom should have a communication center. Use inexpensive organizers to create mailboxes for each staff member. Many newsrooms also use whiteboards or blackboards to leave phone messages. Boards can also be used for editorial budgeting to keep track of stories.

Think about adding furnishings and equipment that will make the newsroom comfortable for your staff. Get a small refrigerator, a microwave oven and a table and chairs and encourage staff members to eat their lunch in the newsroom. (But if you do, make sure people are responsible about throwing out their garbage; leftovers will quickly attract rodents and insects.) A sofa, even a bedraggled one, can make a room cozy and provide an oft-needed space for power naps during marathon production sessions.

You should also have a television and radio to keep up with breaking news. Consider buying a police scanner, which will help you monitor police and fire calls on your campus and in your community.

Many student newspapers invest in photo and recording equipment—cameras, lenses, tripods, video cameras and audio recorders—that staffers can check out as needed. If you do, it probably pays to get insurance in case of loss, breakage or theft.

Publicity

When you're ready to publish the first issue, get the word out. Put up fliers and banners announcing the new publication. If your school has a campus radio or TV station, ask them to publicize the new publication. (In fact, you could establish a trade arrangement by which you run ads or a regular guide to their programs and they run public service announcements about your paper.) Staffers advertised the launch of the *DoG Street Journal* at the College of William and Mary, which started as an online newspaper, by donning T-shirts with the paper's launch date.

Don't just drop stacks of your first issue around campus and expect people to pick the paper up. Have staffers pass them out in classes, cafeterias, dorms, the student union and the library. Come up with a catchy slogan and announce it over a megaphone.

Reach out to professors as well as students. Brian Vander Kamp, co-founder and editor in chief *of The Flip Side* at the University of Wisconsin-Eau Claire, said, "The first issue we had a handful of professors come over to our table and ask for twenty or thirty copies to take to their classes. One batch I delivered myself and overheard the professor announcing some assignment based on *The Flip Side* for the next class period. Right there, I was able to go back to my room and cross one of my journalism fantasies off my list. It was so great."

To Do:

1. When starting a new newspaper, study which publications already serve your campus, including professional newspapers, faculty newsletters, university magazines and publications put out by your public affairs office. Ask yourself: What's missing? What's not being covered? What could we do better?

2. Study mission statements. To get ideas, browse other student newspapers on the Web. Then assign a group of staffers to write a mission statement for your new newspaper.

3. Create a launch campaign for your publication. Get ideas from marketing professors or marketing students on campus. You might even get a marketing class to take your newspaper on as a project.

To Read:

Ridgley, Stanley K., ed.. *Start the Presses! A Handbook for Student Journalists*. Wilmington, Del.: Intercollegiate Studies Institute Books, 2000.

To Click:

The Campus Alternative Journalism Project
http://www.indypress.org/programs/cajp.html

The Collegiate Network
http://www.isi.org/cn/

Campus Progress
http://campusprogress.org/

Question & Answer

Why did you want to start a new campus newspaper?

Originally the *DoG Street Journal* was a joke. A friend of mine and I took an International Relations course together and every week, we'd toss around the idea of starting a new paper because we weren't really happy with the options that existed. Midway through the semester, that joke turned into a real desire to try and build a publication. As freshmen, we figured we had little to lose so we began meeting and started to spell out what we wanted to accomplish and how best to do so.

How did you get the publication together?

We went to friends of ours and just shared with them what we wanted to do. To our more witty friends, we asked if they'd be willing to write a column. To those who loved photography, we asked them to join the photo staff. To those who'd shared stories at some point with us about high school journalism, we asked them to climb aboard, too.

What has been very rewarding is to see how many of those people, nearly all, who came out to the first interest meeting we ever had are still actively involved and encourag-

■ **George Srour**

In 2003 George Srour and Dan FitzHenry, two sophomores at the College of William and Mary in Williamsburg, Va., launched the DoG Street Journal, an online publication, to compete with The Flat Hat, the campus weekly. The following semester, the DSJ staff began publishing a print edition of the newspaper. More than 100 students contributed to the effort in the publication's first two years. Srour describes the joys and challenges of starting a new college paper.

ing others to join in and take a position at the paper.

How did you come up with the name?

The name is derived from Duke of Gloucester Street, the main throughway of Colonial Williamsburg that ends at the tip of the college's campus. Everyone on campus refers to it as "DoG Street," so we thought we'd take it a bit further and have a little fun with a name that everyone on campus could relate to.

How is the *DoG Street Journal* different from *The Flat Hat*?

The main difference is that we're an online daily newspaper, which is what we really wanted to accomplish when we first started. *The Flat Hat* offers a thorough weekly publi-

cation, but we felt that the demand and talent were there to come out more often in a format more in tune with what students favor.

Another major element that has set the *DSJ* apart from other publications is that the staff has grasped what I believe is an important aspect of journalism—that of using our media outlet as not only a way to cover the less fortunate around us, but to also do something about it. Be it raising money to replace trees lost to Hurricane Isabel or collecting contributions for the construction of a school in Uganda, our staff tries to unite the community in efforts to benefit those we've written about. I think this has helped define the *DSJ* and those who work for the publication.

The *DoG Street Journal* started as an online newspaper. Why did you start that way? When did you add the print edition?

Money. After we took some time to look at the costs involved in a print publication, we realized that it would be far easier to start online, and if that met some success, to go ahead and venture into the print edition. When we got started, we didn't have a dime to our name, a computer for ourselves, let alone a place we could meet. Going online made more sense to start.

The print edition came in after our first semester of online publication. Originally it was produced twice a month with plans to increase our frequency. We had to modify our plans because of the resources available to us—an office that can fit three people at one time and just two computers. Coming out more often, and even twice a month, was simply too much of a strain.

That said, our current print edition, a monthly magazine, has been a big hit. We've seen an increased number of advertisers per issue, and more importantly, the readership rates are far higher than they were for the initial publication. I think that's a combination of being around for more than two years now and being able to discern our exact niche in the print world.

Figure 15.3. The *DoG Street Journal* at the College of William and Mary started as an online publication. *DoG Street Journal,* College of William and Mary

How did you publicize the online newspaper?

We had about 25 people when we got started and we had shirts made through an advertiser with our name and our release date and we sent our entire staff out with fliers to post around campus. It was great fun periodically checking the statistics for Web visits because they started on a steep incline, which we still see to this day when school is in session. Once people knew there was a source for news that was as current and up-to-date as the *DSJ*, many people started logging in and checking out the site.

What were some of the greatest challenges you faced in starting the *DoG Street Journal*?

Our venture was a lofty one. We met administrators, students and even close friends who doubted how successful the *DSJ* could be in the face of a publication that's been around campus for nearly 100 years. Over time, however, I think the very same people who voiced some apprehension would agree that the *DSJ* has become a part of the publications scene at the college and is well-read. We had to show that we were after something different than any other publication and that we had a solid number of people who wanted to get involved and keep things going.

What kind of reaction did you get?

I have a stash of e-mails we printed out during our first week online—friends from all over, alumni, random visitors and many others wrote to say how much they enjoyed reading about college and Williamsburg news online. That said, we also got a handful of suggestions that we looked at and were able to make improvements to the site as a result.

How did you finance the publication? What have your greatest costs been?

Initially, everything was financed through ad sales. We had months where we skimped and made it on $20 and $30 to cover the hosting costs, but once we were able to prove ourselves, more ads came in and helped finance purchasing a computer, furnishing an office and other such things. Our greatest costs are really printing costs, which are offset by ad sales. We also receive a subsidy from the college and we're hoping that in two to three years' time, the paper will be fully independent and not reliant on such funds.

(continued on next page)

Figure 15.4. While maintaining the Web site, the *DoG Street Journal* staff began to put out a biweekly print newspaper. *DoG Street Journal*, College of William and Mary

What advice do you have for other students who want to launch a new campus newspaper?
Take some time to construct a vision. One of the best things that happened to us was that we took almost a year before our first day online to hash out what exactly we wanted to do, who would be able to help us get there and the most efficient means for starting a publication. Even in the face of doubts, we found old advisers, local people and friends who believe in the vision we constructed and by building the *DSJ* around their words of wisdom and insights, we were able to put together a publication that far exceeded any expectations we ever had.

Figure 15.5. The *DoG Street Journal* later switched to a monthly newsmagazine print format. *DoG Street Journal,* College of William and Mary

Figure 16.1. *The Ball State Daily News* at Ball State University is known for its out-of-the-box page designs. *The Ball State Daily News,* Ball State University

Chapter 16

Design and Graphics

Your staff has produced some great stories and eye-catching photos for this issue. But where are you going to put them on the page? How will you entice readers into each story? In fact, how are you going to get people to pick up the paper at all? The answers to all these questions lie in design.

Newspaper design is about getting people who don't want to read to read. It's about making text so effortless, so captivating, so compelling, that they can't help themselves.

Chapter Contents

Newspaper design is governed by a set of basic principles based on studies of how people read type. Once you understand these rules, you can follow them, bend them and even occasionally break them.

Design is Content

The first rule of newspaper design is that design should be dictated by content.

Design isn't about making the paper pretty; it's about making it easier to read and easier to navigate. Good design guides the reader through the paper, showing what's important, where to find things, how to make sense of information.

"Design is journalism," says Amy Emmert, a former page designer for the *Orange County Register* who now advises the *Daily Bruin* at the University of California, Los Angeles. "Visual choices should be about information, not decoration."

Layout and Design

Every publication has a "look." That look is consistent day after day, week after week. *The News York Times* is recognizable among all other newspapers on the newsstand. So are *USA Today* and the *Wall Street Journal*. What gives these papers such distinctive appearances is that they follow the same design for every issue. When they want to change the design after a number of years, they go through a redesign process.

For each issue, page designers place the stories, photos and graphics onto pages; this

The Front Page

Figure 16.2. Elements of a page. *Indiana Daily Student,* Indiana University. Graphic by Eugenia Chien

process is known as layout (Figure 16.2). The designers may change the size of the headline or where the photos are placed from issue to issue, but all their decisions follow the basic design of the paper. Typefaces used for headlines and text, the size of margins and the location of certain regular features should all remain consistent, maintaining the basic design scheme of the publication.

Principles of Design

What are the elements of good design?

Balance. Every element on a page has a visual "weight." In general, large objects are "heavier" than small ones, color elements are heavier than black and white. If you put all the pictures at the top of the page, for example, it will look top-heavy. If all the images are on one side of the page, it will look lopsided. A well-designed page is balanced horizontally and vertically.

Consistency. Consistent design helps build trust and loyalty among readers. They

know where to find what they're looking for and what certain things mean. To maintain consistency, use the same margins, fonts and color scheme throughout the paper (Figure 16.3).

Contrast. While you want to maintain consistency, you don't want to be boring. You can make a page visually interesting by varying shapes, colors and sizes. The key is to provide just enough contrast that a page is interesting without looking cluttered or confusing.

Visual hierarchy. A well-designed page tells the reader what's most important by putting key elements in the most visible positions. Stories with the greatest news value should be at the top of the page and have the largest headlines. As the reader reads down the page, the headlines should become smaller, indicating stories are less important.

Simplicity. Simplicity in page design means fewer elements and more white space. Pages should be functional and uncluttered.

Design Consistency

■ **Publication identity**

Just as a logo gives a product, company or service an identity, the identity of a newspaper begins with its nameplate. It continues into standing heads at the top of each section and even into column heads such as "Letters to the Editor" and "News Briefs." This consistency ensures that readers will know what publication they are reading without even seeing the nameplate. Such consistency also helps establish brand loyalty.

Daily News (Ball State University, Muncie, Ind.; Justin Hesser, editor, Vince Filak, adviser)

The Shorthorn (University of Texas at Arlington; Amber Tafoya, editor; Lloyd Goodman, adviser)

Technician (North Carolina State University, Raleigh, N.C.; Rebecca Heslin, editor; Bradley Wilson, adviser)

Figure 16.3. Design consistency. Graphic by Bradley Wilson.

one size, style and weight (such as lightface, heavy, extra bold).

Font family—a group of related fonts with a variety of weights (lightface, regular, boldface) and styles (roman, italic, condensed).

Serif type—a font with tiny strokes, or serifs, at the tips of each letter. Most body text is set in serif type.

Sans serif type—a font without serifs. Sans serif type is slightly harder to read than serif type, so newspapers generally use sans serif fonts for larger type, such as headlines, reverse type (white type on a black or colored background) or small blocks of type, like photo captions.

Type size—all type is measured two ways. The face of each letter is measured vertically in points, with 72 points to the inch. The width of a line of type is measured horizontally in picas, with 6 picas equal to 1 inch. So a headline set in 72-point type across an 18-pica column would be one inch high and 3 inches wide.

Leading—the space between the lines of type. Body text is generally set with 2 points of leading.

Body type—small type, usually 12 points or smaller, used for text.

Display type—large type, usually 14 points and larger, used for display information, such as headlines.

Agate type—the smallest point size type (usually 5 or 6 points) that can be read, often used for sports scores and stock quotes.

Alignment—The way type starts and ends on a line. Left aligned means the type starts on the left margin and ends in an uneven arrangement on the right. Centered type is set to the middle of the line. Justified type lines up on both the left and right edges. Computers can force justify a line of type by adding spaces between words or letters.

Typography

Ever since Johannes Gutenberg started printing Bibles in the 15th century, people have been playing with type. They've scrunched it, stretched it, curled it and twirled it, all with the hope of making the 26 letters of the alphabet more interesting or fun to read.

But as a newspaper person you have to remember that the primary function of type is to make reading easy. Type should be clear and legible. It may look cool to use funky typefaces or run words up one side of the page or run pink text on a black background, but if people can't read the text, you've failed.

Here's a typography vocabulary that will help you talk about type (Figure 16.4):

Typeface, or font—a set of characters (letters, numbers and punctuation marks) in

Tips for Good Page Design

1. **Select a dominant visual element for each page.** The lead art should be at least twice as big as any other visual element on the page.
2. **Divide the page into rectangles.** Each story, including art, should fit into a rectangle.
3. **Shoot for a 2:1 text-to-art ratio.** That means each page should be about one-third art.
4. **Think in terms of packaging.** Group related stories together.
5. **Try to have a visual element for each story.** If you don't have a photo or infographic for a story, use an infobox or pull quotes to break up text and create another point of entry.
6. **Avoid jumps as much as possible.** When you do jump, run at least 4 inches of the story before the jumpline and at least 6 inches after jumping. Don't jump a story more than once.
7. **Use graphics to explain complicated information.** Even if you don't have a gifted graphic artist on staff, you can use maps and simple charts to convey information visually.

Type Vocabulary

■ Type has its own language
Typography, the study of type, is a field with its own unique vocabulary. Understanding this vocabulary makes it easier to communicate expectations to designers.

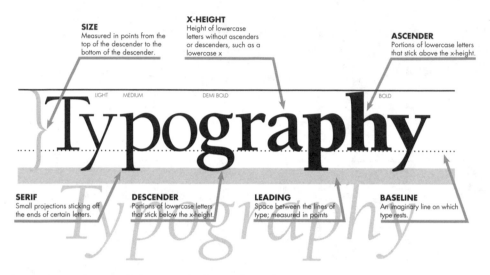

SIZE
Measured in points from the top of the descender to the bottom of the descender.

X-HEIGHT
Height of lowercase letters without ascenders or descenders, such as a lowercase x

ASCENDER
Portions of lowercase letters that stick above the x-height.

SERIF
Small projections sticking off the ends of certain letters.

DESCENDER
Portions of lowercase letters that stick below the x-height.

LEADING
Space between the lines of type; measured in points

BASELINE
An imaginary line on which type rests.

Figure 16.4. Type vocabulary. Graphic by Bradley Wilson

The Building Blocks of a Page

Every newspaper page is made up of four basic building blocks:

Headlines—the oversized type that labels each story

Body text—the stories themselves

Images—graphics or photos that complement the stories

White space—the space around the text, headlines and images.

Let's examine each of these building blocks in more detail.

Headlines

As we discussed in Chapter 10, headlines are designed to grab the readers' attention and give them a sense of what the story is about. They also help organize the page and anchor each story.

Headlines are written in larger type than the stories themselves. The general rule is the more important the story, the larger the headline. And since the most important stories generally run at the top of the page, headlines usually get smaller as you move down the page.

Small headlines range from 12 to 24 points, midsize headlines from 24 to 48 points and large headlines are above 48 points.

Many papers also include a deck under the headline. This smaller headline generally has more words than a main headline and can offer a more complete explanation of the story.

Body Text

Body text in newspapers is generally 9 or 10 points and set in columns.

Text is hard to read if it's set in columns narrower than 10 picas or wider than 18 picas; most newspapers set columns at 12 to 15 picas across.

Long columns of type also tire the reader. The best depth for text is between 2 and 10 inches per leg of type.

Art/Photos

Newspapers use art—photos, graphics and illustrations—to break up columns of type and help tell stories in a visual way. Photographs provide emotional depth; graphics explain complicated concepts. These visual elements also serve as a nice contrast for the eye to long columns of gray type.

Each page should have one dominant piece of art—a single large photo or graphic. The dominant art should be at least twice as large as any other piece of art on the page.

White Space

What's left? White space. These empty areas give readers a break. But white space isn't just space that's left over after all the other elements are put on a page. It should be planned like any other element on a page. White space should be treated like a visual element in itself.

White space is best used in the corners or outer areas of a page. Large areas of white space in the middle of a page can get "trapped" and distract readers from other elements—like body text, photos and headlines.

Like other elements of a page, white space should be consistent throughout your paper. Gutters, the vertical spaces between columns, should be the same size, usually about 1 pica, unless you're using a special design treatment.

Modular Design

If you look at a newspaper from 50 or 100 years ago, you'll see a clutter of stories and photos. You'll have a hard time figuring out what's most important or where you should look first.

The 1970s and '80s ushered in a new style of newspaper design, one marked by simplicity and organization. One of the most important results of this revolution was the development of modular layouts.

In modular design (Figure 16.5), each element—photo, headline, cutline, body copy—is treated as a rectangular building block. These blocks are then packaged together to form larger rectangles.

Modular design makes a paper easier to read and navigate. It helps readers know which photos, stories, sidebars and info boxes go together and where to find the next column of type.

Multiple Points of Entry

To attract readers to a story, newspapers increasingly rely on multiple points of entry—different doors readers can use to enter a story. Some readers, for example, might enter a story through a headline; others might be attracted by a photo, while someone else might start by looking at a graphic (Figure 16.6).

Designers have a number of tools to help create multiple points of entry. Among them:

- Information boxes summarize information such as key points of a story, details of an upcoming event, actions at a meeting, biographical details about a key person in a story.
- Refers guide readers to a related story or stories on a different page or on the Web.
- Information graphics, such as pie charts, bar graphs and maps, help explain the story in a visual way.
- Pull quotes, also known as pullout quotes and liftout quotes, are quotations from the story that are set in larger type to attract readers to the story.

Modular Design

■ Make it easy for the reader

In each of these modular units, the headline covers the entire module, captions touch the photos; the upper left corner of the story touches the headline; copy blocks form L shapes, U shapes or rectangular blocks; and white space is to the outside. With consistent internal spacing (1 pica), the reader will perceive each of these units as a package of related elements. And in no case does the reader have to jump over any elements.

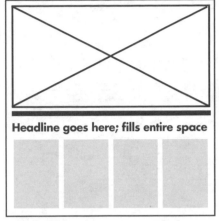

Headline goes here; fills entire space

Vertical Module • photo (on top), caption, headline, story

Story in block

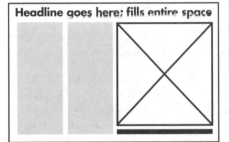

Headline goes here; fills entire space

Story in L shape around art

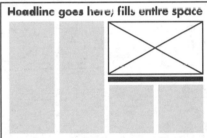

Headline goes here; fills entire space

Story in U shape around art

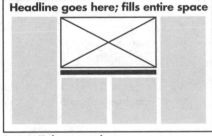

Headline goes here; fills entire space

Story in block • photos (on top), caption, headline, story, white space to outside of module

Figure 16.5. Modular design. Graphic by Bradley Wilson

The Designer's Toolbox

The designer's toolbox should also include tools to make pages easier to read and visually attractive. Among them:

- Subheads are bolder than regular type and are used to break up long stories. They're usually set every eight to 10 inches, usually where there's a shift in topic.
- Rules are lines that are used to isolate or organize elements on a page. Rules can be used to create boxes, separate stories or indicate which elements go together, such as which story goes with which photo.

- Screens are background tints, either in gray or a color, that can be used to add contrast to a page. They're particularly effective for highlighting sidebars and infoboxes, but they should be used sparingly. Screens should be light—no more than 10 percent or 20 percent—and you may want to use slightly larger or bold text to compensate for reduced legibility.

Broadsheets and Tabloids

Newspapers come in two formats: broadsheets and tabloids. Broadsheets are full-size papers, usually about 22 inches long and 12 to 13 inches wide. Tabloids are roughly half that, 11 inches wide by 13 to 15 inches deep. Broadsheets generally run five or six columns across; tabloids generally have four or five.

In a 1999 study of more than 250 American college newspapers, researchers Lillian Lodge Kopenhaver and Ronald E. Spielberger found that nearly two-thirds of college and university newspapers were tabloids. In Canada, the vast majority of college newspapers are tabs.

Tabloids tend to be easier to design, because they offer fewer options and generally include fewer stories on a page. Because of their smaller size they're handier for students to read on a bus or at a desk. They're also thicker; a 16-page tabloid becomes an 8-page broadsheet, which might strike some readers as thin.

Broadsheets offer the advantage of greater flexibility and some think they look more like professional dailies. In addition, broadsheet newspapers can generally charge more for a full-page advertisement because the format is larger and that can help bring in more revenue.

Some newspapers offer a mix of formats. *The Exponent*, the newspaper at Purdue University in Indiana, for example, publishes a broadsheet five days a week during the school year and a tabloid three days a week during the summer months.

The Role of Designers

At many college newspapers (and even some professional papers), the work of the designer doesn't begin until after the stories are written and the photos are shot. This is a mistake. Designers need to be part of the planning process from the beginning. Design shouldn't be the last consideration at a newspaper; it should be among the first.

Emmert, the *Daily Bruin* adviser, challenges student newspapers to ask themselves these questions:

- Do designers and/or design editors have a voice in planning coverage?
- Do they attend budget meetings?
- Do they read stories and regularly contribute their own ideas about story quality, placement, photography, etc.?
- Do your designers consider themselves to be journalists?

If the answer to any of these questions is no, you're underutilizing some of your greatest resources.

Emmert says designers must think of themselves as journalists—and everyone else in the newsroom should, too.

Style Guides

Designing a single newspaper page from scratch can take hours—or even days. Each

Figure 16.6. Information boxes, graphics, decks, photos and teasers give readers multiple points of entry to stories on this page. *Indiana Daily Student,* Indiana University

inating better ideas for illustrations and graphics."

Models

Nearly every designer interviewed for this book had the same advice for student designers: learn from other publications. When you find a newspaper you like, try writing a style sheet for that newspaper. Then, modify the style sheet for your particular publication. You can add, subtract or modify elements that you think will give your paper a distinctive look that reflects something about your campus. And while everyone should look at mainstream daily newspapers, don't stop there.

Tim Harrower, a newspaper design consultant and author of *The Newspaper Designer's Handbook* (a must-buy for newspaper designers), says too many college newspapers "have the same bland personality as the big dull daily down the street. You have to update your design vocabulary so that you're as modern looking as the publications you yourself read."

Alternative weeklies, magazines and foreign newspapers can be excellent sources for design ideas, Harrower says.

Drawing a Dummy

While most newspaper pages are put together on computers using page layout programs such as Quark Xpress or Adobe InDesign, designers usually start on paper with a dummy, or sketch. Dummy sheets are grids that represent newspaper columns. They are generally smaller than the actual paper but proportional.

Dummying saves time and helps you see your mistakes before they get into print. By drawing a sketch you can figure out in advance what kind of headline you'll need, how photos should be sized and cropped and whether you need more information for an information box. A dummy can save you hours of computer time. While moving an element on a computer can mean major rearrangement and take lots of time, a dummy can be changed with the stroke of an eraser.

Infographics

Increasingly, newspapers use graphics to visually explain information; these are called information graphics, or infographics for short. Pie charts, maps, bar charts and diagrams are all examples of infographics (Figure 16.7).

Infographics help readers process complex or hard-to-understand information, such as statistics, geography and dollar amounts. A locator map, for example, can show where a fire happened and put the event into context. A pie chart can quickly show readers what proportion of their tuition

page involves an infinite number of decisions, from the size and font of the headlines to the placement of the stories to the size of the rule under the flag.

That's why newspaper designers generally work from a style guide. Ron Reason, a Chicago-based designer, educator and consultant, says any newsroom larger than two people should have at least a basic design stylebook. "It will reduce questions of style relating to your design and production for newcomers and old-timers alike and reduce inconsistencies in the paper. A stylebook will also allow your staff to focus on more important issues, like writing better headlines, selecting and cropping better photos, and orig-

Case Study: *The Harvard Crimson* Redesign

In 2003, the staff of *The Harvard Crimson* decided to add color to the newspaper, which—despite its name—had been black and white for 130 years. The staff commissioned Ron Reason of Garcia Media, the design firm that helped bring color to *The Wall Street Journal*, to redesign the entire newspaper. (See Figure 16.8 for the "before" version and Figure 16.9 for the "after" version.)

In addition to creating nearly 100 prototype pages for the consideration of the editors, Reason presented a number of formal and informal training sessions to bring the staff up to date on modern editing, planning and visualizing techniques.

"Ron left *The Crimson* with more than just a new style—he spread the Gospel of Visual Thinking," Michael Conti, one of the paper's design chairs, wrote in a column for the newspaper on the redesign. "From the early stages of a story, reporters, photographers and designers have started working together to display our content in a fashion that is both exciting and easily accessible to our readers. The results have been absolutely astounding. 'Visual thinking' has become the catchphrase of *The Harvard Crimson*."

The redesign brought together a nice mix of the old and new, Conti says.

"In terms of its design, *The Crimson* has always been relatively conservative," Conti says. "With our redesign, we were looking to maintain some degree of conservatism, while introducing some important modern design elements."

A big priority was making the content more accessible to readers. The old *Crimson* relied simply on headlines, pictures and text to tell its stories. With the redesign, the paper added new elements, such as infographics, story labels for recurring topics and front-page teasers and an index to guide readers to inside stories and sections.

"We wanted to give our readers more entry points to our content, so that when they scanned the pages important information would jump out at them and pull them into the stories," Conti says.

Reaction to the redesign was overwhelmingly positive. In fact, the paper won two design awards from Associated Collegiate Press in 2004.

Conti offers this advice to other student papers undertaking a redesign: "Take your redesign very seriously and give a lot of thought to every change you make. The smallest details, from colors to fonts, can make or break a page design. Most importantly, think about your changes from the perspective of your readers; the goal of any redesign should be to make content more attractive and accessible to the reader."

Figure 1. Before undergoing a redesign in 2003, *The Harvard Crimson* relied primarily on headlines, text and photos to tell its stories. *The Harvard Crimson*, Harvard University

Figure 2. The redesigned *Harvard Crimson* uses infographics, story labels for recurring topics and front-page teasers to lure readers into stories and guide them to information. *The Harvard Crimson*, Harvard University

Steps to Designing a Page

STEP 1. Assemble and measure the elements of your page. That includes text, headlines, photos, cutlines, information boxes and graphics. Decide which elements are related and how to group them.

STEP 2. Rank your stories. Generally, the editors will decide the lead story, and sometimes the secondary story for each page. If there are other stories for the page, rank them, considering their importance and reader appeal.

STEP 3. Select the dominant art. It may be a photo or an infographic, but you must have one dominant image for each page. "You need something to draw your reader in," says Matt Garton, a designer at the *Cleveland Plain Dealer* who got his start at the *Oregon Daily Emerald* as a student at the University of Oregon. "You are establishing a hierarchy on your page. Lead art tells them where to start."

STEP 4. Place the dominant image on the upper half of the page. It may be in the middle or to one side. The dominant photo will usually run at least three columns if it is a vertical shot and four columns if it is a horizontal shot.

STEP 5. Select and place your secondary visual element. Be sure to vary the sizes and shapes of your photos and graphics. If your dominant photo is a large horizontal photo, try to use at least one vertical shot on the page. The dominant image should be at least twice the size of any other visual element on the page.

STEP 6. Place your lead story. The lead story may or may not correspond to the lead art. Lead stories are generally placed across the top of the page or down the right-hand column, but some papers run them down the left side. Give your lead story the largest headline. Package the story, headline and accompanying elements (photos, graphics, cutlines, info boxes) into a rectangle.

STEP 7. Build more rectangles out of the other stories and photos. Remember that your most important stories should go on the top half of the page and have the largest headlines. Don't forget to leave room for cutlines, jump lines, photo credits and other necessities.

Tips for Creating a Design Style Guide

Every newsroom should have a design style guide—a manual that sets in place the rules and policies of how the newspaper is produced. This may be packaged with an editorial stylebook or exist as a separate document.

A design style guide typically has the following elements:

An index. This makes it easy to find things.

A statement of philosophy. What is the design of the paper trying to do?

A font palette. Most newspapers have one font for text, one or two others for headlines. You may choose one other typeface for special touches, such as logos and section flags. Some newspapers also select a separate font for special text, such as sidebars, graphics, jump lines and cutlines.

A graphics policy. This should explain how graphics get done at your paper and lay down the rules for type fonts and sizes for infographics and other graphical elements. This section should include a copy of your graphics request form.

A photo section. This should include policies on cropping, cutlines, running text over photos and other issues related to photography. This section may include your photo ethics policy and a photo request form.

goes toward faculty salaries, facilities and other expenses.

Certain types of information are best conveyed with particular sorts of infographics.

- A line chart, or fever chart, shows how quantities change over time. These are useful in showing a trend, such as falling numbers of foreign students or rising tuition rates.

percentages of students from different ethnic groups on your campus.

- Timelines are great for showing a chronology, such as the major events in the tenure of a university president or the life of a school.
- Diagrams illustrate how things work or explain a process.
- Maps show readers where events have taken place and may offer context.

To Do:

1. Invite a professional newspaper designer to critique your paper. Ask for specific suggestions on how to make the paper more visually effective. The Society for News Design has a database of speakers that allows you to search by state and topic (typography, ad design, redesign, etc.). See the Web site listed below.

2. If you don't already have one, create a design style guide for your newspaper following the steps listed in this chapter.

3. Send a delegation from your staff to visit the design department of your local or regional newspaper. Ask if you can sit in on a planning meeting. And don't just send designers. Invite at least one reporter, photographer and editor so they can see how the design process works, too.

4. Arrange a one- or two-day design workshop for your staff. Invite designers to lead sessions and allow time for group discussions about how you want your paper to look.

5. Create a design library for your newspaper. It should include a wide range of newspapers and magazines as well as books on design, and design annuals from the Society of News Design and the Best of Collegiate Design series.

6. Send a delegation of students to attend a design seminar sponsored by the Society for News Design, the Poynter Institute, the Society of Publication Designers or your state newspaper association. Most groups list training opportunities on their Web sites.

To Read:

Ames, Steven E. *Elements of Newspaper Design.* New York: Praeger, 1989.

Berry, John D. *Contemporary Newspaper Design: Shaping the News in the Digital Age: Typography & Image on Modern Newsprint.* West New York: Mark Batty Publisher, 2004.

Bohle, Robert H. *Publication Design for Editors.* Englewood Cliffs, N.J.: Prentice-Hall, 1990.

Conover, Charles. *Designing for Print: An In-Depth Guide to Planning, Creating, and Pro-*

- A bar chart uses horizontal rectangles to represent amounts, while a column chart uses vertical rectangles to represent figures. These are best used to compare two or more items, such as student fees for last year compared to student fees for this year.

- Pie charts allow readers to compare the parts that make up a whole, such as the

Graphs & Charts

■ Display data graphically

Numbers confuse and scare away readers. But a simple graph can show a trend in a way that numbers embedded in a story can't.

- A pie chart divides a "whole" into "parts" such as the university into colleges. Even without the numbers present, a reader can determine what is the largest piece of the pie.

- A bar chart shows the relationship between items with differences conveyed by the height, color and/or shade of the box. They can also display trends such as the increase in enrollment.
- A line graph is a quick way to display a trend usually with time on the horizontal axis.
- A chart displays the data and leaves it up to the reader to identify the trends.
- Identify the source of all data.

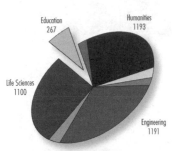

DEGREES CONFERRED
The number of degrees conferred in the graduation year ending in May 2005. The colleges of Engineering, Life Sciences and Humanities awarded the most degrees. The College of Education awarded a record number of degrees, nearly 25 percent than the number of degrees that college awarded last year.

SOURCE: University Department of Planning and Analysis

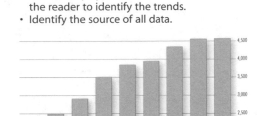

ENROLLMENT INCREASES
Driven by lack of tuition increases, state population increases and increasing demand for a college degree in the workforce, college enrollment has more than doubled in just under a decade.

SOURCE: University Department of Planning and Analysis

FACULTY AND TEACHING ASSISTANTS
There are almost two graduate assistants for every faculty member. The number of graduate assistants has been increasing at a rate faster than the number of faculty. And the university reports that more undergraduate courses are being taught by graduate assistants than ever before — 36 percent this year.

SOURCE: University Department of Planning and Analysis

STUDENT STATISTICS	2005	2004	2003	2002	2001
1. Total Headcount Enrollment	30,149	29,957	29,854	29,637	29,286
2. Total Undergraduate Enrollment	22,879	22,754	22,971	22,780	22,418
3. Total Graduate Enrollment	7,270	7,203	6,883	6,857	6,868
4. Female Percent of Enrollment	43.5	43.2	43.3	42.8	42.7
5. In-State Percent of Enrollment	86.4	86.8	87.1	87.0	86.3
6. Black Percent of Enrollment	9.1	9.7	9.8	9.7	9.7
7. Number of Entering Freshmen	4,253	3,847	3,851	3,628	3,831
8. New Freshman Average SAT	1186	1192	1195	1193	1175

CAMPUS TRENDS
Both undergraduate and graduate enrollment have increased steadily as has the percentage of female students on campus. The percentage of Blacks on campus has remained relatively constant, declining in 2005. During the last five years, the average SAT score has been 1188 varying by only 20 points.

SOURCE: University Department of Planning and Analysis

Figure 16.7. Graphs and charts. Graphic by Bradley Wilson

ducing *Successful Design Projects*. New York: Wiley, 2003.

Garcia, Mario R. *Contemporary Newspaper Design: A Structural Approach, 2nd ed.* Englewood Cliffs, N.J.: Prentice-Hall, 1987.

Graham, Lisa. *Basics of Design: Layout and Typography for Beginners*. New York: Thomson Delmar Learning, 2001.

Harrower, Tim. *The Newspaper Designer's Handbook, 5th ed.* New York: McGraw-Hill College, 2002.

Moen, Daryl. *Newspaper Layout and Design: A Team Approach, 4th ed.* Ames, Iowa: Iowa State University Press, 2000.

The Society for News Design. *The Best of Newspaper Design.* Gloucester, Mass.: Rockport Publishers, Inc. (annual)

White, Jan V. *Editing by Design: For Designers, Art Directors, and Editors—The Classic Guide to Winning Readers, 3rd ed.* New York: Allworth Press, 2003.

Williams, Robin. *The Non-Designer's Design Book: Design and Typographic Principles for the Visual Novice, 2nd ed.*, edited by Nancy Davis. Berkeley, Calif.: Peachpit Press, 2003.

To Click:
American Press Institute
http://americanpressinstitute.org

College Front Page
http://collegefrontpage.com/

Design/Graphics at Poynter.org
http://poynter.org/subject.asp?id=11

News Page Designer
http://www.newspagedesigner.com

Ron Reason
http://www.ronreason.com

Student Society for News Design, University of Missouri-Columbia Chapter (sponsors national student design contest)
http://www.missouri.edu/~wwwssnd/

The Society for News Design
http://www.snd.org

The Society of Publication Designers
http://www.spd.org

Today's Front Pages
http://www.newseum.org/todaysfrontpages/

Question & Answer

What do you see as the role of design at a college newspaper? Is it any different from the professional world?

The question I always struggled with as a student was "What is the role of a campus paper?" Is it the same as a professional paper, that is, to deliver the news best suited to the readership in the form best suited to the readership? Or is it to give student journalists practice writing, reporting, editing and designing as they will in the "real world"? Those are two different audiences we're talking about—the 18- to 24-year-old college audience and your average newspaper editor.

In my mind, college journalists should be crafting their papers for their readers, not their future employers. With that attitude, it's evident that shorter stories, use of infographics, breakouts, alternate story forms and all of the things that design can lead the way on are integral to the fabric of what a college newspaper should be.

■ **Emmet Smith**

As a designer at The Ball State Daily News at Ball State University in Muncie, Ind., Emmet Smith won design awards from the Society for News Design, Indiana Collegiate Press Association and the Columbia Scholastic Press Association. In 2002 he was named the College Designer of the Year by the University of Missouri's student chapter of the Society for News Design. Smith, who also served as editor in chief of The Ball State Daily News, graduated with a bachelor's degree in journalism in 2003. After interning at The Virginian-Pilot and the Detroit Free Press, he got a job as a designer at The Plain Dealer in Cleveland, Ohio.

How can students with little design experience put out attractive, visually compelling newspapers? What can designers do to encourage people on campus to pick up their paper?

That's easy. Hire someone to set up a solid, clean base design for you and follow their rules. There are a ton of people that can do this affordably; you don't need Mario Garcia. Look at good design; the Society for News Design annuals are a great place to start. Edit well, write smart headlines. Someone (who?) once said that a great headline set in Cooper Black looks a million times better than even a mediocre one set in a beautiful face. Use photography well. Great pictures can make or break a page. And above all, keep it simple. Make everything earn its way onto the page.

What are some of the challenges you faced as a student designer?

Resources and time are the two great scarcities in college journalism. Your paper has no money and not nearly enough staff. What do you do? Work all the time, which is rough because there are classes, not to mention the rest of life. Plus, the entire staff is learning. They're going to come up short and make mistakes, even when all of the things necessary for success are there.

What were some of your greatest accomplishments as a student designer?

Our greatest accomplishments were the days when you couldn't tell that we were a college paper, or better yet, that you could because we took a risk that no professional paper would and pulled it off.

What do you wish you had known about design when you were in college?

That there are a million approaches and the only right one is the one that works for your readers. Not everyone can or should be *The Washington Post, San Jose Mercury News, Hartford Courant, Virginian-Pilot,* etc. Stop emulating and start looking for the things that work for you.

What other advice do you have for student designers?

Look at professional newspapers as much as possible, talk to as many people as possible. Develop relationships with professionals who could become mentors and advocates. Try things, be crazy. You've gotta go there to come back. And besides, it all ends up in the trash the next day.

Figure 2. Emmet Smith designed the cover of this holiday supplement for *The Ball State Daily News.* Design by Emmet Smith, *The Ball State Daily News,* Ball State University

Figure 17.1. A newspaper Web site should do more than deliver the print edition online. It should have unique content, including Web-exclusive stories, photo galleries and interactive features. The *Northern Star* at Northern Illinois University has won numerous national awards for its innovative Web site. *Northern Star,* Northern Illinois University

Web Sites

I t's a Wednesday morning in February, and torrential rains are pummeling San Francisco State University. Several buildings on the campus flood, lights flicker out, the main parking garage is closed after water rises in the basement level. The staff of the student newspaper, *Golden Gate [X]press,* is poised to spring into action.

But there's one problem. Production of the weekly print newspaper has already begun. The front page has been delivered to the printer and can't be recalled. Editor in chief Christine Yee isn't worried, though; the staff, she decides, will use the newspaper's Web site as the primary vehicle for breaking the news. (Fortunately, the electricity in the student newspaper offices isn't affected.)

At 9:51 that morning, just minutes after the university president decides to cancel all classes, [X]press posts its first story on the deluge. Over the next few hours reporters, photographers, editors and online producers create and publish an extensive multimedia package on the floods. One team produces an audio report and slideshow on the damage to the student health center, capturing the hum of the vacuum cleaner as the staff cleans up. Others collect anecdotes from students who gathered in the student union. One enterprising reporter snags an audio interview with a student who finds his Honda Prelude half submerged in the flooded basement of the parking structure (Figure 17.2).

With the flood package, the [X]press news staff gained a new appreciation for its Web site. Students were able to publish many more stories and photos than could possibly have fit in the newspaper (about a third of the text and a tiny fraction of the photos made it into the print edition the next day). Reporters and photographers got the thrill of covering the news as it was happening—and the satisfaction of disseminating vital information in a matter of minutes. In addition, the staff made use of the Web's multimedia capabilities, finding innovative ways of telling the story.

Web sites offer newspaper staffs a host of new opportunities for covering news. Unfortunately, many college papers fail to take full advantage of the medium. Some student newspapers simply "shovel" stories and photos from the print paper without updates or enhancements. This chapter will teach you some of the basic principles of online journalism and help you make your Web site an indispensable resource for your campus community.

The Online Medium

To begin, let's look at some of the important ways in which the Web differs from print (Figure 17.3).

Immediacy. Stories and photos can be posted minutes after news breaks and be updated any number of times as a story changes.

Space. There's virtually no limit to what you can run.

Multimedia. In addition to text, photos and graphics, the Web offers the ability to transmit audio and video, allowing you to tell stories in new and creative ways.

Interactivity. Polls, quizzes, reader feedback and discussion forums can all enhance

Figure 17.2. When a major rainstorm and flood hit San Francisco State University just as the weekly newspaper was being sent to the printer, the staff used the paper's Web site to break the news. *Golden Gate[X]press*, San Francisco State University

news coverage, engage readers and help the newspaper gauge interest in particular issues.

Linking. By connecting readers to other parts of your site and to other sites you can add context and depth to your stories.

So how does all this apply to your online newspaper and your stretched-to-the-max staff? Let's go over each of these elements in more depth.

Immediacy

There's nothing like having a big story break just after deadline and being forced to wait for the next issue to deliver the news. If you work for a daily, it means holding the story till the next day—and possibly getting scooped by your professional competition. If your newspaper publishes weekly, or even less frequently, it means your story is old news even before it sees print.

The Internet, the ultimate breaking news vehicle, has revolutionized the news cycle for countless publications—from the small college weekly to *The New York Times*. But taking advantage of this 24/7 medium requires some planning. Large professional newspapers have staff assigned to night and weekend shifts. The majority of college newspapers don't. In addition, most students are juggling classes, homework, jobs and social activities with their newspaper commitments—and the newspaper doesn't always come out as the No. 1 priority.

This means that editors need to plan for

breaking news. Editors need to know how to get in touch with staffers when news breaks—and reporters and photographers need to know to check in when there's a crisis. If the staff is large enough, you may want to assign people to night or weekend shifts or at least have certain people on call.

You also need to make sure that editors can publish Web stories and photos quickly and easily. Many student newspapers have content management systems that allow reporters and photographers to file copy and photos and editors to publish stories on the Web without even being in the newspaper office. If you don't already have such a system, consider creating one or find ways to handle breaking news by e-mail.

Space

As we've discussed, the Web offers virtually unlimited space—a true luxury in times of shrinking newspaper budgets and rising paper and printing costs. But this doesn't mean that you should publish photos and stories that aren't good enough to appear in your print paper. Web reports should meet the same standards for accuracy and readability that you have for your print edition.

Think, too, about creative ways to use this extra space. If, for example, you can't print all the letters to the editor that you receive in your paper, print them all online. (Make sure you put a note on your print letters page referring readers to the online letters section.)

Newspaper Web Site

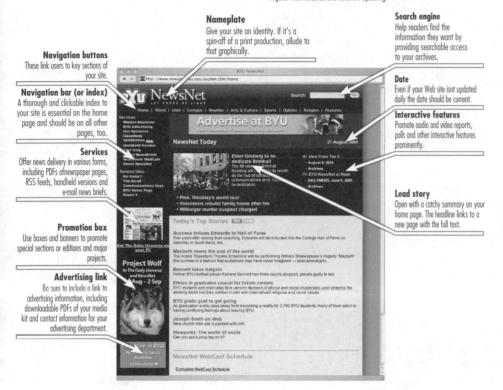

Navigation buttons
These link users to key sections of your site.

Navigation bar (or index)
A thorough and clickable index to your site is essential on the home page and should be on all other pages, too.

Services
Offer news delivery in various forms, including PDFs of newspaper pages, RSS feeds, handheld versions and e-mail news briefs.

Promotion box
Use boxes and banners to promote special sections or editions and major projects.

Advertising link
Be sure to include a link to advertising information, including downloadable PDFs of your media kit and contact information for your advertising department.

Nameplate
Give your site an identity. If it's a spin-off of a print production, allude to that graphically.

Search engine
Help readers find the information they want by providing searchable access to your archives.

Date
Even if your Web site isn't updated daily the date should be current.

Interactive features
Promote audio and video reports, polls and other interactive features prominently.

Lead story
Open with a catchy summary on your home page. The headline links to a new page with the full text.

Figure 17.3. Elements of a Web site. NewsNet, Brigham Young University, graphic by Bradley Wilson

---

If you have a great collection of photos from an important campus event, create a digital slideshow or photo gallery. During football season, the *Collegiate Times* Web site at Virginia Polytechnic Institute and State University publishes a gallery of each week's game photos. Editors say it's one of the most popular features on the site.

You can also use the Web site to publish documents related to your story. The online editor of *The Otter Realm* at California State University, Monterey Bay did just that when a group of students "kidnapped" the university president's plastic lawn flamingo. The newspaper got hold of the e-mail "ransom" note and published it on the newspaper's Web site along with the tongue-in-cheek story (Figure 17.4). More serious documents—letters, police reports, audit reports—that back up news stories can also be scanned and published this way, adding credibility and depth to your stories.

The *Northern Star* at Northern Illinois University is one site that takes full advantage of this unlimited space (Figure 17.1). By

including everything under the sun, from campus, national and international news to bus schedules to local restaurant menus and movie listings to MP3 files from local bands and video clips from Huskies football games, the site has made itself an indispensable resource for the entire campus community.

Jeremy Norman, the paper's online editor from 1999 to 2003, explains the philosophy behind flooding the audience with material: "Sure, students can find residence hall menus on our university Web site, but where? Sure, they can find information regarding utility hook-ups for apartments, but there's no central location. Sure they can find a calendar of events for our community, but how many sites should one have to go to find local band dates, CD releases, late-night talk shows and university events? With us, it's just one."

Norman took over as online editor in his freshman year. At the time, the newspaper's Web site, which simply posted campus news from the *Northern Star*'s five weekday editions, attracted about 400 hits a day, mostly from alumni.

He revamped the site completely, looking for models not in other college newspaper Web sites but in CNN.com, washingtonpost.com and nytimes.com. By 2004, the site, with its eclectic mix of news, information and entertainment, was attracting more than 80,000 unique visitors a day and garnering national awards from Associated Collegiate Press, *Editor & Publisher*, College Media Advisers and the Student Society for News Design.

Norman's advice to others who want to enhance their Web site: "Don't be afraid to go crazy. Chase those stories that happen in your community and abroad, then add what you can to make them more important than a standard article template. You can add important stats, photo galleries, interactive surveys and local resources to a multitude of stories each day. You will become the source for all news and entertainment in your community."

Multimedia

Photos, video, audio, text. Multimedia means telling stories using several media at once. It may be an interactive graphic, a slideshow with an audio track or a video clip that runs on the Web.

Some multimedia reports are produced by converged news operations. At Brigham Young University's NewsNet site, visitors can read stories from *The Daily Universe*, watch video news reports from the cable television station and listen to "News from the Y" audio reports. The school's media outlets merged in 1996 to create the first converged student newsroom in the nation.

A few student news media operations have followed suit, including the S. Gale Denley Student Media Center at the University of Mississippi. The staffs of *The Daily Mississippian*, the college radio station, television station and Web site discovered the power of convergence—the coming together of multiple media—in August 2004 when the campus was gripped by the deadly fraternity fire described in Chapter 1.

But even newspaper Web sites without such vast resources can produce multimedia narratives. Reporters who take a digital audio recorder with them, for example, can add sound clips to their stories on the Web. Photographers can collect ambient sound—chants at a demonstration, music from a rehearsal room—to enhance a slideshow.

Interactivity

The Web's interactive capabilities are part of what makes it such a fun and engaging medium, particularly for today's tech-savvy generation of college students. Many college newspaper editors understand this and have given polls, bulletin boards and other interactive features space on their sites.

Tips from a Pro
■ **Jake Ortman**

A newspaper's Web site shouldn't simply be an online repository for material that's already appeared in print. It should be a dynamic online publication with original content, breaking news, blogs and other cool stuff. Here are some tips for making your newspaper's Web site all that it can be:

1. **Put someone in charge.** Have a dedicated online person on staff—be it somebody with computer or news experience—or, better yet, both. While many publishing systems allow easy uploading of story content, you want that person around if something goes wrong or if you want to do something more advanced. This person will also act as a liaison for the online edition—attending newsroom editor meetings, putting pressure on editors and reporters to consider online possibilities and suggesting additional content for the Web site.

2. **Color, color, color.** In the print world, you can only publish color if a) you can afford it, or b) you have an advertiser pay for it. On the Web, color doesn't add to the cost and it really brightens up the site. Have photographers shoot color and make sure the color version is scanned, even if the photo only runs in black and white in the paper.

3. **Class up your classifieds.** Classifieds should be online and searchable, and people should be able to submit classifieds via your Web site. You can mark up your classified ad rates for this privilege and make a few bucks.

4. **Promote your staff.** Put their pics online with their beats or titles and e-mail addresses (use professional-looking, non-personal addresses, like JoeBlow@yournewspapername.com). Add some personal biographical details and plug your staffers'

accomplishments, such as awards they've won, big stories they've covered, etc. This kind of information also helps them land internships and jobs.

5. **Break news online.** If an important story is breaking before the next issue goes to print (and this is especially the case with non-dailies), get it online. Now. Faster. Even if a story isn't fully written, get a blip on your Web site about it. If your site is set up right, you can get a story online anywhere with an Internet connection. I've posted stories from hotel lobbies, my parents' house, the library, even a gas station on a mountain pass. Get it up, and make a spectacle out of the local media who get thrown off guard. Scooping the pros will give the staff a jolt and will keep readers checking the site and the next morning's paper for more information.

6. **Get personal.** You're in college. You know who your readers are. You share in-jokes and frames of reference. Bring that personal connection to your Web site. Be it a daily note from the editor(s), a random quote, a funny picture, whatever, give your site a personality.

7. **Experiment.** Another perk about being in college and not on some major corporation's dime is that you have a lot more leeway. Take advantage of it. Experiment—don't be afraid to screw up. This applies to the print edition as well. Figure out what works and what doesn't and what you can and can't do now, and bring that enthusiasm to the real world.

8. **Interact.** Give folks reasons to come back to your site. Local weather, polls, surveys, events, forums, whatever—the news can't be the only thing that brings people to your online edition. Give people an option to express their voice, and they will—

Some newspapers, such as the *Indiana Daily Student* at Indiana University and *The Oklahoma Daily* at the University of Oklahoma, post daily or weekly polls, asking such questions as "Were you able to get all the classes you registered for?" or "Do you think grade inflation is a problem here?"

Other polls link directly to breaking news. For example, the day *The Chronicle* at Duke University reported that the university's longtime basketball coach Mike Krzyzewski had been offered an $8 million contract to coach the Los Angeles Lakers, the paper ran a poll: "Will Coach K leave Duke for the Lakers?" Within hours nearly 1,000 votes had been cast—and this in the middle of the summer on the eve of a holiday weekend.

Visitors to the Web site of Auburn University's *The Auburn Plainsman* can submit a story idea, play a game or pick someone up in the chat room. Want to find an easy elective or see who the most popular teachers are? Check out one of the myriad message boards on campus issues, sports or politics. If the sophisticated Web site is a little too high-tech for you, you can click on a detailed FAQ page for the answers.

Monitoring your Web site and checking interactive features, such as polls and feedback forms, gives you a sense of which stories are creating a buzz among your readers. Duke's *Chronicle* drew more than 1.2 million hits in September 2003 when Matt Drudge linked to a story, "Sigma Chi Party Outrages Latinos," on his Web site. The story described reaction by the university's Latino community to a Sigma Chi fraternity "Viva Mexico" party that featured invitations made to look like expired green cards and a 'border control' at the door. More than 500 people posted feedback on the story.

Linking

Adding links is the easiest and most obvious way to turn a conventional newspaper story into an online story. By linking to other Web pages, you can enhance the story, providing more information and giving the reader a fuller, deeper understanding of the issues, people and events you write about. That, in turn, makes your site more useful and valuable. (For tips, see Linking Do's and Don'ts in this chapter.)

Web Service Features

With its vast space, multimedia capabilities, immediacy and linking opportunities, the Web offers many opportunities for service features. For example:

- Students at the University of Washington, Seattle who have a hankering for pizza can click on the PizzaSquad feature on *The Daily* online (Figure 17.5). The page offers reviews and vital information (hours, numbers, actual delivery times) for a dozen local pizzerias.
- At Georgetown University, students looking for the inside dope on particular courses can go to *The Hoya's* "Course Review" section and find out how other students rate the course. There they can find a statistical analysis of such key points as the number of exams, studying time required per week and whether students felt they learned much.
- Students at the University of Pennsylvania looking for an expensive French restaurant to take the parents to or a cheap Indian place for a first date can browse the *Daily Pennsylvanian's* restaurant database.

either via a simple letter to the editor feedback form, or via comments on individual articles. This is especially important if you don't update your site's content on a daily basis. You have to keep people interested.

9. **Run next-day teases.** Along the same lines as the breaking news, put up next-day teases the day before—a "here's what's coming in tomorrow's issue" type of thing. These don't need to be detailed, just little blips to entice people to pick up a paper or come back to your Web site the next day.

10. **Get an RSS/syndication feed.** If you use some sort of content management system for your Web site, this will be a trivial thing to produce, but it's very important. Why? Traffic and exposure. If you set up an RSS (which can stand for Really Simple Syndication, Rich Site Summary or RDF Site Summary) feed, your headlines (and even story summaries, if you like) can be subscribed to and syndicated all over the Web in feed readers and portal sites. That way, every time you post a story, all these sites and feedreaders will be updated with your new headline. When breaking news hits, this is a great way to get people to come to your site.

11. **Post online exclusives.** This is a no-brainer. Put content online that readers can't find in the print edition. Be it an exclusive column, more letters to the editor, more photos, a longer story, full details on a senate vote, or whatever, it's not too hard to get at least one online exclusive per issue. Tease your exclusives in the print edition with a nifty little icon.

12. **Search engine submission.** Submit your site to as many search engines and directories as you can think of. If you can't find yourself on a "(insert college name) news" search on Google, you have some work to do.

13. **Advertise.** Put your paper's URL on everything—Fax cover sheets, T-shirts, letterhead, business cards, the front page of the paper (in type larger than 12-point font), receipts, tearsheets, office doors, distribution boxes ("Are we out of papers? Find the news online at www.campusnewspaper.com"), etc. . . . Anything that leaves the office should have it on there.

14. **Market your site.** Do promotions to get people to visit your site. Advertise an online contest in your print edition with some sort of college-student-friendly prize (pizza, beer, money and sex will get their attention 99 times out of 100). Give out bumper stickers with your Web address on them. Form a partnership with the local student-run TV or radio station; have them plug the site in exchange for a free newspaper or Web ad.

15. **Get your link everywhere.** Your campus has a ton of student organizations, university offices, alumni groups, and fan groups that have Web sites. Get your Web address on them. This will not only bring you more traffic via those links, but it will increase your search engine rankings. Be sure you give people an easy way to link to your site.

16. **Name that site.** Get an easy-to-remember URL—I've seen too many URLs for college newspapers that look like the *Emerald's* old one did: http://darkwing.uoregon.edu/~ode. How are people supposed to remember that? Talk to your folks on campus and see if they will host a domain for you, or give you a more friendly URL (like http://ode.uoregon.edu). Most domain registrars will point domains to an existing URL for free or very low cost.

Jake Ortman was the online editor and technology columnist for the Oregon Daily Emerald at the University of Oregon in Eugene from 1997 to 2000. During his tenure, the Web site won awards from the Associated Collegiate Press, College Media Advisers, Society of Professional Journalists and the Oregon Newspaper Publishers Association. He is a Web designer and marketing manager for Sunray, Inc., in Sunriver, Ore. and writes a popular Weblog at http://www.utterlyboring.com.

- At BruinWalk, UCLA's student-run Web site, students can read ratings on professors and buy and sell used textbooks.

Blogs

Web logs, better known as blogs, can add personality and vitality to a student newspaper Web site. Staff writers and editors can use blogs to report up-to-the-minute and/or personal observations on campus events and issues. But as professional newspapers have found, the most engaging blogs often come from outside contributors rather than staffers.

To add blogs to your Web site, launch a contest inviting readers to submit a sample blog. You may set categories—sports, Greek life, dating/relationships, first-year students, particular dorms or academic departments—or ask for general musings on college life. Another strategy is to invite specific students—the head of a campus group, a player on one of your teams, a student studying abroad for a year—to share their reflections with your readers.

As many professional newspapers have found, blogs should be edited. There's no

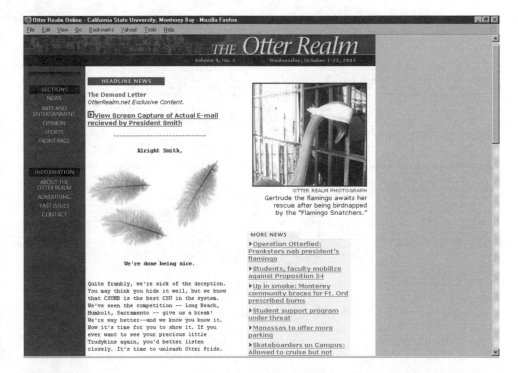

Figure 17.4. Use the Web to publish documents, such as police reports, court documents and "ransom" notes. *The Otter Realm,* California State University, Monterey Bay

Case Study: *The Badger Herald* Web Site Redesign

In 2004, the editors of *The Badger Herald*, one of two daily newspapers at the University of Wisconsin, Madison, decided it was time for the newspaper's Web site to join the 21st century (Figure 1).

"There were a lot of problems—it was slow, ugly, and hard to update," says John Zeratsky, who led the redesign. "The design was a hindrance to communication and we didn't have a sufficient degree of control over the site."

At the time the newspaper was part of the Digital Partners network. The home page had no art—just text on a white background and a gray border. Content came primarily from the print paper.

Zeratsky, who had been a designer for the paper for two years, led the redesign (Figure 2) using Movable Type, a content management system that gives Web publishers flexibility and control. In addition to changing the way the site looked, he created a plan to change the way the site was put together. The Web site added columns, events calendars, sports stats, blogs, photo galleries and other Web-exclusive material.

Under the new design, each story has a place for reader comments and links to related stories and other pieces by that writer. Photos and graphics enliven the pages. The paper also added online comics.

"One of the most interesting things we've done is post late-breaking stories that couldn't get into the paper due to printing deadlines," says Charles Parsons, who was Webmaster in 2004-2005. "The death of Christopher Reeve broke on our Web site hours before it was posted or printed in any other Madison paper, and running tallies of undecided states were continually updated during the days after the 2004 election."

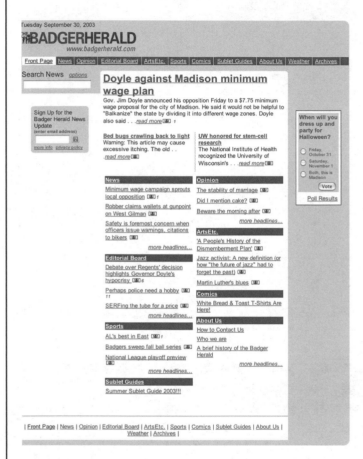

Figure 1. The old *Badger Herald* Web site was simply text pulled from the print newspaper. *The Badger Herald*, University of Wisconsin, Madison

Figure 2. The redesigned *Badger Herald* Web site has photos, original content and interactive features. *The Badger Herald*, University of Wisconsin, Madison

point in showcasing writing with misspelled words and sentences that don't make sense. But edit lightly. Correct obvious errors and check for potentially libelous statements, but be careful to keep the writer's voice. After all, that's the whole point of running a blog.

Publishing Options

Student newspapers can publish independently or use the services of digital publishing companies. College Publisher Inc., which joined forces with its competitor, New Digital Group, in 2005, has emerged as the leader in the field. With the company's software you can post text, photographs and graphics; supervise forums; conduct polls; and post advertisements.

The company doesn't charge college newspapers to use its services. In exchange for putting the papers online, the company sells online and print advertisements in the publications.

College Publisher's content management system is appealing to many college newspapers because its simple templates allow students to create professional-looking Web sites without a lot of technical know-how. The company offers technical support and a selection of templates. And because you're part of a national network, you may actually get more advertising revenue.

However, many student editors and Webmasters complain that the software limits what they can do. Even though the templates can be customized, the sites don't have the fresh, individual look of a tailor-made site.

Linking Do's and Don'ts

While links can take just a few minutes to post and they enhance stories, you need to think carefully about what you're linking to and whether the links truly add value to the story. Before doing your Google search, think about what search terms you want to use and what kind of site you want to connect your readers to. Here are some tips on adding links:

DO add links that provide additional information about an event, exhibit, show, etc. Virtually every arts and entertainment story can benefit from links. On sports stories, think about linking to athletics department home pages, particularly if they include game schedules and other useful information. However, check the site out first. If it doesn't contain helpful or interesting information, don't bother making the link.

DO add links to sites that will give readers information about related events. If, for example, your story is about an exhibit for Black History Month and your school has a Web page listing other commemorative events, link to it.

DO link to sites that offer multimedia elements that you may not have access to, such as music clips for a band you write about or video clips of a film you're reviewing.

DON'T link to the Web site of every business, program and person you write about. Check out the site to see if it will give the reader useful information. Avoid linking to commercial sites for products or businesses unless the reader can truly gain added information. There's no reason to link to Amazon.com if you're writing about a book or Toysrus.com if you're writing about a new board game.

DO link to sites you mention in your story. If you're writing about a dating Web site or a teacher review site, put in the links. Sure, your readers can do a Web search to find these sites but it's so much easier if you link them.

DO link to related stories and photos on your own site, particularly if this is part of an ongoing issue such as faculty contract negotiations or student government elections. By connecting your readers to previous reports you can add background and context to the story.

DON'T link to your competitor's stories.

DO link to published studies or journal articles about research you're writing about. If, for example, you're writing about a study a professor has just published in a scientific journal, link to the study if it's online.

DON'T, however, link to the press release about the study. Press releases are secondary sources. Stick to primary sources for links.

Creating a New Web Site

If you're putting your site online for the first time or planning a redesign, talk to editors and Webmasters at other student newspapers that you admire. Cruise the Web looking for neat features you want to replicate. Spend a day with one of the online editors at your local professional newspaper.

When you're getting ready to launch, put out the word. Plaster the campus with posters about the new Web site. Put ads in the campus paper. Pass out fliers in the quad. Issue a press release to the local media. To bring users to the site, put up a quiz and give prizes to the first winners.

If your newspaper doesn't already have a cooperative relationship with the campus television and/or radio stations, this is the time to build one. The Web offers myriad opportunities for media convergence. Even if you want to keep your media entities separate, you can link to one another's sites, offer ad exchanges and promote one another's special features.

To Do:

1. Look at other student newspaper Web sites (see list below) to get ideas about design, navigation, use of photos, interactive features and story placement. When you find a site you like, send an e-mail to the online editor or Webmaster and ask for ideas about your site.
2. Invite an online editor from your local newspaper to critique your Web site in front of the staff. Ask for constructive criticism about how you can improve the site.
3. Assemble a focus group of students from your campus and ask them to discuss what they like and what they don't like about your Web site. Reward them with cookies or pizza.
4. Review how your staff is presented on your Web site. Do you include short bios and photos? Are staffers labeled by position or beat? Can readers send e-mail to

Figure 17.5 *The Daily* at the University of Washington offers user-friendly ratings on pizzerias, cafes, bars and other student haunts on its Web site. *The Daily*, University of Washington

The Newspaper Web Site

In setting up or evaluating your newspaper's Web site, ask yourself:

1. Does it have a clear and easy navigation system? Can readers get around easily?
2. Does it have contact information for the newsroom, including street address and phone number, and e-mail addresses and phone numbers for top editors?
3. Does it include information for advertisers, such as a rate card or contact information for the advertising department?
4. Does it have a search function?
5. Does it have an easy-to-access archive?
6. Does it offer readers ways to interact, such as response forms, polls, forums, chat rooms?
7. Does it make good use of photos, such as slideshows and photo galleries?
8. Does it take advantage of multimedia storytelling techniques?
9. Do you use the site to break news?
10. Can you update the site easily?

kets with your site's URL and hand them out at campus events.

7. Check out winners of the latest Online News Association contest (http://www.journalists.org/). For each winning entry, jot down a few ideas that you could apply to your newspaper Web site.

8. Take one of the Online News Association's training modules, which are available for free through the Poynter Institute's News University (http://www.newsuniversity.org/). The modules offer tip sheets, instructions, examples and resources. Each module is based on one of the projects honored in the 2003 Online Journalism Awards competition.

To Read:

Garcia, Mario R. *Redesigning Print for the Web.* Indianapolis: Hayden Books, 1997.

Harrower, Tim. *The Newspaper Designer's Handbook, 5th ed.* Boston: McGraw-Hill, 2002.

McAdams, Mindy. *Flash Journalism: How to Create Multimedia News Packages.* Burlington, Mass.: Focal Press, 2005.

Williams, Robin and John Tollett. *The Non-Designer's Web Book, An easy guide to creating, designing, and posting your own web site, 2nd ed.* Berkeley, Calif.: Peachpit Press, 2000.

To Click:

Interactive Narratives
http://www.interactivenarratives.org/

Online News Association
http://www.journalists.org/

The Poynter Institute's News University
http://www.newsuniversity.org/

The Digital Edge
http://www.digitaledge.org/

Online Journalism Review
http://www.ojr.org/

Check out these award-winning campus newspaper Web sites:

Arizona Daily Wildcat, University of Arizona
http://www.wildcat.arizona.edu/

The Auburn Plainsman, Auburn University
http://www.theplainsman.com

The Heights, Boston College
http://www.bcheights.com

Golden Gate [X]press, San Francisco State University
http://www.xpress.sfsu.edu

Hard News Café, Utah State University
http://www.hardnewscafe.usu.edu/

The Harvard Crimson, Harvard University
http://www.thecrimson.com

Indiana Daily Student, Indiana University
http://www.idsnews.com

The Maneater, University of Missouri
http://www.themaneater.com

NewsNet, Brigham Young University
http://nn.byu.edu/

The *Northern Star,* Northern Illinois University
http://www.northernstar.info

Red & Black, University of Georgia
http://www.redandblack.com

The Sentinel, North Idaho College
http://www.nic.edu/sentinel/

The Shorthorn, University of Texas-Arlington
http://www.theshorthorn.com

You can find links to other college newspaper Web sites at Newslink (http://newslink.org/statcamp.html), which lists campus newspapers by state.

the sports editor, for example, or the reporter who covers student government? Make sure your staff is accessible.

5. Create special projects for your Web site that take advantage of multimedia, interactivity, linking, immediacy and other online attributes discussed in this chapter.

6. Set up a publicity team to promote your Web site. Sponsor a contest or giveaway. Make up amusing bumper stickers, pencils, keyrings or other inexpensive trin-

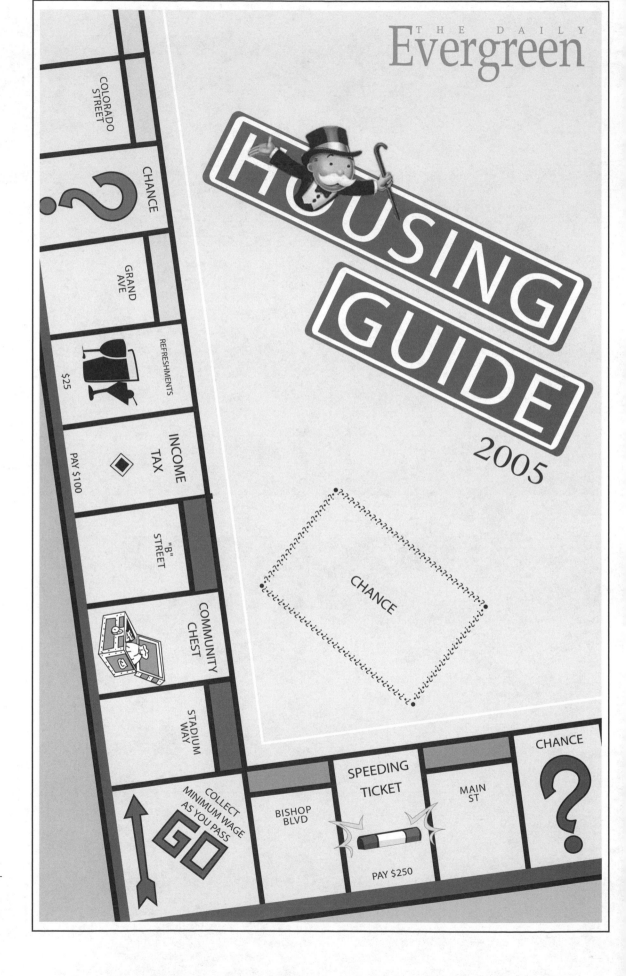

Figure 18.1. Special issues and special sections—such as housing guides, sports preview sections, back-to-school handbooks and graduation editions—are attractive to advertisers and readers alike. *The Daily Evergreen,* Washington State University

Chapter 18

Advertising

For most college newspapers, advertising is vital. While a few papers exist solely on student government or journalism department funding, most are reliant, at least in part, on a steady flow of advertising dollars. Without advertisers, many college papers would cease to exist.

But advertising isn't just a necessary evil. It also provides a community service. Your readers want to know where to get a good deal on housewares for their new apartments or what bands are playing at the local bars or which pizza places offer student discounts. They want to know where to find apartments and jobs and tickets to the upcoming Bright Eyes concert. Running ads is another way to serve your readers and help students become part of the community where they live, work and go to school.

Recruiting Your Sales Staff

Some student newspaper advertising departments have only professional, non-student employees; others employ only students. The majority have a mix, usually a professional business manager and/or advertising director and a student sales staff.

Whatever staffing model you use, recruiting and hiring good employees is key.

To recruit student staff, run ads in your newspaper and on the campus radio station; post fliers around campus; and announce job opportunities in business, marketing, communications, advertising and graphic design classes. Make it clear that advertising sales positions offer flexible hours, excellent pay and valuable work experience that can prepare students for professional careers.

Screen applicants carefully. You don't want someone who will spend a few weeks making contacts and then quit. Advertising sales can be a lucrative job, but it takes persistence, motivation, creativity and hard work. A flaky sales person who drops the ball can lose hundreds, even thousands of dollars in revenue for your paper.

The Purdue Exponent, the daily newspaper serving Purdue University in Indiana, puts new student advertising sales representatives through a rigorous interview and an eight-hour unpaid training program before hiring them. At the end of the training, students must show they can put together an effective sales presentation. "That tells us if they have the perseverance and drive it takes to sell ads," says Advertising Director Christy Harrison.

Training Your Staff

Once you have a sales people in place, you need to train them. Normally the business and/or advertising manager oversees training.

Whether you're training a single new sales rep one on one or conducting a workshop for a dozen or more, training should include:

Basics of professional behavior—appropriate dress, phone etiquette and the importance of meeting deadlines.

How your department works—who's in charge of what, what forms need to be filled out when, deadlines, record keeping.

The rate card—how to figure out the cost of an ad, how to calculate discounts, whether color is available and what it costs.

How to submit ads—procedures for layout, design and copywriting.

Advertising policies—what sort of ads your newspaper does and doesn't accept, what to do with a potentially controversial ad.

Collection and credit policies—who handles collections, the procedures for establishing credit for an account.

Ad copy and layout basics—how to put an ad together, including headlines, illustrations, body copy, logo and contact information.

Understanding your market—demographic information on your campus, media usage and shopping patterns among your readership.

The competition—how your newspaper compares to other media in the area and what advantages you offer in reaching the college student market.

Selling techniques—developing a sales presentation, how to respond to objections, building customer relations.

If you don't have the resources or personnel to train employees, see if a professional newspaper will help out. Local newspapers will often let a student sit in on a sales meeting or training session or shadow a sales representative. You can also contact your state or provincial newspaper publishers association in search of a mentor.

College Newspaper Business and Advertising Managers, Inc. (CNBAM) is probably the best training resource for student newspaper advertising departments. This membership organization sponsors a national training conference each spring and offers a 150-page training guide to new members. The organization's listserv and Web site (listed at the end of this chapter) offer support and networking opportunities to student and professional advertising employees.

Motivating Your Staff

Most sales representatives are paid on commission—usually somewhere between 6 percent and 20 percent of the revenue they bring in. Some newspapers also pay a small base salary.

To motivate your sales reps and keep them selling, you've got to provide incentives. Most newspapers set goals for each sales rep and many offer higher commissions or bonuses to those who make or exceed their monthly sales goals. Some papers also pay bonuses for landing a lucrative contract or a major advertiser.

At the *Mustang Daily* at California Polytechnic State University in San Luis Obispo, General Manager Paul Bittick promises all-expenses-paid trips to the national CNBAM convention to reps who meet their sales goals. "This year (2005) we spent $10,000 to take 11 students to New Orleans," Bittick says. "But these people sold nearly $200,000 in ads so it was worth it."

Types of Newspaper Advertising

To sell ads you have to understand what you're selling:

Getting to Know Your Client

Before you can sell an ad, you need to get to know your clients, their businesses and their needs. Some questions to ask:

1. When did the business open? How did you start in this line of work?
2. What do you enjoy most about your work?
3. Who is involved in making decisions about advertising?
4. How do you try to promote your business?
5. Where do you currently advertise? Why did you chose those media?
6. Who are your customers?
7. Are you trying to reach the college market?
8. What percentage of your customers are male? What percentage are female?
9. What is the age breakdown of your customers? Income level?
10. How far do your customers travel to do business with you?
11. Are you satisfied with your customers? If not, what changes would you like to see?
12. What are your top five products?
13. Do you foresee any major inventory changes over the next year?
14. What's your best month for gross sales? Which is generally your worst month?
15. Which media are working best for you? Which are not working well?
16. Who are your major competitors?
17. What are your competitive advantages?
18. Do you have a slogan or motto for your business?
19. What are your feelings toward our newspaper?
20. What else should I know to understand you and your business better?

Tips from a Pro

■ Kami Smith

You walk into a business, ready to sell an ad, and the owner or manager shuts you down. Kami Smith, president of College Newspaper Advertising and Business Managers, Inc., 2005-2007, offers these responses to common objections.

I won't advertise because I didn't get any response from my last ad.

Advertise items that people want when they want them and in a price range they are willing to pay. Lack of results is not necessarily the medium. Look at the ad. Is it attractive? Easy to read? Is your store identification clear, your price right? Do you feature a benefit?

Other advertisers say they are satisfied with their advertising, so maybe we should take a look at your ad(s) and see how we can improve them.

I don't advertise because I don't have the money to advertise.

As a merchant you must invest money to make money. One of the best investments you can make is advertising in the newspaper, because it creates sales. The secret of good advertising is frequency, not size. Let's work on developing a consistent campaign.

I won't advertise because it isn't the right time of year.

Advertising is designed to build business, and it works best when repeated regularly. You have items on your shelves to sell, so you should still want/need customers to come in your door.

I don't need to advertise because I have enough business.

Advertising is an investment in your future. An advertiser may have too much business today, but what about next month or next year? Competitors are constantly trying to take business away from you. People switch their business to different stores all of the time and college students are especially selective.

Also, there are 20,000 students at the university, plus 4,000 faculty/staff, and new potential customers are moving into the area all the time. Each year there are more than 3,000 new students at the university and the faculty and staff are changing all the time.

Kami Smith is the assistant director of student media for advertising and marketing at Oregon State University.

Display ads—bordered or boxed ads that run in the newspaper.

Classified ads—ads sold by the word under classified headings such as "help wanted" and "apartments."

Classified display ads—bordered display ads positioned in the classified section.

Pre-printed inserts—advertisements that have been prepared and delivered to the printer to be inserted in the middle of the newspaper.

Advertising Policies

If your newspaper accepts advertising, you should have an advertising policy in place. It may be as simple as a one-sentence statement—"We reserve the right to accept or reject any advertisement"—or a detailed notice explaining what sort of ads are acceptable and which are not. Many student newspapers, for example, don't accept advertisements for tobacco and alcohol products; some Catholic school newspapers won't advertise birth control or abortion services.

Keep in mind the First Amendment **doesn't** mean you have to print everything that comes your way; it simply means the government can't censor the press. You may reject any ad that your editors or advertising department finds offensive, discriminatory or inappropriate.

When a controversial ad is submitted to a college newspaper, the decision on whether to publish it must be made quickly, so you should have a procedure in place. Some student newspapers leave that decision to the advertising manager; others see it as an editorial decision to be made by the top editor or the editorial board. A few leave it up to a publisher or publisher's representative, such as an adviser.

Whoever decides, it is helpful to have standards in place for what is acceptable. Among the reasons for rejecting an ad are:

- It's potentially libelous
- It will offend some readers
- It's false, misleading or inaccurate
- It violates community standards or university policies
- It discriminates against a certain group of people

- It contributes to a significant health or societal problem, such as smoking or alcohol abuse.

If you don't already have a policy and procedures for dealing with controversial ads, form a committee to draw up guidelines. Nearly every newspaper has to deal with some kind of advertising challenge at some point; you might as well be prepared.

Advertising Rates

Advertising rates at student newspapers vary widely, depending upon many factors, including the size of the school and the readership, frequency of publication and the economics of the community. If you're setting new rates, don't feel you have to reinvent the wheel. Study rate cards of the professional daily and weekly newspapers serving your community. Then look for student newspapers that are comparable to yours in circulation, frequency of publication, student population and type of community (rural, college town, small city, big city). To find rates, look for rate cards, which are usually available on a newspaper's Web site, or call other advertising departments.

Rates are generally calculated in column inches. Ads are measured by the width in columns and the depth in inches. For example, a 3X5 ad is 3 columns wide and 5 inches tall for a total of 15 column inches. If the rate is $10 per column inch, the ad would cost $150.

Ads can also be sold by the page and its fractions—a full-page ad, half-page, quarter-page, one-eighth page, etc. Newspapers often offer discounts as incentives for advertisers buying full- or half-page ads.

Most student newspapers have a two- or three-tier system with one rate for national advertisers and reduced rates for local businesses and university-affiliated or non-profit advertisers. That's because national ads usually come from agencies that take a commission. If your rate is $100 for a quarter-page ad and the firm takes a 15 percent commission, your paper will only receive $85 for the ad.

The tiered system takes this into account. If the national rate is $10 per column inch, the rate for local advertisers may be $9 and the rate for university groups and non-profit charitable organizations may be $8. That way your paper doesn't lose anything to the national ad reps and gives a break to campus advertisers.

Newspapers generally offer discounts for frequency. You should offer a lower rate to advertisers who run an ad multiple times or who sign a contract to advertise a certain number of inches during the academic year.

Media Kits

Every newspaper that accepts advertising should have a media kit, a package of materials that gives potential advertisers all the information they need to buy an ad. A good media kit helps sell the publication and its readership to the advertiser and works as a reference source that your sales reps can use when making presentations. A media kit also acts as a "silent salesperson," answering questions when your sales reps aren't available.

Media kits can range from a couple of photocopied sheets to a glossy, professionally designed, full-color brochure. Small publications may think they don't need a sophisticated media kit. But keep in mind that the more professional-looking your kit is, the easier it will be to sell ads. You may be students, but you have a valuable product—a newspaper read by hundreds or thousands of people.

A media kit should include, at a minimum:

- A detailed rate card that explains ad rates for different sizes and types of ads, discounts for frequency, and deadlines (Figure 18.2)
- A publication calendar that lists publication dates for the entire year, as well as special sections (Figure 18.3)
- Advertising policies that spell out what kind of ads you do not accept and your policies on cancellations, errors, etc.

You may also want to include:

- Demographic information for your campus community, including enrollment figures; spending patterns; numbers of students who live on campus, with parents, at fraternity or sorority houses, etc.
- Statistics from readership surveys
- Photos of your campus
- A list of awards your newspaper has won
- A map or list of distribution sites
- Other key information about your school or your newspaper that would sell it to potential advertisers.

The Sentinel
the kennesaw state university newspaper
Schedule & Rates
2005-2006

We're your best friend.

Figure 18.2. A basic rate card should include rates for display and classified advertising, a publication schedule, advertising policies, specifications on submitting ads and contact information for your advertising department. *The Sentinel*, Kennesaw State University

Designing Ads

Many student newspapers offer advertising design and photography services, either for free or for an extra fee. Such newspapers generally have student designers who can translate an advertiser's concept into an effective advertisement.

Sales reps should also understand the basics of advertising copy and layout. Every ad should have:

- A catchy headline that draws the reader's attention

- A graphic element, such as a photograph, an illustration or a graph
- Body copy that explains the product or service being advertised
- Logo and contact information, including the name, street address, phone number, Web address and business hours.

Advertising sales reps and designers should study ads in other newspapers to get a sense of what makes them effective. Some ad reps even design (or have a designer design) an ad "on spec" (before the client

agrees to advertise) to give an advertiser a sense of what it could look like.

Ten Steps to Selling Newspaper Advertising

Selling is an art, but there's a science to it, too. Most sales reps can't just walk into a business and sell an ad. To make a successful sale, follow these 10 steps:

Step 1 Prepare before you call. Do some preliminary research on your prospective client. Has this business advertised or been approached by your paper before? Have you

Display Rates

Local/Open Rate: $6.50 per column inch
BUY 3 DEAL: $5.00 pci* (Save over 20%!)
University Affiliated: $4.60 pci
Student Group: $3.10 pci

Display Reservation deadline is 7 days prior to the requested issue. Copy deadline is 2 days prior.

The Buy 3 Deal!

*If you commit to three run dates - ANY three - and prepay in full, we'll give you the special rate of $5 per column inch. Same ad, same great service, 3 times the exposure - and save over 20%!

Color & Inserts

Spot color:	$85 per color (front & back)
	$160 per color (inside pages)
Full/four-color:	$230*
Insert rate:	$85 per 1,000 (Contact us for rates over 8 pages). 2,000 insert minimum.

* Inside pages will cost more. Contact your ad representative for prices & details.

Classified Rates

$9.10 for 240 characters (about 40 words). Classified ads require advance payment and are handled by Universal Advertising, a Website contracted by the newspaper. To run a Sentinel classified - or an ad with other college newspapers - go to:

www.ksuads.com

Run your ad 4 times and your 4th run is FREE!

Deadlines for classified ads are Sunday prior to (2 days before) the Wednesday issue. Keep in mind that payment must be received before ad will run.

Payment

Check or money order. Credit cards may be used with classified advertisements.

Premium Advertising: new!
Full Color Strip Ads

Do you allow front page advertising?
Yes! Front page advertising is the best branding opportunity in the marketplace. With only one position available on each section front, your four-color ad will have complete page exclusivity. Your ad can run on the front of Page One, Campus Life, Sports, and Classifieds.

All premium strip ads run the full width of the page (6 columns; 11.5"), are 1.5" tall, placed at the bottom of the page, and are full color at no extra charge.

Due to the exclusivity, strip ads are first-come, first-serve. Discounts and B&W options are not available. Please see your Account Executive about premium strip ads.

Numbers

Advertising:	770-423-6470
FAX:	770-423-6703
Editorial:	770-423-6278
Adviser:	770-499-3083

Mailing Addresses

Sentinel Advertising

Bldg. 5, Rm 277
Kennesaw State University
1000 Chastain Road
Kennesaw, GA 30144-5591

For Inserts:

Star Printers
Attn: Sentinel inserts
4140 Southside Drive
Acworth, GA 30101
770-974-6495

Web Addresses

Classifieds: www.ksuads.com
Editorial: www.ksusentinel.com
Email:
• sentinel@students.kennesaw.edu (editorial)
• ebonza@kennesaw.edu
(adviser; and for electronic delivery)

Figure 18.2. (continued)

your idea, offering facts and examples that bolster your case. Show how your solution has helped other businesses in similar situations. Explain how this approach might work for the client.

Step 6 Evaluate the client's response. Listen carefully to concerns and questions the client raises. Try to determine if the person is open to persuasion or if you should try a new tactic.

Step 7 Respond to objections. Many potential advertisers will raise concerns or objections. The person might say it's not the right time of year for an ad or it's too expensive. Remember that an objection is better than a flat "no;" it opens the door to more conversation. Offer a polite but persuasive response. Or suggest a different approach—a smaller ad or a different sequence or timing.

Step 8 Close the deal. Once you see the client is ready to buy an ad, stop talking. Don't oversell. Look for buying signals, comments and body language that suggest the client is ready. Pull out the contract and get a signature. A little reassurance is fine but don't do a lot of unnecessary chatting.

Step 9 Wrap it up. Thank the client for advertising with your paper and confirm the agreement—the size of the ad, the start date, whatever details bear repeating. Invite the customer to call if questions arise.

Step 10 Follow up. Make sure you get a final proof to the advertiser, leaving plenty of time for corrections. When the paper comes out, hand deliver the ad—or, if time doesn't allow for that, send a tearsheet the same day. Later on, ask how the ad worked out. The better service you provide, the more the

seen the company's ads elsewhere? What do you know about the client? What do you need to know? Rehearse what you want to say and jot down some questions.

Step 2 Find the decision maker. In most businesses, one person is responsible for making advertising decisions. It may be a store owner or manager or a media buyer at corporate headquarters. Find out who that person is and introduce yourself and your newspaper. Present your media kit and discuss the benefits of advertising with your paper.

Step 3 Collect information. Before start-

ing your sales pitch you want to find out as much as you can about the business from the client. What are the client's most popular products and brands? When are the best and worst times for sales? What challenges does the client face? What does the client need?

Step 4 Form a proposal. Find a solution to the client's problem. If sales are weak in the late summer, suggest advertising in your back-to-school issue. If a restaurant isn't getting enough customers on Sunday evenings, suggest offering a student discount that night or running an ad in your restaurant guide.

Step 5 Present your proposal. Explain

client will want to buy another ad in the future.

Customer Service

Landing a new client is great, but keeping one is even more important. The key here is to provide top-notch customer service. That means returning e-mails and phone calls promptly, turning ad designs around quickly, delivering proofs when promised.

"It's about speed, but it's also about quality," says Mike Spohn, advertising manager for the *Arizona Daily Wildcat* at the University of Arizona. "That means looking over a proof before it is sent to catch any obvious errors before the client does, etc. A sales rep who has a client that says, 'Wow, I can't believe the level of customer service and attention I get from my rep' is going to be the account executive who is successful."

Special Issues and Special Sections

Some of the most effective and lucrative sales opportunities at college newspapers are special issues and special sections. Bittick at California Polytechnic State University in San Luis Obispo says nearly one-third of his paper's advertising revenue comes from four special issues—the back-to-school, freshman welcome, open house and graduation editions.

"There isn't a school around that can't do a back-to-school issue," says Bittick. "It's a no-brainer. It's really easy to sell. And by doing that back-to-school issue, you've created a customer. They may not be in every issue, but you may get them three or four more times over the course of the school year."

Some of the common themes for special issues and special sections are:

- Freshman orientation
- Back to school
- Homecoming week, alumni weekend, founders day (or other special events that bring alumni, parents or other visitors to school)
- Valentine's Day
- Housing guide
- "Best of" guide (with results of reader polls on best pizza place, best bookstore, best coffee shop, etc.)
- Career guide or summer jobs guide
- Commencement
- Sports supplements or special sections to preview a season or a big game

Be sure to plan special sections in advance. Set dates by the spring or summer before the academic year so you can present them in your annual media kit.

Classified Advertising

While online sites like Craigslist and eBay have cut into classified advertising at all pub-

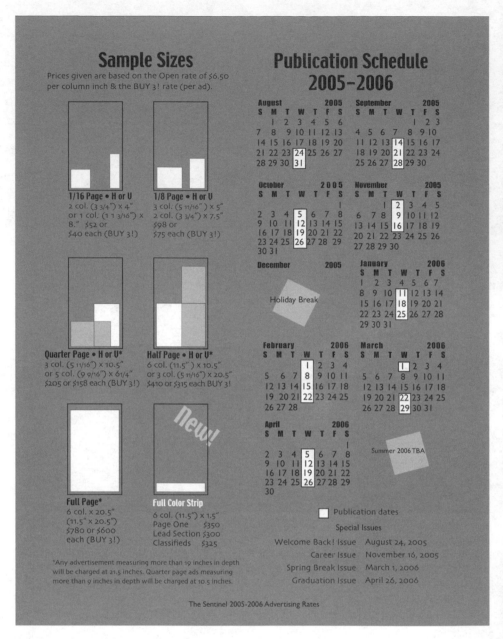

Figure 18.2. (*continued*)

lications, student newspapers remain an important forum for help wanted, housing, personals and other classified ads for your campus community. Most college newspapers have a classifieds section in their print editions and many now include classified ads on their Web sites.

At the *Daily Egyptian* at Southern Illinois University at Carbondale, for example, students can submit a classified ad online one morning and read it in the newspaper and on the Web site the following day. The paper charges an extra $5 over the print price to put the ad online; about one-third of the paper's classified advertisers buy an online ad.

"Online advertising has been especially popular with landlords," says *Daily Egyptian* Advertising Director Jerry Bush. "Students who aren't on campus—they're on break or they haven't even started school yet—can see the ads from home."

Online Advertising

In recent years the Internet has changed the way many student newspapers sell advertising, giving papers a new product to sell and a new way to communicate with potential advertisers. Most newspaper Web sites have an advertising information page that may include:

About KSU

Kennesaw State University, a 4 year public residential institution, is the third largest university in Georgia, with 18,000 students in over 55 academic programs.

About The Sentinel

Published every Wednesday in broadsheet format, approximately 5,000 copies are printed. The Sentinel is free at over 30 distribution points, including the residence halls and apartments.

About Our Readers

- 40% of Kennesaw State's undergraduate student body is considered nontraditional by age; the average reader is 25. The youngest KSU student is 15, the oldest is 77! Six out of 10 students at Kennesaw State are female.
- Over 2,000 students live on campus.
- Almost 60% of students live within 10 miles of campus (we do, however, have over 1,500 international students representing 132 countries!).
- Over 10% of Sentinel readers are professionals and work at least part-time.

Ad Delivery: Digital

The Sentinel's Prepress process is 100% digital, operates on a Macintosh platform and supports the following formats: PDF*, TIFF, EPS, and high quality JPEG. Contact your Ad Representative for other supported formats and applications.

*When preparing a PDF, please do not crop the ad image and do imbed all fonts.

The Sentinel prints at 85 lines per inch. Photographic images should be prepared at a resolution of 170-250 dpi at full size. Higher resolution will not increase quality. Line art, such as logos or scanned text, should be prepared at 600-1200 dpi at full size. Color images should be prepared for CMYK printing.

E-mail ads to ebonza@kennesaw.edu or call for other delivery options.

Acceptance Policies

The Sentinel reserves the right to reject any advertisement which it deems objectionable due to subject matter, illustration, phraseology or setup. The Sentinel will not guarantee positioning or placement under any circumstances, but will honor requests when possible. Policies may change due to programmatic or editorial decisions. Complete policies are at www.kennesaw.edu/student_life/sentinel/advertising2.html or contact The Sentinel Advertising Manager or media adviser. The Sentinel is the registered newspaper of Kennesaw State University.

Mechanical Specifications & Column Conversions

- 6 column broadsheet
- 1 13/16 inch column width
- 20 1/2 inch printable page depth
- 11 1/2 inch printable page width

1 column	= 1 13/16 inches wide
2 columns	= 3 3/4 inches
3 columns	= 5 11/16 inches
4 columns	= 7 5/8 inches
5 columns	= 9 9/16 inches
6 columns	= 11 1/2 inches

The Sentinel
THE NEWSPAPER OF KENNESAW STATE UNIVERSITY

_____
Your Advertising Representative

Phone 770-423-6470 :: Fax 770-423-6703
Phone: _____
E-mail: _____
Ad info online: www.kennesaw.edu/student_life/mediaad.shtml

Figure 18.2. (continued)

- Media kits and rate cards in downloadable PDF files
- Interactive features that allow potential advertisers to contact the advertising department directly
- Information about theme issues, promotions and other special products and services
- Classified advertising forms that people can download or fill out on the Web.

You need to have good usage data on your Web site to sell online advertising. You should be able to tell your advertisers how many readers visit your site, how many of those readers come from your university and other details on usage patterns. Stress that your Web site offers access to a different, wider audience that may include alumni and potential students, as well as family and friends of current students.

Once you've collected usage statistics, you should have a simple, easy-to-understand advertising program. Don't offer too many options; that just confuses advertisers, some of whom may be venturing into online advertising for the first time. Come up with a few standard sizes and pricing packages.

The most common types of online advertising are:

Banner ads—horizontal rectangles that usually run across the top or bottom of the page.

Tower ads—vertical rectangles that run on one side of the page.

Tile or button ads—smaller rectangles or square ads, usually stacked in the right or left margins.

Text link ads—ads that use text hyperlinks to take readers to the advertiser's Web site.

Online advertising may be sold by the week, month or number of impressions (the number of times the ad is shown). *The Badger Herald* at the University of Wisconsin, Madison, for example, sells ads in units of 1,000 impressions.

In addition to selling your own ads, you can generate online revenue by subscribing to an online advertising service such as Google AdSense. Such services place relevant ads on your pages and then send a monthly check based on the number of hits. Programs like this can bring in hundreds, even thousands of dollars each year, without taxing your sales staff.

To Do:

1. Review and update your media kit. Make sure the statistics are up to date and the design and content of the kit represent your paper well.
2. Look over your advertising policies. Do you have a procedure for handling potentially controversial or offensive ads? If so, is it sufficient? If not, assign a committee to develop guidelines and policies.
3. Ask local professional newspapers if your new ad sales representatives could sit in on a sales training session or shadow a professional.
4. If your newspaper is not already a member, join College Newspaper Business and Advertising Managers, Inc. The organization's training conferences, listserv and online resources will soon pay for the membership fee.
5. Review your training procedures. Are new ad sales representatives prepared to go out and sell? Would more workshops or training help? Look into training options from CNBAM, College Media Advisers, your state college media association or state newspaper publishers association.

To Read:

College Newspaper Business and Advertising Managers, Inc. *Advertising Sales Resource Guide.* (Available at http://www.cnbam.org)

Blakeman, Robyn. *The Bare Bones of Advertising Print Design.* Lanham, Md.: Rowman & Littlefield Publishers, Inc. 2004.

Figure 18.3. The publication schedule should include deadlines and publication dates for special sections and guides, as well as your regular newspaper. *Arizona Daily Wildcat,* University of Arizona

York: John Wiley & Sons, 2003.

To Click:
College Newspaper Business and Advertising Managers
http://www.cnbam.org

Newspaper Association of America
http://www.naa.org/

National Newspaper Association
http://www.nna.org/

Western Association of University Publications Managers
http://www.waupm.org/

College Marketing Firms
Campus Media Group, Inc.
http://www.campusmediagroupinc.com

MJS Communications
http://mjscommunications.com/

360 Youth
http://www.360youth.com/

Campus Party, Inc.
http://www.campusclients.com/

Corbett, Michael. *The 33 Ruthless Rules of Local Advertising.* New York: Pinnacle Books, Inc., 1999.

Fowler, David. *Newspaper Ads That Make Sales Jump: A How-to Guide.* Cardiff-by-the-Sea, Calif.: Marketing Clarity, 1998.

Koren, Leonard and R. Wippo Meckler. *Graphic Design Cookbook: Mix & Match Recipes for Faster, Better Layouts.* San Francisco: Chronicle Books, 2001.

Larkin, Ernest F. and Susan Schoebel Larkin. *Campus Newspaper Advertising Managers Handbook.* Minneapolis: Associated Collegiate Press, 1994. (This book is out of print, but Associated Collegiate Press will e-mail PDF versions to member publications upon request.)

Sullivan, Luke. *Hey, Whipple, Squeeze This: A Guide to Creating Great Ads, 2nd ed.* New

Sample Job Descriptions

Advertising Manager

1. Generates advertising for student newspaper
2. Hires, trains and supervises advertising sales and design staff
3. Develops and updates account and prospects lists
4. Checks and proofreads all display ads
5. Assigns ads to individual production pages
6. Delivers camera-ready ads to the production manager or other designated person
7. Handles customer inquiries and complaints
8. Develops and updates advertising sales materials, including rate card and media kit
9. Sets and updates advertising rates
10. Plans special advertising sections and issues

Advertising Sales Representative

1. Solicits advertising accounts assigned by telephone and in person
2. Seeks out new accounts
3. Works with designers to design ads when necessary
4. Writes or assists the advertiser in writing ad copy
5. Creates layouts for advertisers and submits them to the production department at the appropriate deadline
6. Informs the advertiser of all charges
7. Proofs all ads and notifies production staff of errors or changes
8. Provides tearsheets to accounts
9. Prepares all ads for production, including rough layouts, art and copy
10. Completes all necessary forms for production and completes billing accurately and on time
11. Keeps accurate records of clients and prospects for regular submission to the advertising director

Classified Advertising Manager

1. Takes responsibility for classified advertising section, including entering ad copy, accepting orders, reserving space, making necessary copy changes, proofing, assisting with billing
2. Notifies production manager of status of classified section for dummying purposes
3. Maintains and/or develops online classified advertising section
4. Solicits classified advertising accounts

Question & Answer

What was your experience like selling advertising for the *Rocky Mountain Collegian*?

During my time selling advertising for the *Collegian*, I grew more confident in my abilities, gained direction for my education and career, and earned a ton of money. To be honest, I think that I learned more at the *Collegian* than in my four years of college! I had no idea what I was getting into when I applied for a sales job, but once I overcame my initial fears, I enjoyed every minute of it.

What was it like going out on your first sales calls?

I remember sitting in my car in front of the business going over exactly what I planned to say. I was surprised to find that of the few business owners that actually showed up for my appointments, most only had about two minutes to spend with me. I'm sure that my nervousness showed as I rushed through my presentations, forgetting necessities, such as a calculator or business cards. I somehow managed to come out with a few signed contracts, which gave me the confidence I needed to keep trying. Looking back, I laugh at the silly mistakes I made during my first few calls.

What was challenging about the job?

At times I felt overwhelmed by all of the numbers I had to memorize: rates, column inches, marketing stats, and, worst of all, deadlines! At first, I took every rejection personally. Over time I realized that a "no" is not the end of the world, and it's not completely my fault. Also, it was hard for me to schedule my time. Between classes, exams, sales appointments and looming deadlines, it was easy for priorities to slip between the cracks.

What did you enjoy about the job?

I loved the individual responsibility and freedom that I had. As a sales rep, I determined the most efficient use of my time and decided which clients to call on. I had opportunities to be creative as I developed ad campaigns and dreamed up new answers to common objections. I also enjoyed establishing relationships with business owners across town; I was always in the loop about new business openings, upcoming events and great deals.

What did you learn over your time with the newspaper that helped you become a more effective salesperson?

The most valuable thing that I gained was an improvement in my communication skills. I

■ Leigh Sabey

Leigh Sabey was an outside advertising representative for the Rocky Mountain Collegian at Colorado State University for two and a half years and was honored as Salesperson of the Year for 2002-2003 and 2003-2004. She was the student advertising manager for the 2004-2005 academic year and was named Advertising Manager of the Year by College Newspapers Business and Advertising Managers, Inc. (CNBAM). Sabey was the student representative to the CNBAM executive board for the 2004-2005 academic year and helped coordinate the annual conference in New Orleans. After graduation, she took a job as an advertising representative for the Northern Colorado Business Report.

went from stumbling through phone messages to feeling completely confident that I deserved each client's time and attention. I learned to be prepared for every single sales call. It's amazing how much more smoothly a call goes when you arrive with a typed proposal, spec ads and examples of their competitor's ads printed in your paper. I also learned customer service skills. Sometimes, it's easy for salespeople to get so excited about a signed contract that they forget to follow through with their promises. Long-term relationships are built on simple things like thank-you notes and correct ad copy.

Selling can be very frustrating. What do you suggest ad sales reps do when businesses come up with objections?

Believe it or not, you will hear the same exact objections over and over again, just with slightly different wording. Memorize responses to your most common objections. That way, you won't get stumped every time a client says that their budget is already spent or they don't believe that college students are their prime market. If you can't talk them through an objection immediately, always call back later. You will usually hear several "no's" before you finally get a "yes." I remember calling on our local bowling alley every month for about a year before I finally got anywhere. Suddenly, they changed owners and completely remodeled the building. Thanks to my persistence, the first ad premiering their new image ran in my paper, later followed by ads in our local daily and alternative weekly publications.

How did your experiences working for the *Rocky Mountain Collegian* prepare you for the professional world?

My experiences at the college paper helped me develop a resume that was very impressive

to potential employers. Words like "Salesperson of the Year" can really make one applicant stand out amongst hundreds of recent college graduates. Because of my time at the *Collegian*, I was able to secure a summer internship at a Gannett newspaper after my sophomore year. They invited me back the following summer to cover the territory of a rep on extended leave, and then offered me a great territory after I graduated. I ended up accepting a position at a business publication, which gives me the opportunity to combine my passion for sales with my interest in business. Several of my clients offered to provide references for me during my job search.

What advice do you have for student ad sales reps working for college newspapers?

1. Find a mentor, whether it's a more experienced rep, your ad manager, or even a professional ad rep at your local newspaper. Regular meetings with someone who has been through it all will give you a broader perspective.

2. Look beyond your Rolodex! I held the same territory for two years, and my major clients at the end of that time were completely different from the ones I started off with. You never know when clients will go out of business or change decision makers, so it is important to constantly seek new advertisers. The best place to turn for new prospects is in competing publications. These businesses already understand the value of print advertising, so it should be an easy sale.

3. Maintain balance in your life. It's easy to become overwhelmed by all of your responsibilities as a student and as an ad rep, so make sure to set aside time for relaxation and fun.

Contests for Student Journalists

Associated Collegiate Press

2221 University Ave. SE, Suite 121
Minneapolis, MN 55414
(612) 625-8335
http://www.studentpress.org/acp

Contests are free but open only to ACP member publications. Contests include the Pacemaker awards for college newspapers, online publications, yearbooks and magazines. ACP also awards individuals in categories such as Story of the Year, Photo Excellence, Design of the Year and Reporter of the Year. In addition, ACP co-sponsors a cartooning contest with Universal Press Syndicate and an advertising contest with Larson Newspapers of Arizona. The deadline for the Online Pacemaker award is in February; the deadline for the yearbook/magazine Pacemaker award is in January; the deadlines for the Newspaper Pacemaker Award and the individual awards are in June. College publications attending the ACP spring convention may also enter the Best of Show contest. The Pacemaker awards have no prize money attached; prize money for the individual awards varies.

Black College Communication Association

Valerie White
School of Journalism & Graphic
  Communication
Florida A&M University
Tallahassee, FL 32307-3200
(850) 599-3379
http://www.bccanews.org

The Excellence in Journalism Student Newspaper Contest honors the finest work of student-produced newspapers at historically black colleges and universities. Awards are given out for newspapers and individual work in multiple categories. The annual deadline is in December.

The Chronicle of Higher Education

1255 23rd Street, NW
Washington, DC 20037
http://chronicle.com/help/milleraward.htm

The David W. Miller Award for Student Journalists is an annual competition for excellence in journalistic writing. The award consists of a $2,500 prize and a certificate. The deadline is in June.

College Media Advisors

Best of Collegiate Design
c/o Bob Adams
1906 College Heights Blvd. #11084
Western Kentucky University
Bowling Green, KY 42101-1084
(270) 745-6278

College Media Advisors' annual Best of Collegiate Design contest honors the best work produced by student media designers in more than 20 categories for college newspapers, magazines, yearbooks and online publications. Winners are showcased in an annual publication distributed at the Associated Collegiate Press-College Media Advisors National College Media Convention in October and mailed to CMA members. The annual deadline is in May.

College Photographer of the Year

Rita Reed, director
109 Lee Hills Hall
University of Missouri-Columbia
Columbia, MO 65211
(573) 882-2198
http://www.cpoy.org

The College Photographer of the Year awards recognize outstanding student photographers in nine single-picture categories and seven portfolio categories that include news, sports, features, portraits and photo stories. The winner of the first-place portfolio competition receives a camera, an internship and $1,000. Other winners receive fellowships, or other prizes or certificates. The deadline is in October.

Columbia Scholastic Press Association

Columbia University
Mail Code 5711
New York, NY 10027-6902
(212) 854-9400
http://cspa.columbia.edu

The Columbia Scholastic Press Association Crown and Gold Circle Awards recognize excellence in student media. The Collegiate Crown awards honor newspapers, magazines and yearbooks. The Gold Circle Awards recognize outstanding writers, editors, designers, cartoonists and photographers. It is the largest national competition for individual achievement in college and university publications in the United States. The annual deadline for Golden Circle awards is in November; the deadline for the Crown awards is in October.

The Fund for American Studies

Traci Leonardo, director
Institute on Political Journalism
The Fund for American Studies
1706 New Hampshire Ave., NW
Washington, DC 20009
(202) 986-0384
http://www.tfas.org

The Thomas L. Phillips Collegiate Journalism Award recognizes "excellence in well-sourced news stories of analytical reports in collegiate publications that demonstrate an understanding of the basic ideas that support a free society, including freedom of the press, freedom of speech and free-market economic principles." Judges recognize stories or a series of stories that show initiative, original reporting and superior writing skills and an appreciation for the traditional constitutional values of free speech and free markets. Entrants must be undergraduate students who are currently enrolled in a four-year college or university in the United States. First-place winners receive $5,000; second-place and third-place winners receive $2,500 and $1,000, respectively. The deadline is late January for work published in a print or online student publication the previous calendar year.

Hearst Journalism Awards Program

William Randolph Hearst Foundation
90 Montgomery Street, Suite 1212
San Francisco, CA 94105
(415) 543-6033
http://hearstfdn.org/hearst_journalism/

The Hearst Journalism Awards program includes six writing competitions, three photojournalism competitions and two broadcast competitions. Finalists compete at national championships held each year in San Francisco. Students must submit entries through their schools of journalism. The awards range from $500 to $2,000, with the schools receiving matching grants. Deadlines for entry vary from November to March each year.

The Independent Press Association

The Independent Press Association
65 Battery Street, 2nd Floor
San Francisco, CA 94111-5547
(415) 445-0230
http://www.indypress.org/cjp/

The Independent Press Association's annual Campus Independent Journalism Awards competition recognizes socially engaged journalism on college and university campuses. The awards honor progressive alternative publications as well as progressive writers at mainstream campus publications. Individual categories include investigative reporting, political commentary, feature writing, artwork/cartoons, environmental coverage, race coverage, gender/women's coverage, GLBT coverage and labor/economic coverage. The annual deadline is in March.

Institute for Humane Studies

Institute for Humane Studies at George
  Mason University
3301 N. Fairfax Dr., Suite. 440
Arlington, VA 22201
(703) 993-4880
http://www.theihs.org

The Felix Morley Journalism Competition awards full-time students or young writers (under 25) whose journalistic writing is inspired by liberty. The application can include published articles, editorials, essays, or reviews. Cash prizes range from $250 to $2,500. The deadline is in December each year.

Investigative Reporters and Editors

138 Neff Annex
Missouri School of Journalism
Columbia, MO 65211
(573) 882-6668
http://ire.org/

The IRE Student Award recognizes outstanding investigative reporting by a student in a college newspaper, magazine, specialty publication or internship. The winner receives a $250 cash scholarship for Outstanding Investigative Reporting. The deadline is in January each year.

Association of American Editorial Cartoonists

3899 North Front St.
Harrisburg, PA 17110
(717) 703-3069
http://info.detnews.com/aaec

The AAEC/John Locher Memorial Award recognizes undergraduate editorial cartoonists between the ages of 17 and 25. The winner receives an all-expenses-paid trip to the AAEC convention. The annual deadline is in April.

National Lesbian and Gay Journalists Association

1420 K. Street, NW, Suite 910
Washington, DC 20005
(202) 588-9888
http://nlgja.org

The Excellence in Student Journalism award recognizes outstanding coverage of lesbian/gay/bisexual/transgender issues. Work must be published by a college or university news organization. Winners receive a $500 award. The deadline is in June.

National Society of Newspaper Columnists Education Foundation

P.O. Box 156885
San Francisco, CA 94115-6885
(415) 563-5403
http://www.columnists.com

The annual College Columnist Scholarship Contest awards scholarships to two outstanding student newspaper columnists who write for U.S. college or university undergraduate newspapers. The contest is open to undergraduates who write bylined general interest, editorial page or op-ed columns. First prize is $1,000 and free registration at the society's annual conference. Second prize is $500. The annual deadline is in March.

Payne Awards for Ethics in Journalism

University of Oregon
School of Journalism and Communication
1275 University of Oregon
Eugene, OR 97403-1275
http://payneawards.uoregon.edu

The Payne Awards for Ethics in Journalism honor "the journalist of integrity and character who reports with insight and clarity in the face of political or economic pressures." Students eligible for the University/College Media Awards must be enrolled in a two- or four-year college when the nominated work is published. Work must be published in a regularly distributed medium (e.g. a student or professional newspaper, magazine, broadcast or cablecast news program or an edited Internet publication). The winners of the student and professional awards each receive a $1,000 prize. The deadline is in February for material published or broadcast the previous year.

Religion Newswriters Association

P.O. Box 2037
Westerville, OH 43086
(614) 891-9001
http://www.rna.org

The Chandler Award for Student Writer of the Year honors excellence in writing on religion. Emphasis is placed on "reporting skill and a grasp of religion issues that is fair, balanced and in accordance with journalistic standards." Named for Russell Chandler, former religion writer for the *Los Angeles Times,* this student contest is made possible through the Chandler Legacy Fund. First-place winners are awarded $500 plus up to $500 to travel to the RNA conference. The annual deadline is in May.

The Robert F. Kennedy College Journalism Award

The RFK Memorial
1367 Connecticut Ave. NW, Suite 200
Washington, DC 20036
(202) 463-7575
http://www.rfkmemorial.org

The Robert F. Kennedy College Journalism Award recognizes college journalism that includes accounts of the disadvantaged in the United States and around the world. The winner receives $500 and a trip to Washington, D.C. to attend the awards ceremony. The deadline is in February each year.

Scripps Howard Foundation

P.O. Box 5380
312 Walnut Street
Cincinnati, OH 45201
(513) 977-3035
http://foundation.scripps.com/foundation/

The Scripps Howard Foundation and the School of Journalism at Indiana University offer the Roy W. Howard National Reporting Competition for in-depth reporting of campus or community issues. Scholarship amounts range from $1,000 to $3,000. The student newspaper of the scholarship winner receives a $1,000 grant. The annual deadline is in April. The foundation's National Journalism Awards also includes the Charles M. Schulz Award for college cartoonists. The deadline for the college cartoonist award is in January.

Society for News Design at Michigan State University

c/o Cheryl Pell
305 Communication Arts Building,
East Lansing, MI 48824-1212
http://snd.jrn.msu.edu/

The Michigan State University Design Contest for College Students awards work done by students for classes, student newspapers, jobs or internships. Categories include newspaper sections, art and illustration, infographics and advertisement. The annual deadline is in March.

Student Society for News Design at the University of Missouri-Columbia

203 Neff Hall
Missouri School of Journalism
University of Missouri-Columbia
Columbia, MO 65211-1200
http://www.missouri.edu/~wwwssnd/

The College News Design Contest awards student work in more than 20 categories for both daily and non-daily newspapers. The Designer of the Year winners receive travel grants to the annual Society for News Design national workshop. The annual deadline is in April.

Society of Professional Journalists

Eugene S. Pulliam National Journalism
  Center
3909 N. Meridian St.,
Indianapolis, IN 46208
(317) 927-8000
http://www.spj.org

The Mark of Excellence Awards offers 45 categories for print and online collegiate journalism. Entries are first judged on the regional level, then forwarded to the national competition. The deadline is in January each year.